THE INVENTION OF LITERATURE

THE INVENTION OF LITERATURE

From Greek Intoxication to the Latin Book

BY FLORENCE DUPONT

Translated by Janet Lloyd

THE JOHNS HOPKINS UNIVERSITY PRESS
BALTIMORE AND LONDON

This translation was prepared with the generous assistance of the French Ministry of Culture.

Originally published as *L'invention de la littérature: de l'ivresse grecque au livre latin* Published 1999
Printed in the United States of America on acid-free paper
9 8 7 6 5 4 3 2 1

The Johns Hopkins University Press
2715 North Charles Street
Baltimore, Maryland 21218-4363
www.press.jhu.edu

Library of Congress Cataloging-in-Publication Data will be found at the end of this book.
A catalog record for this book is available from the British Library.

ISBN 0-8018-5864-X

For Emmanuelle, Pierre, Raphaelle, Thierry, Catherine, Arnaud, Sandrine, Stéphane, Romain, Estelle, Emmanuel, Françoise, Franck, Marie-Danny, Marc, Florence, Michèle, Nathalie, Damien, Sophie, Eric, Claire, Claire-Akiko and the many other participants in the seminars held on first Tuesdays, then Wednesdays.

I thank them for their patience and for their objections and also for their works on reading, epistolarity, the invention of the poet, masculine love, the theater, the plague, gardens, memory, and exile. I have made constant use of them all.

CONTENTS

NOTE TO THE READER

BOTH THE METHOD and the purpose of this book may surprise readers accustomed to more academic works, for it is not a university thesis but represents research that addresses contemporary questions. Historical anthropology and ethnic studies have cast doubt on the supremacy of a Western, mainstream culture founded in particular on book learning, schooling, libraries, and museums. In the current debate about minority cultures, antiquity is often cast in the role of the founding myth of our own Western culture. The present work examines the question of whether that role is historically justified or whether the culture of antiquity has been distorted in being represented as the "cradle of the arts and literature." But the raising of these questions is really not at all revolutionary: it is a direct development from the initiatives of Jean-Pierre Vernant and Pierre Vidal-Naquet when they set about dismantling the myth of the "Greek miracle."

The method adopted in this book involves, first, a return to the documentary evidence, a philological analysis of the texts, a systematic study of the use and significance of certain terms that refer to specific cultural practices, such as the Greek verb *prooinein* and the Latin verb *osculare*. Linguistic and cultural idioms such as these serve as guiding threads in an exploration that strives to follow a path that is not determined from the outside but, rather, emerges from within the cultures under scrutiny themselves. So this book is neither a history of ancient literature nor a monograph proving a particular thesis. Each chapter provides an in-depth analysis of a particular text that I judged to be essential for any reconstruction of the symbolic network that I was studying—that is to say, the relations between orality and writing-reading in the ancient world. I have made extensive use of not only philological analysis but also pragmatics in the linguistic sense, and cultural anthropology.

In some quarters eyebrows may be raised at the liberties I have taken with the bibliography. It is true that I have not systematically listed all the works written on each subject tackled in the book. With the advantage of age and experience, you learn that you never find more than one or two points of view expressed in academic works, and these are repeated in book after book. So, if you adopt a position outside the mainstream tradition, it is enough simply to cite some telling examples of each. Sometimes those studies converge with others, which, however, use different methods: in such cases I have indicated this but without going into the matter at length.

Those who take an interest in antiquity know that there have always been two possible types of intellectual relations with Rome and Greece. You may endeavor to perpetuate the "humanities," as though you were preserving our common patrimony, without entering into any dialogue with the present day: such *academic* humanism is eminently respectable work so long as one is content merely to be learned. Alternatively, you can accept the challenge of a dialogue with the present day, as did Vico and Nietzsche, accepting the risks always implicit in speculative thought: in *living* humanism, an understanding of antiquity equips us with a "long-distance" perspective on ourselves, using time in the way that anthropologists use space.

The translations of classical texts used are from the Loeb Classical Library (London and Cambridge, Mass.: Harvard University Press):

Apuleius, *Metamorphoses*, tr. J. Arthur Hanson, 1989.
Aristotle, *Poetics*, tr. W. Hamilton Fyfe, 1946.
Athenaeus, *Deipnosophists*, tr. Charles Burton Gulick, 1971.
Aulus Gellius, *Attic Nights*, tr. John C. Rolfe, 1967.
Catullus, tr. Francis Warre Cornish, 1988.
Horace, *Odes and Epodes*, tr. C. E. Bennett, 1968.
Juvenal, tr. G. G. Ramsay, 1918, 1990.
Maximus of Tyr, in *Lyra Graeca*, tr. J. M. Edmonds, 1924.
Petronius, tr. Michael Heseltine, 1979.
Pindar, tr. Sir John Sandys, 1946.
Plato, *Ion*, tr. W. R. M. Lamb, 1952.

Pliny, *Letters*, tr. Betty Radice, 1969.

Quintilian, tr. H. E. Butler, 1968.

Seneca, *Epistulae morales*, tr. Richard M. Gummere, 1962.

Tacitus, *Dialogus*, tr. W. Peterson, 1970.

Virgil, *Eclogues*, tr. H. Rushton Fairclough, 1977.

F. D., 1998

THE INVENTION OF LITERATURE

INTRODUCTION

Toward Another Use of Antiquity: A Recreative Otherness

Invitation to a Journey

IN THESE LAST YEARS of the twentieth century, geographical journeys seldom take us elsewhere. Soon, the only different journeys that remain, on which to recognize that "I" is "Another," will be journeys through time. Our Western history is rich in exoticism; and medievalists, in particular, excel at rediscovering the many worlds swallowed up in our past. To resuscitate the humanity of those ancestors who seem so unlike us is to discover that we are related to other civilizations that we believed to be totally foreign, across the board from deepest Africa to the shores of the Pacific.

Today Greece and, even more, Rome are once again in fashion with publishers, but it is a somewhat suspect fashion when it insists at all costs on exalting what is claimed to be the modernity of the ancients. The likelihood is, I fear, that in celebrating its Greek and Roman origins this age of ours is seeking comfort for the uncertainties of the present. Antiquity, which is claimed to have invented literature, philosophy, and history, humanism, human rights, and democracy, is called upon to vouch for us, the Europeans of today, in the face of the passing centuries, by demonstrating that our own civilization cannot possibly be mortal since it is civilization itself. Sophocles and Socrates, Seneca and Cicero are all claimed as our contemporaries and their eternity is claimed to be ours also.

But there is another, more disorienting way of using antiquity. The present work would like to suggest a rediscovery of the alienness of the ancients, for this would be a way of rediscovering ourselves in all our repressed diversity. A journey through the Mediterranean of two thousand years ago would introduce us to quite different human realities among those Greeks and Romans whose heirs we claim to be. We should be hard put to it to recognize ourselves in people whose daily life was a tissue of rituals and for whom religion meant not a faith but an accumulation of sacrificed animals and the manipulation of bloody innards through which to communicate with the gods. For some ancients, to believe in life in another world after death was a superstition befitting only barbarian Gauls, a fable that their priests spread among naive souls so that warriors should not fear death. What understanding should we, to whom introspection comes more or less naturally, have of people without inner lives, for each of whom a personal identity was mediated by a reflection in the eyes of another, the only mirror available in which an individual might come to know himself? What understanding could we have of the Roman city in which a man's identity, both personal and civic, was constituted by interpersonal relations? Rome was not a legally constituted state as we understand the expression, for an individual there was not defined solely by his position vis-à-vis the law. What are we to think of the Athenian nobility for whom drugs and pederasty were superior forms of culture and a prerogative of the elite? What are we to think of the Romans who considered hope to be a weakness and for whom true courage in a shipwreck was not to cling on in order to survive but to allow oneself to sink as soon as possible?

The peculiarities of the ancients are inexhaustible. The present work, following up an earlier book devoted to the Homeric banquet and the song of the bard,[1] will limit its explorations to the no less peculiar uses that the Greeks and Romans made of orality and writing.

Writing or Orality: Utilitarian Reasons and Symbolic Reasons

In *Homère et Dallas* I showed that the rediscovery of archaic Greece prompts one to criticize any history of writing that is based on "utilitarian" reasons[2] and that represents writing as a technique whose discovery revolutionized the culture of those with access to it and whose progress from ideograms to syllabaries and thence to the alphabet went hand in hand with the progress of civilization.[3] Thanks to writing, it was claimed, men arrived at democracy, history, literature, and philosophy—in short, at reason. It was thus writing that had wrested first Greece, then Rome from myth, the irrational, religion, subjection, barbarity—in short, from the famous Greek Dark Ages. The monuments to this miracle, at the dawn of civilization, were the *Iliad* and the *Odyssey*, the tragedies of Sophocles, the *Odes* of Horace, the *Eclogues* of Virgil, and the comedies of Terence.

Historians and linguists have already for some years been questioning that view of writing: the history of graphic signs is a history not of a technique but of the different roles that different civilizations chose to entrust to memory that was given objective form by inscriptions of various kinds.[4] Thus, the tablets discovered in Crete and Pylos, the archives of royal storekeepers, did not constitute hesitant precursors of Solon's laws or poems, the Greeks having "forgotten" about writing during the decades of invasions (?) and cultural regression (?) identified as the Dark Ages, in which the Homeric epic is also situated. It is not as if a human group that uses a form of writing for one domain of activity automatically uses it in every domain in which we of the twentieth century use it. We need to switch from a utilitarian concept of writing to a symbolic one.[5]

In *Homère et Dallas*, I tried to show that the Homeric epic was altogether on the side of orality, in the sense that a bard's song was always a recomposition improvised on the spot in the course of a banquet. The Homeric epic, which was certainly the highest form of speech of archaic Greek culture, could not be preserved in the form of a unique, fixed, and definitive statement—that is to say, in the form of a text—short of losing its raison d'être.[6] For the archaic Greek epic put human beings in contact with Mnemosyne, the divine Memory of the world, within the framework of a sacrificial banquet, through the intermediary of a bard, a singer of epics, a lyre player and priest of the Muses. The divine knowledge to which they thus acceded was not a human knowledge, knowledge of the same kind as a list of goods drawn up by a storekeeper in Pylos, as he counted implements used for plowing and jars of cereals or oil. No, this was an ephemeral, musical knowledge, accessible to human beings only in a ritual banquet, not something to be stored like material goods. Writing was a language that was different from speech. The reason why the Homeric culture was oral, and solely oral, was not that no writing was available; it was because of the role that was at that time conferred upon writing, namely a secular and economic role—unlike, say, that of the Egyptian hieroglyphs, which constituted a sacred language. That is why, in Greece, men's relations with the gods were mediated orally.

However, the Homeric poems, the *Odyssey* in particular, may not be the best choice when it comes to reflecting on orality and writing in ancient Greece, since the text that we possess is not a transcription of a real performance but an arrangement of a number of bardic performances designed to produce a written text for solemn recitations. The *Iliad* and the *Odyssey* that have come down to us had thus already been transformed into monuments of Hellenism by an Athenian tyrant, even if that arrangement does not appear to have affected the techniques used in the composition of the poems, the evolution of which stemmed from traditional epic speech acts. When I refer to Homeric epic in the present work, what I mean is epic as it was practiced in the Homeric poems, not in the *Odyssey* and the *Iliad* as they have come down to us. The text of Homer is thus at once too oral and too written to be the best starting point for the present analysis: too oral in that bardic song stemmed from a traditional orality that owed absolutely nothing to writing, an orality that had already disappeared in the classic or even the archaic city; and too written in the sense that the epic statements that we possess do not really constitute traces of any actual epic speech acts.

We should stop imagining a misleading break between a pre- or protohistorical Greece without writing and a historical Greece equipped with writing, moving forward from an oral tradition characteristic of primitive peoples to the written kind of memory that characterizes civilized peoples. The Greeks and the Romans, like ourselves, if in different ways, always made use of orality and writing simultaneously, albeit in different proportions and for different purposes, according to different periods. We should not, in any case, make sweeping judgments since in the course of time and at different dates every type of speech must have changed in its relation to writing.

In the case of epic, the break does not come between an archaic, oral culture and a developed, written one produced by a historical mutation ("the Greek miracle"), with the former reciting and the latter reading the same Homer. Rather, the break comes between, on the one hand, a culture that chose to entrust to inspired singers a shifting memory that it regarded as divine while using writing in other domains and, on the other, the point in the same culture when it distanced itself from that tradition and fixed some of the words of those singing priests by means of the same graphic system as it used for making its laws public. To be sure, that shift cannot have taken place without a measure of upheaval in both the oral and the written domains, for such a mutation in the epic memory presupposes a change in the use of writing, which, having initially been used for inscriptions, later came to be used for transcriptions. The Homeric song of the Greek banquets was not set down in the *Iliad* and the *Odyssey* and subsequently preserved thanks to the papyri of the grammarians of Alexandria. In reality, there were three stages to what took place: first, a ritual song was performed by a possessed singer, impossible for writing to seize upon; next, two texts fixed in writing were solemnly recited in Athens; finally, a book was consigned to the depths of the palace of the Ptolemys.

Overall, post-Homeric culture was just as oral as the culture of Homeric Greece, and also just as written, albeit perhaps in different ways. Each case needs to be considered separately, for there are many kinds of writing and many kinds of orality, and they all correspond to different symbolic functions. Here is just one example: we should beware of confusing inscription writing, used for making dumb things speak—objects, the dead, the people in general—and transcription writing, used for recording live words and preserving them.

Orality, Writing-Reading, and Greek Culture

The aim of the present work is to rediscover the double tradition at the origin of our European culture: a tradition of writing, more recent and probably more limited than is sometimes claimed, and a tradition of (oral) poetry, a ritual poetry that was part of men's relationship with the gods and, like sacrifice, defined their identity as civilized Greek or Roman human beings. As we shall see, within this double tradition, orality was always given symbolic priority, writing often being considered merely an auxiliary to it. Poetic culture was oral in more than a purely technical sense: it involved the entire bodies of the singers and listeners—who were often the very same people—mobilizing all their senses and creating a social link, albeit sometimes of a fleeting nature, between all the participants.

How far did the sphere of orality extend? Far beyond poetry. It lay at the very heart of the "Greek miracle." Philosophy was an oral teaching: Pythagoras rejected all forms of writing; Socrates spoke but did not write, as the famous passage in the *Phaedrus* testifies.[7] Furthermore, this philosophical teaching took place within a particular ritual space and implied certain religious practices.[8] Aristotle himself, when he founded the Lyceum, created a cultural association: his Peripatetics had a sanctuary, held sacrificial banquets, and formed a religious college—a *thiasos*. Of course, Aristotle's teaching was twofold: for the profane, it was exoteric and written (but those books of his consisted merely of classified knowledge); and, for the initiated, esoteric and oral (whatever has come down to us from the latter category consists solely of notes taken by his listeners). It is as if writing could only serve to provide an archive of a storekeeper's type of knowledge; it could not be used to transmit complicated discourse that constructed real understanding.

Greek democracy was itself based on an essentially oral political speech,[9] writing being used only for ambassadors' letters, evidence for trials, and the publication of laws. Once again, the famous historical cleavage between human, written laws and divine, oral laws turns out to be no more than an attractive story that belongs to a land of dreams.[10]

In general, classical Greece was distrustful of writing that claimed to transcribe and preserve the words of the living, and of reading that subjected the reader to the will of the writer, for the most ancient function of Greek writing was not to record the words of men but to get mute things, funerary cups or stelae, to speak, using a reader to read the inscription aloud.[11] The distrust was justified, since in the time of Alexander writing was certainly seen as an instrument of power and domination, a means of conquering the world; and the promotion of books, the vehicles and transmitters of Greek culture, was intimately connected with the end of liberty: the library of Alexandria represented a triumph for Macedonian imperialism.

Once again, we should be wary of associating the presence of increasing numbers of books throughout the Mediterranean, in Alexandria, Pergamum, and Rome—a folly denounced by Seneca under the Roman Empire[12]—with an increasing number of readers. Nor should we assume that literature began in the reign of Alexander, for to do so it would be necessary first to prove that those potential readers were "literary" readers.

We know of many examples of "literatures without readers." In the library of Assurbanipal, for instance, a corpus of texts was discovered which, to contemporary eyes, might have passed as "literary," until, that is, it was shown to contain prophylactic texts, intended to be recited ritually on particular occasions. "*We* may read an account of the plague simply as an account, but that was not what it was supposed to be. Its true function was that of a conjuration."[13] Writing is but a first step, whose purpose is only revealed by the subsequent one that it usually implies, namely reading, and reading can take many different forms. A prophylactic text cannot be read as a literary work unless its true historical background is suppressed. Here is another example: although book 13 of Martial's *Epigrams* could be purchased in Roman bookshops, it was in fact a collection of short poems designed to accompany the presentation of gifts, *xenia*. The Romans bought Martial's book not in order to read it, but to extract from it a poetic dedication for their offering, whether they simply copied out Martial's verses or produced an imitation of them that suited the circumstances.

So in truth, the question of whether a culture was oral or written, in ancient Greece or anywhere else, is not a matter of dating that takes into account only the act of writing, since writing presupposes reading, of which there are many kinds. No book ever constituted a dramatic announcement of "the beginning of literature." Any study resolutely determined to adopt a historical perspective needs to reconstitute the reading practices of the ancients, in order to discover whether, at one moment or another, reading a book or an inscription really did give a Greek or a Roman as complete a pleasure as he derived from "oral" cultural practices that associated words with music and other physical delights.

The Invention of Literature

We should thus be wary of those "literatures without readers," writings that were not intended for a literary public. And this means that we need to define literature simultaneously from the point of view of not only its production but also its reception: for any piece of writing presented as such conditions and prepares for its reception and suggests the preordained way in which it is to be read. The existence of literature presupposes a sequence begun by a specific reading of it. In other words, there can only be literature where there is an expectation of a literary institution.

That is one of the points made by Michel Charles in *La rhétorique de la lecture.*[14] He criticizes the generally accepted idea that in *every* written text, whatever it may be, literature is "already there."[15] He explains that "how it is read is part of the text, an integral part"; it cannot be imposed from outside if it is not already implicit in it. Not every text is readable. "It is in the reading, through the reading, that particular texts become literary; this may seem to ascribe an exorbitant power to reading, but that is compensated for by the fact that the text itself 'decrees' its reading" and "if what makes a text literary is our reading of it, that reading is incised within the text itself and, as such, can be discovered."[16] Consequently, no reading can transform oral speech recorded in writing into a literary text, "since a readable text implies textual procedures that make its reading possible." Equally, reading Homer or Plautus as a literary text is strictly a matter of invention, pure fabrication, a kind of distortion, even if it is always possible to justify it as such and even if that distortion produces creative effects in the readers, as any other imaginative procedure may.

The institution of literature establishes a social contract between the absent writer and his reader, a contract that provides the only way into the text. That contract is written into the text and makes it possible for the text that is read not to be a message from no one to just anyone. The rhetoric of a literary text dictates a very particular type of speech act that already exists, thanks to the institution of literature, and that alone can give life to what is said. The text will persuade the reader that it belongs to literature, that it is worth preserving once read, so that it can be read again. "The model for the reading of a literary text must constantly recreate the process of transformation [that reading is], presenting itself as a model not only for reading, but also for rereading."[17] For a literary text presents itself as incomplete; it is speech that it lacks, "a father," as Plato would say or, as we might put it, a statement being made by nobody. But instead of this absence constituting a deficiency, the effacement of the subject of the statement now ceases to signal the absence of the subject of this speech act and, instead, makes it possible to introduce another subject and another speech act, the reader and the reading. The reader appropriates what is said according to rules indicated to him by the rhetoric of the text, here and now.

Literature thus finds a position in between meaninglessness and multiple meaningfulness; for that is the double destiny of any recorded speech, which, by itself, says nothing, yet which the reader can get to say anything that he wishes. What literary writing in effect does is indicate to the reader what paths to follow in his own hermeneutics, since he alone can produce meaningful discourse from whatever is stated in writing. But there are many paths to choose from and it is up to the reader to decide on one for himself. This is quite different from what happens in letter writing, which takes the form of a monologue, because of the particular definition of the two actors in this kind of speech act, a definition that makes it possible to establish between them a communication situation that is clearly defined in the social context.

Literature thus establishes a speech-act situation that must be constantly renewed, thereby to recover an immediacy characteristic of orality. But it will have replaced two people who confronted one another face-to-face in total transparency by the infinite quest for meaning and the perpetual frustration of the reader. "The effect of literature is both to keep alive the desire to read and, at the same time, to fail to satisfy it. The reading must be motivated but it must also be disappointed."[18]

The invention of literature, in the historical sense of "invention" consists in exactly that: the writing of texts that not only demand to be read (for all the inscriptions designed to make mute things speak make the same demand) but also place the reader in the position of being the subject of the speech act, rather than an instrument for the oral expression of a text. Given that the reader becomes the father of the writing that is read, he becomes capable of defending it and commenting on it; since he can master the language that produced it, he can also master its meaning. One comes to understand that all other models of reading lack this literary effect, and what the present work is intended to help us to recognize is that, although the ancients knew of many ways of reading a book, it would seem that they never discovered this kind of literary reading except perhaps in the form of a rewriting, or what we might call a "remake." For Virgil, to write the *Aeneid* was probably the only literary reading of Homer that was possible, the only way for him to assume the position of the subject of the speech act.

A Systematic Doubt

Why have I undertaken this inquiry? Why should I suspect that literature did not exist in antiquity? As a result of working with the ancient Greek and Latin texts and teaching them and seeking to reconstruct how they really operated in antiquity, a worry arose in my mind, a worry that increased as the years passed. All these texts turned out to be too malleable: with a little practice and a little skill, it was possible to make them say absolutely anything one wanted, as with the prophecies of Nostradamus. The more they lent themselves to a serious historical exegesis, the more any literary reading of them smacked of pure artificiality. And so a doubt took root: perhaps the literatures of Greece and Rome were a purely modern invention.

Perhaps we had twisted into a purely fantastical literary history shreds of words intended for quite different purposes? After all, the institution of literature is relatively recent in our own history and there are no a priori grounds for believing that it also existed at the time of Thucydides or Maecenas. There are no a priori grounds for claiming that reading was the preferred mode for the transmission of common values and common knowledge in Greece and Rome. Even if books and libraries did exist, how were they used? We ought to find out exactly what it was that the ancients chose to entrust to books and, equally, what it was that they expected from them.

This systematic doubt of mine is bound to clash with a number of convictions. It is true that in recent years the notion of an author has been seriously undermined, so that it is easy enough to break away from the concept of a literature that confides, a literature with a message. It is harder, however, to get rid of the idea of writing itself. Having discarded the biographical reading of literature, our age has instead acquired a whole range of different ways of reading texts; once works were no longer regarded as the outpourings of exceptional souls, they became machines for conveying meanings. On top of all this, my contemporaries are understandably somewhat loath also to accept the loss of the author and the meaninglessness of writing; they are disinclined to give up textual semiotics and, even more so, to revise the very notion of textuality. In short, not many are prepared to use the categories of orality in connection with the monuments of Western culture that are preciously preserved in their libraries. Yet that is indeed what the present study will suggest, since this will lead to the discovery that the ancients disliked finding themselves in the position of readers and that the writings of Greece and Rome were forever mourning the loss of orality.

Methodological Questions

Our inquiry begins by examining three exemplary texts whose "authors" are regarded as founding heroes of Western literature: an ode by Anacreon, a poem by Catullus, and a novel by Apuleius, three statements made in the first person, which moderns have seen fit to regard as three texts that their authors had addressed to humanity in general, hence also to themselves, across the centuries, thanks to writing and reading. The first question to ask is the following: are these writings still readable today? Can they be read as literature in such a way that the reader creates beauty and meaning for himself, and would this be the way that the ancients read them? Can we treat them as we would a poem by Ronsard, La Fontaine, or Verlaine, or a novel by Voltaire or Stendhal?

The present work sets out to show that these three texts are, quite literally, unreadable. Its demonstration begins with a reconstruction of the type of speech act that produced each of them within their respective historical contexts and this leads on to the realization that not one of them was intended for a literary reading such as we practice.

Anacreon's ode has preserved the words of a ritual song that had no reality outside the framework of an aristocratic *symposion*.

Catullus's poem declares that poetic intoxication lies elsewhere, on the side of orality, and that poetic writing can do no more than constitute a transcript of an oral speech act that eludes it; all it can do is testify to an absent body.

Apuleius's *Golden Ass* similarly appears to be a written statement. The preface presents a papyrus covered by Latin letters, as it were a machine for producing tales, probably destined not for consumer-readers but for a single reader–tale-teller who would recompose those characters and compose others too, so as to speak them aloud within the kind of framework in which stories were told. This book that moderns have mistakenly called a novel seems in truth to have constituted an intermediary between two kinds of orality.

To support and extend these three demonstrations—for those three examples are by no means exceptional—the present work associates with each a number of Greek or Roman practices that involve writing, reading, or orality. Alongside Anacreon's ode is set the library of Alexander, alongside Catallus's poem are Hellenistic and Roman compilations, and alongside the stories of Apuleius we consider the public readings that took place under the empire.

I follow the method adopted in *Homère et Dallas,* in which I introduced a number of analytical categories that had helped me to think about the practices of orality. I will set them out here, along with several that I owe to a number of other authors.[19]

I described the song of the Homeric bard as a unique, one-off *performance*, an *event* made possible purely thanks to the *function* of the singer. This event was organized around an *utterance*, a *speech act* that constituted the moment when the *statement* lived. That statement was not *textualized*, that is to say, not isolated from its speech act by being written down, nor was it transformed into a *monument*. In oral culture, each speech act was a *recomposition* or a *saying*, from which it follows that oral performances could not produce any *intertextuality*: the statement was not fabricated on the basis of other statements. What is meant by the speech act and what is meant by the statement are not the same, for we need to distinguish the *pragmatic meaning*, obtained by reconstituting the event (i.e., the speech act), from the *semantic meaning* obtained by analyzing the statement, when this is treated as a text. Let us take a simple example from ordinary conversation: the polite formula "How do you do?" Semantically, it is a question addressed to an interlocutor regarding the state of his health, while pragmatically its meaning is to establish a situation of communication that indicates that the two people involved know each other at least by name (this form of greeting frequently follows on immediately from an introduction). The question is not really a question and is certainly not intended to elicit any real reply that would embarrass the questioner. The pragmatic meaning is always socialized and always presupposes a precise *speech-act situation*, clearly defined within time and space. In other words, orality imposes a *contextualized* use of language, while writing allows for the appropriation of a *decontextualized* knowledge.

This is not to imply that writing must invariably be decontextualized, for that is not the case in letter writing; nor does it imply that orality cannot be decontextualized in other civilizations, for it can be in the case of records declaimed or cited orally. Finally, if writing decontextualizes, reading necessarily recontextualizes what is written. All that the writing does is separate the first speech act that is implied by its production from the second one that is implied by its reception. The only thing that the writing of a text and the reading of it have in common is the statement that is both written and read. The writing-reading sequence may be regulated by a social institution, such as letter writing in Rome or literature in our own contemporary society.

It is perhaps fair to say that a literary text that can be read as such is a statement in quest of a speech act that can add a pragmatic meaning to its semantic meaning by locking into a relationship between the writer and the reader, a relationship that is socially defined in time and space. *Textualization*—that is to say, the implementation of a hermeneutics that enables a discursive sense to be constructed by eliminating ambiguities and dialogisms—can only take place through this speech act–reading. Writing does not produce a text; rather it provides a statement for readings that will turn this into a text. Each new reading, insofar as it constitutes a new speech act for the same statement, since the subject and conditions change, proposes a new pragmatic meaning, provided that this literary reading is appropriate to the statement and provided also that the new pragmatic meaning does not stem from a prior speech act that has already produced one—as happens, for instance, with theatrical texts—and also provided that the statement is (as Michel Charles has put it) "incomplete," not the transcript of a real or fictitious event. The reading of a statement that constitutes the trace of an event can only be a *commemoration* of that event, a *citation*; it cannot be a literary reading. Citation is simply an oralization of a statement: it gives actuality to the signifier without bothering with the signified; it is an oral monument.

The model of writing that serves to record utterances was well known and was used in antiquity to fabricate statements from *fictional speech acts*. The *real speech act* that presided over their reception then became a form of reading that systematically lacked the pragmatic meaning implied by the fictional speech act. This was the case of, for example, Roman or Hellenistic epics written as imitations of the Homeric epics, at a time when no speech-act context existed for them and the singing of epic was no longer practiced. Considered from the point of view of their production, they have the air of pretenses; from that of their reception, they pass as citations. It will be noticed that the very notion of a fictitious speech act contradicts the hypothesis that imitation must necessarily be interpreted in terms of intertextuality. In truth, can one ever speak of intertextuality in connection with ancient texts? For intertextuality is a procedure not only of writing but also of reading. When a Greek or Latin poet rewrote an earlier statement, he applied the ancient principles of imitation, but for there to be intertextuality the reader too would have had to construct his own interpretation of the new text on the basis of the text of reference; he would have had to have the *Odyssey* and the *Iliad* in mind when he listened to the *Aeneid*, for example.[20] And whether that happened still remains to be proved, for it could well be that Virgil's references to Homer were intended as citations, introduced in order to draw attention to the technique of imitation but not designed to produce any semantic effect at all within the text.

These oppositions between orality and literacy, live events and commemoration, speech acts and statements, the spoken and the written registers, recomposition and citation, pragmatic meaning and semantic meaning, all of which overlap but without altogether coinciding, sketch in a nebula organized around two asymptotic poles that I have ventured to call hot culture and cold culture. "Hot culture" comprises the wine and the kisses that enflame Roman drinkers in a *comissatio*, the intoxication that fires the dancers in a *kōmos* and the singers in a *symposion*, the shared pleasure of a Roman public at the theater: hot culture is as hot as a flamenco fiesta. "Cold culture" incorporates tombstones, monument books, where the names of poets may be inscribed, a group of friends attending a public reading of Trajan's panegyric, a treatise of natural history: cold culture is as cold as a reader's solitude.

Mythical Exploration

Finally, in *Homère et Dallas* my study of Homer led me to formulate the idea of "mythical exploration." The Homeric bard told of the truth of a world ordered under a divine warranty, a cosmos in which all individual beings, whether men, beasts, or gods, had their own particular places and received whatever was their due. To tell of the order of the world, an order invulnerable to time and stemming from Being itself, was not a matter of stating laws, defining parts, and enumerating elements; epic was not physics. Human beings could only accede to the truth of the world within their own human reality, through the contingencies of times, places, and peoples. For them, nothing existed short of or beyond the contingency of that reality. So the bard revealed to them the invisible connections in events, connections that organized the culture of human beings. For epic man could accede to what the pre-Socratic natural philosophers were to call Nature only through his own culture—in other words, his own unique way of seeing the cosmos—given that that culture totally defined his status as a man, that is to say his being-in-the-world. But because the hidden connections of which the bard sang were not intelligible through human experience, from within man's culture, the bard, in order to reveal them, coaxed the imagination of his listeners beyond their own cultural experience, inventing impossible situations and fictitious events such as an encounter between sailors and Cyclopes.

The bard recounted tales because he needed to create fictions, improbable stories that the entire audience agreed to recognize as such. The travels of Odysseus, the anger of Achilles, the ten-year war beneath the walls of Troy, and the genealogies of the gods were so many narrative constructions designed to explore the world that lay beyond human experience. But it was not possible for *whatever the bard said*, each time he spoke, to become crystallized into a sequence of sayings, discursive items of knowledge on which men could capitalize in such a way that each epic song was added to and completed the one that had preceded it, with Jason's journey complementing that of Odysseus so as to form a compendium of travel knowledge. On the contrary, each time the bard sang, whatever he had sung last time was effaced; every epic song was the first.

That forgetting of what had been said did not result from a deficiency of memory or the lack of a technique, such as writing, to register what had been said. For the fact is that writing, which created archives, would have registered nothing but emptiness: it was incompatible with circumstantial knowledge, which could not be constructed by accumulating facts devoid of any chronology or setting. Each new truth of which the bard sang on that particular evening was different from all other truths, the one of which he had sung yesterday, the one of which he would sing tomorrow, and the ones of which other bards were singing. For each was addressed to a particular public, in particular circumstances, so each was an exploration through Being, unique yet constantly repeated.

Exploratory fiction as a principle of narrativity associates the Greek myths with hot culture, insofar as those myths constituted narrative practices, not accounts treated as models; they were speech acts rather than statements. As signifying productions, myths elude the categories of narratology. The meaning of a myth does not come from the story that is recounted, for that story has no meaning in itself. It acquires meaning from the partial, cultural field to which that story is applied on that particular occasion. Exactly the same story may be repeated time and again, but each new performance of the myth produces a new meaning. Take the example of Electra murdering her mother, aided by Orestes, her brother. Aeschylus's *Choephori*, Sophocles' *Electra*, and Euripides' *Electra* all tell the same story, but are three different myths.

The notion of a mythical exploration offers a model of interpretation for all accounts that are presented as fictions, even outside epic—for instance tragedies, or tales. But it can only be used if one takes into account the reception of the narrative since only those for whom it is destined can distinguish the probable from the improbable according to knowledge that they share with the narrator. Mythical explorations should therefore be studied only once the speech act that produced them has been reconstructed.

Recreative Otherness: To Reconcile Us to the Future

Today, at the end of the twentieth century, our civilization needs to rediscover its origins if it is to avoid succumbing to the sirens of decadence. At a time when disaffection from literature and anything that smacks of a culture of masterpieces is increasing while hybrid types of music in constant mutation gain in favor, it is important to recognize that one way of making that rediscovery might be to revisit our Greek and Roman origins.

In the wake of the nineteenth century, the twentieth began by believing that the institution of literature, which is simply an ephemeral and as it were "other" form of culture, constituted both for our own civilization and for civilization in general, an irreversible gain for human progress and one aspect of its ultimate achievement. So strong was that conviction that it is stamped upon our ordinary ways of talking. When we speak of "poetry," with no further specification, it is taken for granted that we mean texts in verse, preserved in writing. If necessary, we may specify oral poetry or sung poetry, set to music. But, as Gregory Nagy correctly reminds us, at the beginning of *Pindar's Homer*, it is not the case that oral poetry is poetry without writing; on the contrary, if one takes up a position within the overall history of humanity, in which writing is the exception, written poetry means poetry without a voice, just as spoken poetry means poetry without music; the deficiency, if any, would not be on the side of orality and traditional poetry, but rather on that of writing and the poetry of books.

The fact is that literary culture, which has been presented to us as a thousand-year-old culture that began with Greece and Rome, is in truth barely two centuries old and was the invention of the nineteenth century. For it was the nineteenth century that generalized the cult of texts and definitively established the notion of the author that had first emerged in the sixteenth century.[21] As Bernard Cerquiglini summarizes it, the notion of literature is ideological and historically dated. He writes as follows: "The overriding importance ascribed to the author, on which we have seen positivist philology founded, was, after Mallarmé, to be shifted to the text and the writing themselves, thereby paving the way for the ultimate textual epiphany represented for us by the literary theories produced since the New Criticism."

Today we are witnessing a comeback on the part of orality and the transitory; and it does not foreshadow the end of the world. In truth, our culture, crushed beneath its mountain of writings, has surely always been haunted by a certain nostalgia for orality. And did not the institution of literature, as defined by Michel Charles, itself already represent an attempt to reintroduce the dynamic into a culture that was static, an urge to link up again with a lost orality? Is not the practice of producing commentaries, which lies at the heart of our literary studies, not itself a way of pointing out that God is absent from the Scriptures?

What if our historians of culture engineered a Copernican revolution and took to considering our record-obsessed culture from the point of view of orality, instead of the other way about—that is to say, instead of as they did when, for instance, they pronounced (oral) poetry to be a pre-literature? If we recover our oral origins, we can project ourselves forward to the future without breaking with the past, and can link up again with world culture, thereby acknowledging a recreative otherness[22] that will also enable us to conceive of a quite different relationship to writing.

I

THE CULTURE OF INTOXICATION: SINGING WITH NOTHING TO SAY

Greek Shores

LET US NOW SET OUT, as archaeologists, to explore words once pronounced on the shores of the Ionian Sea, at the time of the most ancient Greek cities. The purpose of this return to sources is to ponder what seems to me to be one of the ultimate great illusions of literary history: lyric poetry. The expression designates a corpus of texts in verse, put together by the ancients themselves and considered by our own contemporaries to be readable. Literally speaking, readable means capable of conveying meaning to readers, to book handlers. These texts, which are always expressed in the first person, are thus *read* today as messages sent by their authors to men of all times, everywhere, to communicate to them lived experiences, to express their intimate selves.

Songs have been preserved under the names of Anacreon, Sappho, and a few others, songs in which an "I" speaks of love, wine and poetry, and which the history of literature presents as "romantic" works, the earliest monuments to the expression of feelings and touching confessions, which go right back to the sixth century B.C. Once translated, they are presented, just as they are, to titillated contemporary readers. Just imagine! We thereby meet up with our very own feelings, expressed all those thousands of years ago by ephebes in little skirts! "Anacreon was even then suffering and loving just as we do! Just read, and you'll see!"[1] To be sure, you have to cheat a bit, sometimes change the sex of the loves of Anacreon or Sappho, to make them more orthodox; forget that Eros, Dionysus, Aphrodite, and the Muses, present in these songs, really were gods and not academic allegories; pretend not to know that lyric poetry—as its name certainly indicates—was sung to music played on a lyre. . . . Whoever would today claim to have access to Mozart's opera just by reading the libretto for *Don Giovanni?*

This Western literary view of Greek lyric constitutes one of those famous "appropriations of orality"[2] by writing that are among the greatest cultural crimes of our civilization. It is a crime against ourselves, for if we are seeking roots in Greek antiquity (and why not?), we should at least restore its authenticity to that Greek culture. That is what the present work aims to do. To that end, we shall not be *reading* a text that was not intended for a literary reading, but will be trying to reconstruct the lyric event of which it constitutes a trace, so as to recover its pragmatic meaning.

This endeavor will lead us to discover, through one of Anacreon's songs, that the texts today published as "Greek Lyric Poetry" are, in truth, unreadable. In other words, the reading process to which our contemporaries submit them when they consider them as literary works can produce nothing but emptiness. If the reader does derive some meaning from them, it will be one that he has himself implanted there.

The Symposion

A Greek town. The sun is sinking into the empty, black sea. It is winter. Men are gathered together in a private house, reclining in pairs on beds arranged in a circle, bathed, perfumed, clad in no more than a wrap and crowned with purple headbands. They are holding a *symposion*, a banquet at which they do not eat—they have already dined—but do "drink together."[3] In the center of the room stands a large vase, the krater. In it, wine has been mixed with water. In this form, the god Dionysus is present at all *symposia*. He will possess those who are about to drink, with a divine and dangerous intoxication. The symposion is a collective ritual in which the wine mixed with water serves as a drug. The symposion creates a space for sharing and mingling, into which other actors, too, are received—the flute players and dancers, whom some of the drinkers will beckon to their beds, thereby introducing two other pleasures, music and love, but always in the form of a ritual possession.

Sym-posion 'drinking together': *syn* 'together' is essential. In the banquet of Dionysus everything is done together and that togetherness is the drinkers' safeguard, for it allows for a collective control over drunkenness. To drink alone is to drink like Euripides' Cyclops and to succumb soon to a bestial drunkenness, untouched by any divine possession, and sink into unconsciousness. In a symposion, the drinker is never alone, not with his wine or in his singing or in his lovemaking. His intoxication, desire, and singing are all an integral part of everybody's drinking, and if he goes under he takes the entire banquet with him. So no drinker ever goes through a solitary, personal adventure in a symposion; on the contrary, he seeks a sharing of gestures, pleasures, and emotions: "Drink with me, play with me, love with me, wear a wreath with me, be wild with me when I am wild, and be staid with me when I am staid."[4]

The circulating cup passing from one to another, replenished by the cupbearer, a young boy or *pais*, serves as a model for everything else that comes to pass within the space of the banquet. Love circulates like the wine and the singing, and is the same for all. Even though each individual experiences that love in his own body, the body of an old man or a young one, an obese, bald Silenus or a handsome, curly-haired athlete, and whether for an ephebe or a woman musician, it is the very same god of love, the very same Greek love that possesses him and that is expressed with the very same words passing from one to another. Individuality is effaced along with the cares of life outside, thanks to the wine of oblivion. Far from being an occasion for personal expression, the symposion makes possible "a bursting asunder of the principle of individuation," to borrow Nietzsche's expression.

Dionysus is really, physically present in the bodies of the drinkers. Here intoxication is divine possession. This should not be regarded simply as another way of speaking of the pathology of drunkenness, for the Greeks were certainly familiar with that pathology and did not confuse it with Dionysiac possession. Drinking wine was not always a sacred adventure, in Greece. More often than not, Greeks would "have a drink" as we do, to slake their thirst or for pleasure, and some, who overdid it, would become excessively merry, aggressive, or stultified.[5] Dionysus was not automatically present wherever there was wine: only the ritual of the symposion could call him into the bodies of the drinkers.

The wine-god was not the only deity to be ritually summoned to the banquet. Others were also present and could likewise possess the drinkers. The symposion, like all cultural practices in Greece, took place under the patronage of a number of deities, all of them involved in this particular practice over which they presided as a minipantheon, to suit the occasion;[6] and they were all present in the same manner, installed in the bodies of the drinkers.

Often to be found alongside Dionysus are Eros and the Muses. Just as Dionysus is the god of wine, Eros is the god of desire, who enters the bodies of young men.[7] Like Dionysus, Eros is a brutal and superhuman power whom man cannot cope with alone, outside the ritual. The Muses, the deities of music, are present through the lyre and the flute played either by the drinkers or by the professional female musicians—who are also professionals of love—hired for the occasion. These are the only women present at a symposion. The Muses are song-goddesses, for when the music of the instruments possesses a singer, it makes him or her compose a song that is full of *kharis*, that is to say beauty and seduction, which charms men and gods alike. Unlike the bard who sings epic, the symposion drinker is not a professional of Memory, his speech is not inspired, is devoid of any superior knowledge; and that is why he speaks only of the banquet and its deities. The drinker's song is never mythical. Usually, it does no more than express his pleasure at being at the symposion, drinking, making love, and singing: "Now I am enjoying the works of the goddess born in Cyprus [Aphrodite], Dionysus and the Muses."[8] Banquet songs often have this circular character, for the symposion closes upon itself, simply celebrating its own existence.

However, even if a symposion is always the same symposion in a ritual sense, it is also an event that is each time different. The intoxication that the drinkers take on is a trial, each time new and always perilous. It varies from one banquet to another, depending on the circumstances, the personalities of the guests present, the quantity of wine drunk, and the strength of the mixture, which is prepared according to the instructions of whichever of them has been designated "king of the banquet." The pantheon for each symposion consequently varies; the three deities are not necessarily always present in the same manner. Others may be added or, in some cases, substituted: Aphrodite, the goddess of heterosexual love, for example, or the Nymphs, the water-deities. Only Dionysus is invariably present.

Every banquet is thus an event and adventure for each of the drinkers. Each song bursts forth in a different situation and will be a unique performance in keeping with the manner of the ritual on that particular day. The actors in this speech act are the drinkers, who reconcile the rules of the ritual and the uniqueness of the event. Only the pragmatic meaning of the song invariably remains the same, since it always expresses and realizes the ritual of the symposion. But as for its semantic meaning, that will vary, for what it registers is the uniqueness of this particular banquet: it is a contextual variant.

ONE

The Song for Cleobulus

A Dubious Intermediary

DID ANACREON EVER EXIST? Was Anacreon a poet? Or was he not, rather, an Ionian way of singing and taking pleasure, 2,500 years ago? As explorers going back through time, we discover among some ancient arcane texts a number of songs collected together under the name Anacreon.

One fragment, among the rest,[1] consists of the words of a prayer to Dionysus, cited by Dio Chrysostom,[2] which the latter introduces as "a warning . . . to kings not to address the gods in their prayers [*eukhomenon*] as the Ionian poet [*poiētēs*] Anacreon does":

O Sovereign, with whom invincible Eros
And the dark-eyed Nymphs
And dazzling Aphrodite
Play like children
You who move among the lofty mountaintops
I beg you to favor me and
Come when you hear
My prayer that is pleasing to you
Counsel Cleobulus well
Tell him, Dionysus
That he must accept my love.[3]

Dio Chrysostom reckons this is a vulgar poem, demeaning to whoever recites it, like the drinking songs and drunkards' refrains that would be bawled out in the drinking dens of Athens: uncouth poems, in his eyes, hardly worthy even of tipsy peasants and the annual banquets held in men's clubs.

But what was actually known of Anacreon and the Dionysus of banquets, in the first century A.D.? Dio Chrysostom, our rhetor, had *read* the text that he cites; for him, this song was already no more than a museum piece, an object that he knew of. Dio lived in a world in which the Greek city of the sixth century B.C. was already part of men's imaginary representations of origins. An intellectual of the Roman Empire was not culturally a contemporary of Anacreon's songs; nor was he an innocent transmitter bringing us, as it were despite himself, an intact speech from the depths of the past. He was one of many actors in a chain that had transformed speech that was an event into a text that was a monument, one of those who lent credibility to the anachronistic figure of Anacreon, the poet. In short, he was what the Greeks would have called a "fabricator."

To further the argument pursued in the discourse in which he inserted this citation, Dio Chrysostom needed Anacreon to be the inventor of these words, so that he could proceed to stigmatize him as the author of a piece of impiety. It was necessary to him that there should have been a particular man who, on his own initiative, addressed Dionysus through this dubious prayer and, worse still, gave his prayer the form of a work of art and considered it to be a memorable masterpiece, a monument to Greek poetry. In short, it was necessary to Dio, for the sake of his own argument, that the subject of the statement, the "I" of the song, should be solely responsible for his speech. For if that speech had been the ephemeral speech of a singer celebrating Dionysus in conformity with the ritual that governed all the banquets of his time, Dio would have had to discard his citation for fear of condemning the whole of the Dionysiac religion of the Greece of yesteryear. The same would have applied had Anacreon been a recognized master, a creator of models ensconced at the heart of the tradition. In short, Dio's point of view establishes a connection between the pure subjectivity of the poet's speech and the pretentiousness of his laying claim to the status of an artistic object for that speech. Such behavior would have been inconceivable in antiquity, for it would have carried its own inherent condemnation: to address to the gods a prayer that was not part and parcel of a ritual was a religious and cultural offense. Dio accused Anacreon unjustly.

A case of bad faith on the part of the rhetor? Not at all: for Dio, as for ourselves, these words were already a dead letter (or dead letters), dead in both senses of the term: mute inscriptions on a lifeless material, received as a message addressed to us by a vanished world. By the first century A.D., these words were no more than a text that the rhetor proceeded to analyze, as a stylist would today, in terms of communication, thereby immediately making nonsense of it. Dio regards it as a type of speech that men use to enter into personal dialogue with the gods. And, in his view, if Anacreon was addressing Dionysus, he should have respected the hierarchy and employed all the politeness demanded of men in such circumstances. Further on in his text, he contrasts Anacreon's manners with the correctness of the Homeric heroes.

Does Dio's commentary prompt a smile? It is no more ridiculous than a contemporary literary commentary going into ecstasies over the poetic beauty of Anacreon's verses and the subtlety of his writing. A very recent critic, riposting to Dio across the centuries, thus declares, in connection with this fragment, that the form of the prayer conceals an erotic plea: "The text gently manipulates the reader, but its very self-consciousness produces humor rather than shock or irreverence. But alongside the humor, the derailment is undeniable."[4]

What Dio and this twentieth-century Greek scholar have both done is *read* this song, fully believing that they had every right to do so. The one regards it as a dialogue between a poet and a god, in which what is said is quite enough on its own for him to pass judgment on it; the other sees it as a literary work designed to give pleasure to its readers. Both ignore or try to ignore the ritual function of those words within the context in which they were spoken, namely a Dionysiac banquet.

A Linguistic Shard

I for my part intend to treat these Greek words as an archaeological document preserved in writing, a trace indirectly left by Ionian drinking companions 2,500 years ago, a fragmentary imprint of words spoken in the course of a symposion. For the religious context implied by these few lines of poetry shows clearly that this was a drinking banquet: Dionysus in association with Eros can only be the wine-god of Greeks meeting "to drink together." The musical form of the ode and its attribution to Anacreon, the banquet singer par excellence in the ancient tradition, confirm this religious interpretation. On this point, all the commentators are in agreement. The "I" of the song is a drinker in a symposion.

So our "linguistic shard" is all that remains of banquet speech, most of which has been lost. It was sung speech, the music for which has been lost forever, even though a trace of it is left to us thanks to the way the words are arranged. According to a writing convention from very much later than the sixth century B.C., such an arrangement does indeed indicate that this particular shard was an ode, that is to say, in Greek, "a song executed to lyre music." However, given the extent of our knowledge at present, this still does not make it possible to restore the music. So let us identify this text by the only patronym to be found in it, and call it "the song for Cleobulus."

The origin of the fragment is now roughly sketched in. But that is just the beginning of our inquiry. Given that each symposion was a ritual event, let us try to reconstitute that event—not, of course, by fitting it into a biography of Cleobulus or Anacreon, for that would be pointless, but within the ritual convention for the unfolding of a symposion, and by rediscovering its distinctive features. For it was that distinctiveness that defined the conditions in which the song for Cleobulus came to be sung.

To this end, I shall be following the method of the iconographers who work on the pots used in banquets. What they do is piece together a series of pots, then reintroduce the pot they are studying into the series, on the basis of its design.[5] Let us start by using this linguistic shard as an iconologist would use his shard of a painted pot, before attempting any interpretation. Let us restore this song to its place within the symposion ritual and see if it is possible to relate it to a whole series of banquet songs of the same type.

The Ritual Opening: The First Sharing

Among the banquet songs that have come down to us is a series of odes associated with a well-known ritual formality that served to start the symposion. In Greek the word for this formal gesture is the noun *proposis*, from the verb *propinein*. Literally, the verb means "to drink first, to drink offering half one's cup to another."[6] The ancients have provided a number of commentaries on this, all of which are more or less in agreement.[7] It was a matter of offering the cup of wine to the neighbor on one's right, addressing him by his name and bidding him share it. The proposis constituted a prelude to further formal gestures by which the drinkers passed the cup around as the banquet proceeded, encouraging one another to drink,[8] but it was distinct from those later formal gestures in that it constituted the very first of the sharings. The proposis gesture inaugurated the symposion: the first drinker drank, *posion*, and shared, *sym*, taking the initiative to introduce Dionysus into the collective space, without running the culturally and religiously unthinkable risk of drinking alone:

> Go child, bring us
> A cup so that, with a long draught
> I may open the banquet [*propiō*].[9]

The importance of this gesture of sharing and giving is so great, so essential, that the verb *propinein* also served to designate other gifts that were given within the framework of the proposis, although these were not gifts of wine. Since they belong to the world of banquets, these gifts can only be singing and love.

> O Theodorus, receive this drinking song [*propinomenen poiēsin*]
> Taken from my poems, I first pass it to the right
> To you after mixing in the cup of the Graces
> the graces of love
> And you after accepting this gift, do, in your turn, offer songs
> to adorn the banquet.[10]

The song was introduced into the circle of drinkers, along with the cup of wine. First it was offered to one of them, then it circulated among them all. On the model of the shared wine, the poem was offered as a "drink" and the seductive charm (*kharis*) of its music was "mixed" with the seduction of love, just as water was mixed with the wine. Whoever received it launched a new song, just as the drinker passed on the cup, once he had drunk from it.

The gift offered in the proposis could also be erotic, as can be seen from a fragment of Anacreon:

> . . . but pledge [*propine*] us, friend,
> your slender thighs.[11]

But the very gesture of the proposis already potentially carried an "Aphroditean" meaning: it could set the seal on a loving relationship between the one who proferred the cup and the one who received it. Mixed in, like water, with the wine that was offered was the name of the beloved, through the words of whoever pronounced the words of the proposis. He, drinking from the cup, having offered it, drank in the name of the loved one,[12] and was thus filled by the eros that would unite them. "Drinking love," says one singer, while another urges, "Offer [*propine*] a loving cup of words."[13] The cup of words mingled love with the name of the beloved, the one sweetening the other, like wine and water.[14]

The proposis could create an erotic link because it always established a closeness between the first two drinkers. However, that closeness might amount to no more than a relationship of hospitality or an alliance between two families. In this way, a proposis could be used to conclude a betrothal within the framework of a banquet, although the cup was shared not by the two betrothed but by the young man and his future father-in-law. A passage in Pindar describes one of these nuptial ceremonies in which a golden *hanap* shimmers in the midst of the banquet in the thick hands of an opulent prince, who holds it out to the young scion of the family, full of rising sap and ambition: "Even as when one takes up in his wealthy hand a golden bowl, the prime of his possessions, a bowl that foams with the dew of the vine, and gives it to the youth whom, when betrothed to his daughter, with a friendly draught he welcomes from one home to another."[15]

The proposis automatically established a greater proximity between the first two drinkers. Because the banquet had to be inaugurated by a sharing of wine, thereby showing that no drinker drank alone, this sharing established a special link between those first two drinkers who, at least for the duration of the ritual, had to constitute not two separate individuals but a "couple," thereby prefiguring the solidarity of the other copairs of drinkers in the symposion. This solidarity would be reinforced by the creation of other couples as the banquet proceeded, whether these were couples of lovers or not. All the ritual gestures were made by pairs,[16] as can be seen from the paintings on the vases used in banquets. That is why, when a participant sang, he always addressed one particular codrinker, addressing him by name.

Histories of Greek literature were to classify these songs as "lyric poetry," a literary genre always complemented by a predictable commentary on "personal lyricism." But the real reason why these songs used "I" and "you" was that this fitted in with the social functioning of the symposion. This involved a group consisting of couples, in which each man was the equal of the other participants: their arrangement in a circle reflected that equality. Both "I" and "you" were defined solely by their presence at the banquet and their position within the system according to which speech circulated. Unlike the bard of the Homeric *dais*, positioned at the center of the dining hall who, from this spot, distributed his speech equally to all, as a known bard, designated by his professional bard's name, the symposion singer was an amateur. He remained part of the circle, in dialogue with his bed companion, for he did not offer his song directly to the whole group of banqueters. So it is not apposite to speak of "poetry in the first person," as if it were a matter of the expression of an intimate and unique experience. Quite the reverse. The "I" of the statement is used to engage in a ritual situation, the symposion, circumscribed in time and place, so it detaches the subject from any biographical involvement: the speaker is simply the "I" of the speech act, the drinker, in that place at that time.

The proposis constituted the ritual opening of the symposion. It involved the sharing of the first cup of the banquet between the first two drinkers. This sharing of wine was associated with a gift (or several further gifts), often of an erotic nature, which also took the form of a sharing and which strengthened the link between those two drinkers. This initial sharing served as a prelude to the generalized sharing that was the distinctive feature of the symposion. The ritual gesture was accompanied by words. In particular, the name of the other codrinker taking part in the proposis was spoken aloud by the one offering him the cup.

The Establishment of a Pantheon

Can the ode that interests us be connected with the songs of the proposis? It is true that the verb *propinein* is not pronounced by the singer, but the song for Cleobulus does refer to and is part of this opening ritual gesture. In sum, what does the song tell us? Wine is offered to a certain Cleobulus, along with love. By receiving this twofold gift from the singer, Cleobulus welcomes in Eros, Dionysus, Aphrodite, and the Nymphs and, by so doing, installs them in the banquet in which he himself is taking part, alongside the singer. From these religious effects that the song produces and from the twofold gift to which it refers, we may deduce that, without saying so explicitly, it accompanies the gesture of proposis.

Those religious effects, in other words the pragmatic meaning of the speech act, are worth examining in detail. The first point to note is that the song must be sung at the beginning of the symposion. It summons Dionysus and his train of deities and introduces the gods into the banquet, so clearly those gods were not previously present within the space of the symposion, which, consequently, had not yet been ritually opened. The "I" of the statement invites them in and indicates that Dionysus must come from far away: "I beg you to favor me and come . . . you who move among the lofty mountaintops." Dionysus is in the mountains, that is to say, for the Greeks, in a space culturally distinct from the space where banquets are held, which is a space of the utmost refinement. In general, Dionysus is never present for long in civilized places. He always has to be fetched from the wilderness. That is why the Athenians would bring his statue in from the outermost edges of Attica whenever tragic competitions were held.

This song thus belongs to the time of the ritual opening of the symposion, when the first drinker ushers in Dionysus and the other gods who accompany him: "with [him] invincible Eros and the dark-eyed Nymphs and dazzling Aphrodite play like children." The pantheon installed by the song for Cleobulus endows the event with its distinctive character: Dionysus appears in the company of Eros and Aphrodite.

If Eros is the god of the surging desire of young men, a desire with no precise object, Aphrodite, for her part, is the goddess of couples, of socialized lovemaking, that is to say of the only human lovemaking possible: pure desire, on its own, like pure wine, drives men mad, makes beasts of them. Aphrodite provides an object for the desire of boys, transforms it into love, albeit sometimes of a fleeting nature, for one of the women or one of the men taking part in this banquet. They desire together, just as they drink together.

The Nymphs, who in this instance complete the chorus of gods, are deities associated with springs, as is suggested by the epithet *kyanōpides* 'dark-eyed'. They are the water that is mixed with wine in the krater, but they also preside over the wild lovemaking of beginners. For if Aphrodite is the girl at the moment of her marriage, a *nymphē* is the young woman of the honeymoon.[17] Yet she does retain something of the wildness of pure desire. The Nymphs in the forest represent the feminine version of wild eroticism. They attract young men and drive them mad—*nymphiō* means "to drive mad." We all know what happened to Narcissus. The presence of these Nymphs imparts a disturbing power to the water used in the banquet. To be sure, when mixed with the wine it reduces its fire and moderates the intoxication of the drinkers, but it also kindles their passionate ardor for the young women at the banquet.

A Greek pantheon is always a structure, with each of the domains pertaining to the gods defined in relation to the others. The sophisticated writing of the first two lines of the song indicates that structure. The opposition of the epithets attributed, on the one hand, to Aphrodite and, on the other, to the Nymphs constructs a complementarity between the deities present at Cleobulus's symposion: the dark-eyed Nymphs, dazzling Aphrodite.

May those goddesses protect us from "literary" misunderstandings about blue-eyed nymphs and rosy (*sic*)[18] Aphrodite, and remind us that Greek poetry is not an art of ornamentation and prettiness. In truth, this pantheonic fragment refers simultaneously to two structures, the one cosmogonic, the other cultural: the cosmic opposition between the deep waters welling up in dark forests and the dazzling brightness of the sea is projected on two opposed erotic images of young women, the civilized Aphrodite and the wild Nymphs.

As this minipantheon assembles for the symposion, it appropriates its social categories. The deities "play together" or rather "act as children together." Some commentators have made much of the erotic meaning of that verb.[19] Without dismissing it, I would prefer to draw attention to the "together" (*syn*), which associates these gods with the ritual ethic of sharing, and to "the child" (*pais*), who is also the boy who pours the wine into the cups, and here pours it for the very first time this evening.

The Wine and the Love Offered to Cleobulus

The song for Cleobulus alludes very clearly to the gestures and gifts of the proposis. The "I" singer indirectly urges a fellow guest to establish a loving relationship with him, through the mediation of Dionysus, that is to say wine.

The singer asks Dionysus to counsel Cleobulus well—literally *symboulos* 'to wish with [him]'—so that he will accede to the singer's love-desire, *ton emon erōta*. So Dionysus, whom the singer begs to be Cleobulus's counselor, needs to be religiously present, and within the framework of the banquet he can only be so through the wine that the singer is about to drink. In this way, Dionysus will become present in Cleobulus. In a single gesture the singer, by presenting the cup to his right-hand neighbor, offers him both Dionysus-wine and Eros-desire, so that he and his partner can share both. As we cannot fail to recognize, this constitutes the religious gesture of a proposis. By accepting the cup and completing the symposion's first act of sharing, Cleobulus links himself in love with the singer and inaugurates the banquet.

The song for Cleobulus thus falls into place in the series of "proposis odes." It accompanies and completes the ritual that opens the banquet. First, it serves to invoke the symposion's four deities as they join the banquet, after which it sets up the loving link that is to unite the singer with his neighbor, Cleobulus, at the point when the young man takes the cup from him and drains it. The words of the song accompany a gift of wine and a gift of love and name Cleobulus, the one for whom the first cup of wine is intended, thereby inaugurating the symposion's first sharing and creating its first couple.

We have now restored the song to its ritual place, and by doing so have managed to avoid both biography and anecdote. For in this way the two protagonists are no longer defined by any shared adventure outside the context of the banquet. The love that is to link them will be the effect solely of their respective places in the ritual, as the actor-couple of the proposis.

The Beautiful Song Offered to Dionysus

We have reconstructed the context in which "the song for Cleobulus" was sung, namely the proposis, and listened to the singer's words that accompanied his gesture as he offered the first cup. But although we have listened to the words, we still have learned nothing about the song itself.

Music was a part of the Dionysiac banquet, just as wine and love were, even though, in this particular song, the deities of music, the Muses, are not summoned along with the others. Culturally speaking, a symposion was defined by its lyre and its flute as much as by its wine krater, cup, and handsome boy. In the proposis, a song was offered as the cup was passed, so that songs would thereafter continue to circulate from left to right, just as the wine did.

The song for Cleobulus was the first of the symposion's songs. As much as the first shared cup of wine and the first shared desire, it was an integral part of the banquet ritual. But that was not necessarily true of the songs that were to echo it. We know that singers at banquets could sing of not just epic and war but of more or less anything, even the city laws, when their turn came round.[20] A symposion accommodated all kinds of words, in fact it particularly welcomed citations.[21] In an Athenian banquet, an ability to sing well-known songs, by Stesichorus or others, was an indispensable proof of one's culture. However, the nature of the song for Cleobulus was quite different. It was not a citation introduced in the course of the banquet; it belonged in the proposis and could not be taken out of it.

It was thus a song with a religious function and this was fulfilled not solely through the content of its words, as seen already, but also by virtue of it being a beautiful song, a song "written" differently—or according to different poetics—and with music that gave it its *kharis*, its seductive charm.

The singer was placed in a liturgical position. "I beg you," he says to Dionysus, then declares that the god will respond to his call, or appeal, because that appeal is a prayer (*eukhōlē*) that is ritually correct (as is implied by the adjective *eumenēs* 'favoring me'). This prayer is also, we learn, a song, speech that is beautiful, since it exerts a power of seduction (*kekharismenēs*) upon Dionysus. The term *kharis* evokes both a gift and pleasure: *kharis* is the seductive power of a gift, the pleasure that you feel at receiving a fine object and that fills you with gratitude toward whoever gave it to you.

Our song is thus presented as a religious song addressed to one of the gods of the banquet, an offering to Dionysus, who responds to it because of its charm, which is part and parcel of its ritual perfection. The song for Cleobulus has the status of a sacrificial offering.[22] It is shared by both the gods and men. But instead of the divine and human recipients being apart in both space and time, as during a sacrifice—with the gods above, breathing in the aroma of the roasted meats, above the altar, and the men below, banqueting after the gods, in a dining hall—in this case men and gods savor the same musical pleasures at the same time and in the same place.

The beauty of this song is offered along with the proposis. It is the third gift for Cleobulus, given so that the name of the beloved comes to be intermingled with the seduction (*kharis*) of the song, just as the water is mixed with the wine. Its purpose is to moderate the fires of desire, by fixing that desire upon the singer and thereby creating an Aphroditean couple. Speech is to music what water is to wine and Aphrodite is to Eros, and all three make it possible to master the three kinds of intoxications of the banquet.

Table 1. The Gift of the Song to Dionysus

Gods Invoked	*The Gifts of the Proposis*		*Gods Invoked*
Dionysus	Wine + water (both in the cup)		Nymphs
Eros	Desire (in the body)	+ the name of Cleobulus (in the song)	Aphrodite

A religious analysis of the song for Cleobulus can be represented schematically. Table 1 shows the three ways in which the song functions. It serves to bring the gods into the symposion, to complete the gifts of the proposis, and is itself a sacrificial offering.

In a sense, this song is a fine functional object. The beauty of the song and the pleasure that it gives are assured by its ritual perfection, its perfect suitability to the moment and the gestures of the symposion, and its conformity with the musical mode of composition bestowed on it by the lyre; and furthermore it possesses a complex poetic structure. This song could be said to be a fine (musical) image of the proposis in the same way as a fine, painted cup may be. It is composed in the same fashion, for a Greek image does not represent a particular ritual moment, but displays elements of that ritual, indicating some of their meanings. For example, a red-figure cup shows two women sitting facing each other, reclining on cushions.[23] One is holding a cup in her right hand and another receptacle in her left, the other is playing the flute and, between the two, running from right to left, is the inscription *pine kai su* 'You drink too'. Clearly, this is not a particular scene in a banquet. Rather it is an arrangement to show how wine, speech, and music circulate, couple by couple, in a symposion. The song for Cleobulus functions in the same way as that vase painting. It sets up an association between the gods of the symposion, the person to whom the proposis is addressed, and two gifts offered within the framework of the proposis: the gift of love and the gift of the song. At the heart of the ritual itself, it combines two types of speech, the prayer to the gods, begging them to join the banquet, and the offer of the first cup of wine to one of the participants. It really is an arrangement similar to those to be found in vase paintings. Here, the arrangement depends on the way the poem is written, which adds to its beauty, just as the painting embellishes the vase.

The Double Performance of the Singer and the Love Trap

Our analysis is still not complete. Let us return to the unfolding of the symposion, on one particular day, in order to understand how, in the course of the ritual, the proposis and the invocation to the gods can take place simultaneously, in combination, and also that this poetic arrangement is not gratuitously aesthetic, but has a particular ritual purpose. The two acts are not cumulative; rather, each is conditioned by the other.

Let us return to the words that accompany the ritual of the first cup of wine and also consider the verb *propinein*. This is the technical term that can simply be pronounced on its own by the first drinker, as he offers the cup to the second, calling the latter by his name. It is all that is needed to set the wine circulating in the symposion. Pronounced in the present tense and the first person, *propinō* is thus a performative: it accompanies the ritual gesture—the sharing of the symposion's first cup of wine—describing it and completing the action that it describes.[24] In this case the poet does not actually say *propinō*, but the speech act constituted by the singing of the song has the same effect; it forms an equivalent "performative sequence."[25]

This song is performative because the one who sings it possesses the ritual power to do so. And the necessary and sufficient condition for that is to be the "I" of the situation. And in the song that we are studying, the "I" indeed makes it clear why he is singing the song: he is at once the "I" who is Dionysus's suppliant—that is to say, the poet of this beautiful song—and at the same time the "I" who is in love with Cleobulus, to whom the cup of wine is to be passed. This conjunction of the two "I"s enables the two ritual acts to mesh together.

The Prayer to Dionysus

The only explicit performative in the song, and the expression that gives it its linguistic status as a prayer, is the verb "I beg you." "I" has no name, no history, he is neither priest nor poet; it is enough that he says to Dionysus: *gounoumai se* 'I beg you'; and he becomes his suppliant because he says that is what he is and because the verb he uses to say this indeed does make him that, provided only that he also makes the required gesture. The verb *gounoumai* is a performative, the utterance of which in the first person establishes a particular relationship between the person speaking and the one addressed, provided the former grasps the latter's knees (or chin) (literally, *gounoumai se* means "I grasp your knees") in a gesture of supplication. So the legitimacy of this *gounoumai* stems solely from the ritual posture of the singer in the proposis when he raises the cup in his right hand. In addressing Dionysus, the singer does not lay hold of the altar of this deity, but instead seizes what, in this banquet, stands in for that altar, namely the cup of wine.[26]

Now, of course this gesture of supplication is simultaneously the gesture of the drinker offering the cup to Cleobulus. Two ritual gestures thus coincide: seizing the cup to pass it on to be shared and invoking Dionysus in a supplication become, through the song, one and the same action. Of course this setup makes use of a metaphor, since it ascribes a knee to a cup. But it is a metaphor that is in no way surprising, for terms of human anatomy frequently are used when speaking of the various parts of vases.[27] In some depictions of cups, the cup's stem, for instance, takes the form of a *phallos*. It was a way of illustrating the erotic meaning of the gift of the proposis: whoever received the cup accepted both the wine and the desire of the giver.

What is interesting about the poetic setup engineered by the song for Cleobulus is that such a plea to Dionysus can only be made by the participant who holds the cup at the beginning of the banquet, that is to say in the course of the ritual of the proposis. Furthermore, this prayer, which makes the singer a suppliant, changes the wine into the god, or rather makes the god present in the wine. At the beginning of the song, the singer first addresses the cup, then invokes a distant Dionysus, out in the wilderness, in a periphrase: "O Sovereign, . . . you who move among the lofty mountaintops," telling him to come and take possession of Cleobulus. Only then, in the last lines, does he address the god by his own name, "Dionysus," for now the Dionysus of banquets is present: he is the wine that Cleobulus is about to drink.

The song consists of a single sentence, organized around one verb, the linguistic performative *gounoumai* 'I beg you (grasping your knees)'. The two parts of the song, that which precedes the principal verb gounoumai and that which follows it, correspond neatly to the two parts of a Greek prayer: the first defines the invoked deity or deities within the existing situation, by recalling to mind how they intervene within the cultural space in which they are invoked, in this case a Dionysiac banquet; the second announces the object of the prayer addressed by men to the gods. Pronounced in any other context, however, these words would be ineffective, so meaningless. The only sense in these words is their religious efficacy. The song for Cleobulus is thus truly a prayer to Dionysus—not just a representation of a prayer to Dionysus—even if it is a very particular prayer, the effect of which is to make the wine god come immediately.[28] It is indissociable from the ritual context in which it is pronounced, the proposis.

A Performative Prayer

This prayer to Dionysus is one that is immediately answered, not one for which men have to await a divine response. It is performative—in other words, it brings about what it requests even as it appears to make the request—and that is because it is a song, a beautiful song offered in a proposis.

The fact that it is a prayer should not make us forget that it is also a song of seductive beauty. It is the conjunction of, on the one hand, the seduction of the proferred song and, on the other, the supplication to the wine-god that makes the song a performative prayer. To be sure, the singer formulates a request, "come . . . counsel well," but this request is at the same time a seductive gift, which the god cannot resist. "Listening" to the song, he is immediately "well disposed," out of gratitude for this gift that pleases him, and this implies that he "hears" the singer's request. The fusion of the two meanings of *epakouein* 'to hear'—the one indicating perception, the other acquiescence—expresses the immediacy of the prayer. In fact, failure for the prayer would be unimaginable, for it would be failure for the song because it lacked the musical *kharis* that, as the gift of the proposis, it is bound to introduce into the banquet.

That the singer should sing the song for Cleobulus, holding out the cup to him, is thus enough to ensure that now, at the moment when Cleobulus grasps the cup, Dionysus is there. This performativity, which could likewise be called magic, or enchantment, results from the fusion of the gesture of the proposis and the prayer to the gods of the banquet, and that fusion is brought about thanks to the poetics of the statement that is, in its turn, the linguistic manifestation of the ritual efficacy that constitutes the speech act. The poetics of the statement, in its turn, is indissociable from the musical beauty of the song, and it is the music that gives concrete form to the presence of the Muses at the banquet.

The Other Gods

The same process makes Eros actually present in the desire of the singer (*ton emon erōta*), the Nymphs actually present in the water mixed with the wine, and Aphrodite actually present in the sharing taking place between Cleobulus and the singer.

That is why the singer, through the meditation of Dionysus a supplicant of Eros, can only bring this god into the banquet by receiving him into his own body. Just as the wine in the cup makes Dionysus actually present in this banquet, the sexual desire of the singer makes Eros actually present. So the singer, to render his prayer performative, needs not only to raise the first cup of wine aloft but also to desire Cleobulus physically. Thus, his love is not the expression of a biographical "I," an anecdotal sentiment and, as such, the object of an account given in the first person. This desire is ritually necessary, just as the wine in the krater is. Any lover of Cleobulus, or of some other boy present at the banquet, would have fitted the bill equally well. For this desire for Cleobulus establishes within the person of the drinker-singer a material association between wine and desire.

When this "I" has handed the cup to Cleobulus, his ritual role will be over and he will disappear. Once he has introduced wine and desire into the symposion and has shared them, Eros and Dionysus are installed there among the banqueters.

The companionability of the gods introduced into the symposion is expressed, in accordance with the banquet categories, by the verb *sympaizousin*: "They play, act as children [literally, act as boys] together." This is not simply a poetic metaphor; what is important is the presence of the gods, perceptible in the joyful freedom of the *paides*, the boys at the banquet, intoxicated by the wine and desire in which they share (*syn*), first and foremost among them Cleobulus.

The prayer thus sets the minipantheon of the banquet instantaneously in place. There is no gap between speech and its realization. By asking them to come, the singer instantaneously installs the deities whom he names there, in the wine, the water, and the desire that are already present. He transfers that desire, wine, and water from a profane space to a sacred one, namely the symposion that is instantaneously inaugurated by music, gesture, and speech.

The song that is sung is a ritual operator that sacralizes a number of constituents essential to the symposion: wine, desire, water, couples, and music.

The Proposis

Finally, the song for Cleobulus is a performative of love. The second part of this song-prayer-offering brings about a union between the singer and Cleobulus. The imperative formula with which wine-Dionysus is addressed, "Counsel Cleobulus well . . .," should not be interpreted as a formula of demand, which is its semantic sense (it was the use of that imperative that so shocked Dio Chrysostom, who considered it lacking in the respect due to a deity). Rather, it belongs to the register of the imperatives of official consecration such as "Be henceforth man and wife . . .," imperatives that are performatives in that they themselves create the new relationship or situation: that is the pragmatic sense of this particular imperative. It is a matter of creating the Aphroditean bond that will unite the singer and Cleobulus at the end of the ritual sequence, at the moment when the boy receives from the hands of the singer both the cup and Dionysus, a moment that coincides with the song's last word, *dekhestai* 'receive, accept'. The singer says "receive my love," and Cleobulus accepts the cup. Ritually, the two are equivalent. Here too, the formula is performative. The proposis is a single whole: Cleobulus accepts the wine, the love, and the song, all at once.

Cleobulus had no choice. Placed next to the man opening the banquet, possibly the master of the house, and probably on the same bed, he had to take the cup and share the wine; to refuse to do so would have provoked a scandal, been impolite, an impiety, and the banquet would not have taken place. This gesture of sharing the wine in the presence of the assembled drinkers, which concluded the opening ritual, simultaneously made Cleobulus "officially"—at least for the duration of the banquet—the singer's "loved one," his *erōmenos*. Socially, there was no way of avoiding this. To reject the singer's gift would have been to indicate that Dionysus had not "heard" him and to prevent both the coming of the gods and the exchange of the first cup of wine. It would have been an insult to the other guests, to the singer, to the master of the house.

But it was not just a matter of respecting the rules of social civility (as, today, it is not "done" to refuse to taste one of one's hostess's specialities); for Cleobulus's love was "sincere." It was the immediate effect of his intoxication. By draining the cup, he became filled by Dionysus, for the song had brought about the sacralization of the wine, and also by Eros and Aphrodite. Inflamed by desire by the "invincible" Eros, and incited by Aphrodite to share this desire, he really would "want" (boulos) the singer's love. Had the boy's response to the song not been a consent at once spontaneous and polite, the symposion could not have begun: and that would have meant that the proferred wine was not accompanied by the gods of love, that Dionysus had not accepted the song for Cleobulus. It would have been a religious, erotic, and aesthetic disaster.

An Unreadable Song

Finally, everything in this song that stems from the "writing" of it, or you might say the "poetics," that is to say from play with the potentialities of language, serves to mount a ritual setup, the end effect of which is to bestow on the proposis an undeniable erotic implication. For Cleobulus, to reject the erotic dimension of the singer's song would be to assume the unthinkable responsibility of turning the symposion into a religious disaster. For that reason the song cannot be claimed by literature, as a poem. What is said is empty of any semantic content that can be isolated from the context. It tells only of the engineering of a religious situation, and of nothing else. It testifies neither to the singer's sentiments nor to an ironic distancing of the gods, nor to a manipulation of the public humor. There has been no attempt to distort the form of a religious hymn in order to express a "personal prayer,"[29] nor is any opposition drawn between social speech and individual speech, for both are present and are indistinguishable. Genuine love, here, takes the form of a social convention, a gesture of politeness and a religious act.

It is this ritual scene setting, fused with the poetics of the text, that makes the song so unique. Not that this scene setting is impossible to repeat, for we shall be considering other examples of it; rather, it cannot again be realized in the same terms, or for the same gods, or for the same Cleobulus. The song cannot be reused, word for word. It constitutes a statement that is indissociable from this particular speech act. To return to the water/wine dichotomy: the mixture produced in the krater, which is central to the banquet, is projected in the song as another mixture taking the form of speech/music, and the semantic meaning of the song could be said to be as stale and bland as water. And that semantic meaning is the only meaning that a reading of the song reveals, which is why reading makes Anacreon's song seem so insipid. To put that another way, to read the symposion poem is to reconstruct a symposion without its wine.

Those are two good enough reasons for wresting Anacreon's song from the literary conservatories of today's scholars. The statement itself is all that writing has preserved; its poetic character, its beauty, and its musical *kharis* stemmed purely from the event, since all their force was derived from the erotic desire shared by the singer and Cleobulus. We today cannot, without artifice, attain any aesthetic perception of them, since all we can do is read the song. In fact, the song for Cleobulus is unreadable because the event, that is to say the speech act, is not preserved in the statement, which is the only thing to which the reader has access.

But there is also a third reason for regarding the banquet song as an exclusively oral practice, namely that it expresses a cultural choice. In truth, writing, too, was present in a symposion. Some banquet vases bear inscriptions. Some of these endow the objects with words, in accordance with a well-known Greek custom.[30] One cup declares "Taleidès made me." For the potter or painter, this was a way of signing his work. Another celebrates a boy's beauty: "Kallias is beautiful." A vase may also address a drinker: "Drink me and enjoy yourself." Clearly, in these examples the writing does not serve to register an oral performance later to be reconstituted through being read; instead, it allows something that has no voice to speak. Consequently, in a symposion, writing cannot serve as an alternative to memory, a replacement for an oral transmission. Here, writing is nonorality, serving to convey the absence of a body and a voice; in some cases it constitutes an image of that absence on a vase. One of the uses of writing was to represent speech graphically. On some vases we find strings of letters that form (or do not form) intelligible (or unintelligible) words emerging from a figure's mouth.[31] When these signs *are* comprehensible, their meaning is frequently redundant. A singer announces, "I am singing" or makes some other declaration that is equally unnecessary to an interpretation of who he is or what he is doing: either unintelligible or redundant, these strings of letters simply serve to indicate that speech or singing is going on here; they "sonorize" the image by making that speech visible without, however, making it say anything in the way that a comic strip does.[32]

As Simonides tells us, in a banquet, images and singing were equivalent: "Painting is silent poetry, poetry is painting that speaks." But we should be careful when it comes to the meaning of this statement, often quoted but frequently misunderstood. Silent poetry is poetry that makes no sound, not poetry that says nothing. In this dichotomy, there is no place for poetry without music or for painting without images, that is to say for literary writing. Drawn letters representing the words of a poem only secure a place among the arts of the banquet in painted images, where they represent sound, not sense. "By making the song of the participants visible, painters integrate the dimension of sound within the visual space, drawing attention to the whole verbal and musical side of the symposion."[33]

If lyric poetry does not lend itself to reading, that is because in a banquet the eyes were absorbed with other sights: they contemplated images and derived the same delight from them as their ears did from listening to songs. Reading, even reading aloud, gives pleasure to neither eyes nor ears.

Symposion and Flamenco: Cultures of Intoxication

Song in a symposion embodied to the highest degree what I have suggested calling hot culture. That is why it is difficult to give an account of it in discursive speech, speech that is, furthermore, written. It is impossible to seize upon intoxication amid the silence of dead letters.

The best way of renewing contact with the symposion of over two thousand years ago is to go to Andalusia and be carried away in a flamenco fiesta, far from the perfumed folklore of music hall spectacles and gypsies in flounced costumes, showing off on a stage, and far from official festivals and competitions.[34]

This detour by way of southern Spain may help us to understand what symposion songs were really like, how they were experienced and transmitted, and also how they one day came to be written down and attributed to authors.

Traditional flamenco, too, incorporates wine, singing, guitars, and dancing. Families from the same quarter gather together in the evening. There are no professionals among them, even if some are regarded as great, even very great artists. They are peasants, blacksmiths, basketmakers, mothers, the unemployed. Seated on their chairs, they wait. After one or two glasses of wine, one of them starts off, the rest encourage him, urge him on, as you might blow on a spark to get a fire going: this is the *jaleo*, and it is indispensable. At first it is a rhythm created by clapping hands, a rhythm that defines a particular genre of songs (there are about forty of these to choose from). The rhythm on its own can be enough to start the dancing or singing. It comes from inside the body, moving the dancer even before it becomes audible. Over this rhythm, a flamenco guitar improvises music, a variation that is new but recognized, like all improvisations in what we call oral traditions. In the same way, the cry that suddenly bursts forth from among the listeners: "Aï . . . aï . . . i," which a woman or a man then modulates, masters, models into words and songs, is always the same yet always different. Usually, the singer remains seated, arms gently extended, hands opened to the listeners. Often the words tell of dramatic love affairs, passion, death, exile, prison; the singer's face seems to express feelings that are intense, while the dancer explodes into attitudes that are wildly paroxysmal and provocative. Then both return to their seats, separate from what they have expressed but satisfied with their performances.

The voice that sprang from deep inside them, erupting through a twisted mouth, was not an explosion of repressed passion, not misery yelling of aeons of suffering and the harshness of life. It has nothing to do with the individual: he or she is but the vehicle of an art that invades them from elsewhere and in which they do not express themselves personally. All aficionados agree that the words, the *letra*, are of little importance. "The singer is more concerned with the way of singing, that is to say the rhythm and the form that he gives his song, than with its content, the meaning of the song itself: the message from the *cantaor* to the audience is conveyed not by its semantic content but by its underlying rhythm and melody."[35]

Flamenco is not something that any of them have learned. They will all tell you that it came to them through their family and the best of them may reconstruct long genealogies to show how it was passed down, sometimes skipping out an entire generation. They have not learned the music or even, in some cases, to read or write. But the children are there, in the fiestas, from their earliest infancies, immersed in flamenco. Even before they can walk, they are clapping their hands, as babies also do to Sufi music. And in the streets of Jerez, they play at dancing.

The art transmitted and practiced thus fluctuates with each region of Andalusia, each poor quarter of Seville, proud of its own style. New ways of performing arise, then die, affected by the group's prosperity, opportunities, the impact of a new inventive musician, who leaves his mark, then disappears. Particular families reign for a while. And flamenco, like all popular art, expresses an endless nostalgia. Its evanescent plasticity and the fading memory of past festivals produce a sense of irreparable loss that in truth is simply a consciousness of time, spurring children on to outstrip their fathers, so as to prove to themselves and to others that the present exists.

The tension between, on the one hand, the memories and endlessly repeated stories of the elderly and, on the other, the desire of the young to shine, in their turn, imparts dynamism to this hot culture and strength to its fragility. Popular art, oral traditions are totally socialized. There would be no flamenco without large families in which complex transmissions can take place, from uncles to nephews, and from grandfathers to grandsons. So it is that the innovations of a third or fourth generation turn out to be a return to a tradition that is purer, or claims to be, discovered from some aged relative. Popular art is regulated by society; society is life and death to it, is its living memory. Once the state meddles, slotting it into history, it dies.

"Flamenco is neither a distraction, a spectacle, nor an art,"[36] which is why a written flamenco, a fixed flamenco, noted down, organized by rules, taught in schools, theorized by professors, transposed to theaters, the object of competitions, is not flamenco at all: neither for those who sing and dance it nor for those who listen to it. Flamenco in a theater calls to mind all those "popular ballets" of the former Soviet Union, in which the subjects of the Russian Empire, Caucasians or Tatars, wrenched from their own cultures and disguised as kolkhozians and Soviet labor heroes, were dressed up in multicolored cottons and leaped about to fiendish rhythms. They were all the same, embodying Moscow's idea of popular art, more athletic than cultivated, to the accompaniment of a variety of musics blended by orchestration.

Fixity, rigidity, and restrictiveness do not result from tradition, but on the contrary from popular art being recorded and transcribed. Transcription forces it into another kind of time, a time of stagnation and discontinuity. Conservation in conservatories does not take on the risk of life or oblivion. It hands over to specialists control over an art whose rules are unknown to its spectators.

A traditional art such as flamenco, on the contrary, makes no hard and fast distinction between artists and public. They all, to varying degrees, practice the art, whether or not they are conscious of who is the best at it. The singers and dancers do not perform on a stage. They sing from one of the chairs arranged in a ring, or leaning against a door. An old woman begins to dance as she sits, but may never move into the center of the circle. It all depends on how she feels, the encouragement from the others, a glass of wine more or less. Not that much is drunk in flamenco—at least not to the point where wine takes over—but they do drink regularly, out of thirst, to celebrate, for energy.

But some are recognized as the best and possess a fame that reaches beyond their own quarter and neighborhood. These are much in demand for fiestas. Although not really professionals, they end up devoting more time to flamenco than to their work. The major centers of flamenco organize gatherings and all the best performers go to them, for the sake of encountering a larger public that includes acute connoisseurs. They go there for glory, for the glory of their families. The ritual does not change. The circle of chairs simply expands to the dimensions of a plaza or a large patio. And they know that only the very best will sing and dance. At the end of a performance there is applause. Victory is never formalized. But everyone goes home with the memory of whoever was really the best of all.

The unfolding of a symposion may be imagined along the lines of these flamenco fiestas. A single voice would be lifted in song in the same way from the circle of drinkers and, as with the flamenco singers, that voice came from elsewhere, it was a song for the occasion, a song from tradition; the voice was in no sense used to express the singer. The first song that spurts forth launches the fiesta, and is then answered by others. "Holy Maria, free me from my sorrows. . . . When you are not there, my life is no life, I prefer to die. . . ." The singer, mouth twisted, voice breaking, is a tubby father with a family, well sheltered from the agonies of the heart. "Dionysus, make Cleobulus accept my love. . . ." The prayer of the Greek drinker was just as conventional as that of the gypsy singer. The words were equally unimportant, for the essence of the festivity lay elsewhere.

The parallel between the symposion and the flamenco fiesta is not a full-blown theory. It simply helps us, twenty centuries later, to imagine in some detail the unfolding of that reality in Greek culture, which we have reconstructed intellectually under the generic heading of symposion. What flamenco presents to us is a different way of being human beings, provided we pay attention to the little nothings that constitute as it were the binding fabric of the culture.

Flamenco thus helps us to reconstruct a vivid image of what the sociability of a symposion may have felt like, and how a common memory was created through it. Frédéric Deval tells us that those who have taken part in a fiesta retain an amazingly precise memory of the event. Years after, they recall who was there and who drank, ate, said, and did what.[37] They will speak of it later, with friends, and their common memory creates a unique togetherness. Forgetting implies not having enjoyed it, not having really related to it, having been bored. The important thing is to have been there, with everyone, on that day. This culture of tiny details imparts an intensity to everyday minutiae, magnifying them and imbuing them with an affective memory. That is how it is that flamenco is rooted in the banalities of daily life: there is no separation between the sublime technique of the greatest of singers and ordinary, everyday objects: the rush-seated chair and glass of manzanilla are indissociable from the same culture. In similar fashion, the images of the Greek symposion link together a guest's sandals, the jug of wine, and the inspired song of the drinker.

The flamenco fiesta also helps one to understand how impossible it was to be present without taking part, that to remain withdrawn and politely cold would have been the worst of insults to all present, that everyone there had a duty to be sincere.[38] In a flamenco fiesta, anyone who does not clap to keep the rhythm going or does not interject an *olé* or an *eso es*—"that's the way"—into the song sidelines himself and wounds his friends. He is regarded as too snooty to feel the flamenco, to respond to it, to let himself go with it as if improvising it himself, to be carried away by joy or sadness, nostalgia or grief, depending on the form taken by the soaring song. This is all reminiscent of the code for the symposion drinkers: they had to identify with the flow of the ritual, go along with their companions in the ritual of intoxication. The *jaleo,* the means of spurring on the singer to greater virtuosity in his improvisation, supporting him and guiding him, gives concrete meaning to what we call collective creation. Alone, without the fiesta, the singer could never have produced such a song. All of which shows that linguistic notions of speech acts and speech-act contexts are more than empty ideas.

Finally, the flamenco fiesta enables us to grasp the nature of the ardor that would seize the symposion drinkers, an ardor that enabled them to sing divinely, filling the banqueters with a sense of the sacred. In a symposion, the ardor was not the ritual possession that took over Homeric bards, the priests of the Muses, nor was it that which took hold of Bacchae or dithyrambic choruses[39] assailed by veritable shamanistic visions. Symposion drinkers, like flamenco singers, were neither voodoo priests nor prophetic visionaries. Yet, on occasion, something would happen that was sparked by the sacred. The gypsies call it *duende* 'spirit, divinity, genius'. *Duende* cannot be defined, but will certainly be recalled.[40] Every performance of *cante* is an anticipation: will the miracle happen? Will the ritual create that "obliviousness to time, obliviousness to place, . . . that unforgettable moment when human togetherness is experienced? . . . The respect, almost a holy awe, that seizes you each time, at every moment of true *cante* is a tangible sign of that something that is happening or that might happen . . . that something that does not always happen. Everything is made ready, arranged, set in order so that it will. . . . But Flamenco is not a consequential art: there is no inevitability about it, no amount of meticulous organization can produce that shiver, *duende* never follows automatically. . . . Recipes for success abound; but even when followed, they may not be enough. Conversely, sometimes, even when not wholly respected, they nevertheless do allow something to happen." Ardor either comes or it does not, you do not seek it out for yourself: you can sing perfectly agreeably without *duende*, just as you could drink without intoxication and without Dionysus, but "it's not the real thing." And when that ardor does come, everybody "goes home from the fiesta feeling that he or she has been revealed to his or her true nature."

Frédéric Deval tells of a fiesta in Labriga in which he missed out on the *duende*. The fiesta began, a great singer was there, El Funi—but nothing happened. "People drank, talked, waited, ate, cracked jokes; then there was more playing, singing, dancing"; still nothing. The narrator fell asleep on a couch. He awoke at midday, the next morning, to learn "that at seven o'clock in the morning, in the presence of the entire gypsy community of Labriga, El Funi had suddenly, for the space of a few, long, unforgettable moments, been *really* shattering. Surrounded by the gypsies who loved him and whom he loved, he had truly *represented* the collective soul of Labriga." Nothing remained, or could remain, of the event (*duende* cannot be recorded on a tape any more than it can be written down), nothing but the memories of those who had heard him and supported him and who would never forget. Because of those memories, the other singers present would never again sing in quite the same way and the rest of those present had a new color in their lives.

Literary history has nothing to say about that song of El Funi's on that day in Labriga; nor, similarly, can we do anything with Anacreon's poems written down on paper. A Greek symposion has no literature to hand down to us, just as reading the *coplas* of a flamenco song can be of no more than a purely documentary interest. Furthermore, the *cante* defy analysis as prosody. To borrow Nagy's categories again, flamenco singing precedes the phase when disjunction occurs between (written) music and (written) poetry, a stage that came to pass through Lorca in the case of poetry and Manuel de Falla in that of music. Artificially isolated from the performance by being written down on paper, the texts cannot be analyzed in prosodic terms: flamenco has no poetics, for this is not written poetry. Even if the texts are transcribed in verse, sometimes using assonance (a *copla* contains one, two, or more often three or four lines), the song takes no notice of those divisions, and the breaks that lend emphasis to the dramatization of the short narrative of each *copla*—in four phases or *tercios*, with modulations, cries, repetitions of particular words or syllables—seldom coincide with the ends of those lines.[41] This means that the transcription into verses is simply a writing convention.

"Flamenco cannot be explained or described. It is felt, savored, appreciated, is beguiling, . . . or is boring."[42] The same could be said of the Greek symposion, had it not disappeared from our lives centuries ago. But given that it has disappeared and we can no longer savor it or feel it, what can the Greek symposion have to offer us if it finds a place in our imaginary representation of the history of the Western world? It might reawaken a taste for the shifting, living cultures in which permanent creation is for everyone and in which to be cultivated means not to have read all the books but to be able to play one's part in a traditional fiesta. It might put us back in touch with the magnificence of an everyday life transfigured by collective rituals. Let us hope that the rediscovery of the symposion gets us to reevaluate popular culture and reflect upon the uses of its transfiguring power in the light of this Greek culture of a collective intoxication that linked men together in both space and time, taking them out of themselves and their own little problems to give them, for the duration of the festivity, a different, divine, body.

This association of the symposion song with Flamenco may help us to see that an oral culture can never be pinned down by any linguistic definition that simply opposes it to a written culture: the culture of the symposion was a culture of the entire body, sociability, and pleasure, and the three were indissociable. The poetry for banquets involved not meaning but action. For that reason, no writing-reading could possibly either preserve or transmit the culture to which it belonged.

TWO

The Invention of Anacreon

ARCHAEOLOGISTS OF WORDS are not as lucky as archaeologists of things: the latter are not, in general, expected to explain the survival of a shard of pottery discovered in one place or another. Wars, fires, and exoduses usually leave behind them a number of objects in ruined houses or abandoned tombs. Buried beneath the rubble, then under the dust of centuries, they subsequently reappear by accident in a furrow made by a plow, a ditch alongside a road, or an excavation site.

Oral speech, in contrast, never emerges from oblivion by accident. The Romans petrified in their everyday attitudes by the lava from Vesuvius bear silent witness to first-century Pompei. Archaeologists of words have to deal with the written traces left by their sonorous objects. For the ancients had to play their part, had to decide to transcribe some of those banquet songs, those unique and ephemeral performances normally destined to disappear without trace. Someone must have first memorized them, then—either he or another—written them down, for Dio Chrysostom one day to copy out the song for Cleobulus and include it in one of his own writings, thereby transmitting it over a gap of seventeen centuries. How did this literally unreadable text come to be written down? For what different type of reading was it intended? And finally (and this is the principal puzzle), how did this drinker's improvisation come to be preserved as the work of a famous poet, a specialist—if not professional—of banquet songs? Who invented Anacreon, the author of the Anacreontic songs and inventor of the Anacreontic genre?

City Culture and Panhellenic Culture

The question that the preservation of banquet songs raises is also raised by the rest of archaic Greek poetry, whether epic, choral songs, or lyric monodies. Answering it involves explaining how it is that such a small portion of that poetry has survived and why most of what was produced vocally in Greece disappeared. For neither the loss nor the preservation of such works was a matter of chance.

That, at least, is the opinion of Gregory Nagy, the great American Greek scholar. It is based on a subtle reconstruction of the events that led up to the modern invention of Greek literature.[1] He believes that what happened was as follows.

From the eighth century B.C. to the fourth, Greece, within the framework of community cults—for example, the Olympic Games and the Panathenaea—proceeded to make a systematic selection from among the oral performances of the traditional culture. Singers came from every side to take part in these competitions, category by category. The judges listened to epics, hymns, paeans celebrating Apollo, dithyrambs in honor of Dionysus, choral songs, banquet songs. The victors in the poetry contests won glory for themselves and for their cities, just as the winning athletes did, and their performances became memorable (although that does not mean that they were necessarily written down or even memorized in their original form). They became models in the eyes of all Greeks, the epitome (that year, at least) of the best that could be produced in the genre. A deliberate policy of modelization was thus adopted. A song would be uprooted, wrenched from the event that it would normally have produced, and, for the duration of the competition, would become an object of theoretical assessment. A banquet song presented in a competition was not listened to in the course of a symposion, nor was it sung by a symposion drinker. It was not perceived as a performance, but became the ideal of a particular kind of song.

In technical terms, a festival song was decontextualized from the banquet, then recontextualized in the competition. You could also say that, for the song in the competition, the banquet represented a fictitious speech act, since the competition now became the context of the real speech act.

The first of those two formulations assumes there to be a symmetry between the banquet and the competition, and a textualization of the statement: that is the point of view of writing. The second introduces a dissymmetry, with no textualization of the statement: this is the point of view of orality. Only the fictitious speech act is suited to the statement, so the real speech act has to be defined institutionally in order to make it possible for the statement to be received in this unsuitable situation. As I see it, that is where the historical break occurs: between the statement and the speech act, not between orality and writing.

Gregory Nagy's historical reconstruction is all the more persuasive in that it prefigures, and is not inspired by, the history of the decline of flamenco, beginning in the nineteenth century but above all taking place today, in the late twentieth century. For the great threat to Andalusian gypsy singing lies in its transformation into a spectacle and its universalization. Created amid a rejected minority and restricted to the *gitanerias*, flamenco retained its strength of improvisation so long as it remained an art form unknown to the majority. The singer never sought to please; his relations with his public were those of mutual gratitude—that is, of love and complicity within a small social unit, the family or the quarter where they all lived.

When the gypsies were granted the same rights as other men, in the eighteenth century, the Spaniards discovered their songs and their dancing and "flamencism" became all the rage. Torn from the gypsy fiesta, taken over by respectable people and turned into a form of theater, flamenco lost its ardor, lost its *duende*. A recital was no longer a festivity in which anything might happen. It was reduced to the technical execution of fixed forms, rhythms, and words. The singers exhibited themselves in festivals and competitions. The theoreticians took a hand, wrote the history of flamenco, reconstructed a poetics for the *coplas*, collected texts for fear they would be lost, and produced recorded anthologies. Monumental preservation took the place of oral transmission and, for the second time, after the festivals and competitions, dealt a deathblow to the singers' ability to improvise, for improvisation had lain at the heart of their memories. It reduced the number of models to those in most frequent use, and blocked new creativity. The listeners, seated in serried rows before a stage, as the Greek spectators at Delphi or Olympia used to be seated, were present as an audience but did not take part in this spectacle prepared in advance. There would be no event.

The twentieth-century misfortunes of flamenco give us a better understanding of what may have happened to the traditional songs of Greek culture, not as a result of a transition from orality to writing, but because of a shift from a culture of improvised creations to one of modelization.

Singers of Movement

A Homeric bard was neither a poet nor a musician, but a singer inspired by the Muses: he produced ritual speech acts, thanks to the cithara music that possessed him. Without that context, he could do nothing. And the culture for which he was a vehicle rejected all other forms of music and poetry, for they could only lead men to their doom. That is what the myth of the Sirens told. Any seafarer who sailed by their island and listened to their songs would succumb, irresistibly seduced by their beauty (*kharis*), would forget his duties as a sailor, and would sail straight on to their reefs. His bones would whiten on the beach along with those of all the other imprudent music lovers. Lured by the pure music of voices, without hearing the words of their song, the seafarer shipwrecked on the coast of the island of the Sirens (birds with the heads of women whom nobody had ever seen or ever would, just as nobody had ever heard their songs or ever would) is the mythical reverse of the contented banqueter listening to the bard.

That is why no bard or symposion drinker would ever sing except at a banquet, would never sing in any place where Dionysus or the Muses were not there to inspire the poet.

A bard was not the author of his song, just its vehicle, and what was expressed through him was the voice of the Muse; likewise, the banquet drinker sang only because he was intoxicated or in love, possessed by Eros and Dionysus, who for a few moments allowed him new, ephemeral capacities. The fame of a bard was attached to his person, not to the traces left by his performances. What was expected of him was that he should create an event. And the success of his performance did not depend solely on him; a public with talent was also needed. His song was constructed in an interaction between him and his listeners. Each work was tailor-made for the occasion. Each bard would certainly have his own special subjects and, from the interminable lists of proper names that he stored in his memory—the names of heroes, towns, gods, divine or human genealogies—would propose a particular name and, attached to that name, a narrative unit, such as "Odysseus's return," "Agamemnon's return," "Dolon's exploit," "the anger of Achilles," "the death of Patroclus," "the death of Hector." His public would prefer a story that featured a local god, a nearby sanctuary, a neighboring dynasty. So each performance would take local idiosyncrasies into account.

The tale of the Trojan War was told throughout Greece, but each royal palace expected a different version from the bard, each little king on his own little island would want to hear that one of his own ancestors was the true conqueror of Troy: in northern Greece, they celebrated Achilles' slaying of Hector, around Ithaca and Corcyra they would speak mostly of Odysseus and his horse, in Sparta the blonde Menelaus was the hero, in Argos it was Agamemnon, the king of kings. An episode created for one particular place could never be used elsewhere. So there was a multitude of versions, each making the most of the partialities of its audience. Some were centered on cunning intelligence and were intended for audiences of seafarers (from these the travels of Odysseus have come down to us), others on erotic seduction, others on grief and mourning, on hospitality, on the techniques of archery, on nocturnal warfare or the art of naval carpenters (producing the episode of the wooden horse of Troy). The bards were responsible for the memories of the whole of Greek culture, in all its aspects. But today we can do no more than imagine this wealth of stories and songs that reflected every shade of Greece, for the greater part has disappeared.

This bardic culture was produced by a society that relied totally on the memory of its singers, on their skill passed down in sanctuaries of the Muses, independent of any political institution. A singer, like a prophet or a herald, was protected by the gods and sheltered from the violence of men of power. As a master of truth, the bard would communicate with the mother of the Muses, the goddess Mnemosyne, whose name made her the Memory of the world. His song, in the here and now (or, rather, the there and then) would convey a truth that was always partial, always fleeting, for that was the only kind of truth there was for men. His words applied only to the present moment, so did not need to be preserved. Knowledge was not amassed by capitalizing on partial truths. Rather, men would catch a lightning glimpse of it by acceding to divine Memory for the short space of the singing of a song.

The infinite diversity of epic songs in that very ancient Greece corresponded to the infinite diversity of the social units into which people were collected, and of the cultural forms that organized their lives. It was precisely that double diversity that the city and panhellenism set out to put in order.

The Politicopoetic Order

Around the eighth century, Greek society organized itself according to a different model: the city-state, or *polis*. Each city aimed to be totally independent of its neighbors, was defined by a territory that it prevented others from using, an urban center, and its own sanctuaries and gods, deities identified with the *polis*. In Argos this deity was Hera, in Athens Athena, in Corinth Aphrodite. Each city furthermore had a specific dialect, attached to one or other of the major dialectal families of Greek, such as Dorian or Ionian. Finally, the citizens of a particular town were proud to have customs that were different from those of their neighbors and would boast of their own. Aristophanes draws an amusing caricature of these Greeks all cultivating their own distinctive characteristics: a Spartan was a pederast and sinister, a Theban was stupid and greedy, an Athenian was a liar and loquacious.

The old days had been characterized by an infinite diversity, with each tiny social group differing from the rest in subtle, constantly changing ways, "ways of saying things and ways of doing things" that varied from one place to another, shifting in time, responsive to events, fixed by no rules or institutions. These ways were now replaced by—or, more frequently, had superimposed on them—clear-cut distinctions founded in the first instance on a particular political regime and its laws but thereafter also on collective cultural institutions such as, in Athens for example, theatrical spectacles. City culture replaced a culture of neighborhoods.

By claiming a common identity, each city in effect denied the differences that characterized the various elements—villages, tribes, and clans—of which it was composed, even preventing some from preserving their own traditions. In the absence of laws, public opinion exercised a relentless censorship in order to impose a norm. We know, for example, that Athenian aristocrats had retained the Ionian custom of wearing their hair long, drawn into a chignon and secured with a golden clasp in the form of a cicada. The common folk of Athens poured sarcasm on these knights whom they found it difficult to regard as their fighting comrades. Hoplites from Marathon and oarsmen from Piraeus wore their hair short. Those long-haired men had the look of foreigners: maybe they were plotting treachery. Conversely, a custom peculiar to a particular group or place might spread to the community as a whole, as did the Dionysiac symposion, in Athens. From being the prerogative of the Ionian aristocracy, it came to be adopted by Athenians in general, as a distinctive practice with which they identified.[2]

Every city became a theater of conflict of varying degrees of violence between social idiosyncrasies and state unification. Poetic culture was split in two. While traditional singing persisted in banquets and local festivals, the city promoted synthetic forms of it, put on for the people as a whole, the best-known example being Athenian drama.[3] This was the birth of state culture, as opposed to popular culture. A postulate of this state culture was the existence of a unified public. Socially, this did not exist. The people as a public was a purely political creation.

A Theoretical Greece

In parallel to this centrifugal fragmentation of Greece, in which each city displayed its own particular character, a centripetal movement was creating a Hellenic community around institutions that were common to all Greeks. The most ancient of these were the Delphic oracles, the Olympic Games, and the Homeric poems. Historians call this movement panhellenism. The Delphic oracles fixed the geographical location of a prophetic Memory common to all Greeks. The Homeric poems became the common epic, the poetic Memory, the repository of culture and the sole educative handbook for all Greek children. And the Olympic Games not only created a pilgrimage for Greeks, every four years, but furthermore introduced a common time for them, since the games provided the only means of dating outside the political time of each city: in Athens, for example, a year was designated by the name of one of its archons, an eponymous archon. On this model, other panhellenic sanctuaries, such as Epidauros, were then created, and other competitions, at Delphi and at Corinth; and all the canonical works of poetry became fixed.

By reason of its taste for liberty, Greece did not produce common political institutions, but it did create a unified culture. As we have seen at the level of the city, panhellenism established a self-referential culture, by eliminating differences as though they were deviations from a norm, and thereby elaborated a single, synthetic model. The process is particularly visible in the way that the myths attached to a particular hero or god, all telling the same story, were sifted out. It was now thought that for each hero there was one true, correct version, and all the rest were false, mere fables and stories. One of the tasks assigned to poets was to recover that ideal, single version.

This panhellenic Greece was to produce a theoretical, monumental, and abstract Greece, as it were the greatest common denominator of all the Greek peoples.

The function of the festivals and the competitions was to operate a selection and produce a synthesis of the cultural forms considered to be constitutive of Hellenism, in the course of performances in which the representatives of the various cities competed with one another. Poetry and singing were treated in the same way as racing and wrestling. The spectacle that was presented was a contest before judges (*kritai*), and their decision (*kritis*) picked out the performance most likely to elicit the most widespread consensus from all the peoples of Greece. To be sure, the periodic nature of these competitions implies that the Greeks had not yet reached the point of seeking to establish a canon of exemplary works. The winning performance remained an event: it was the performance that won the crown, not the text that was recited. The latter was not intended to be preserved as a model, although it did sometimes happen that the poet inscribed it on a stele or a bronze and presented it as an ex-voto offering in thanks for his victory, to one of his city's gods, as he would have presented his discus had he won the discus-throwing contest. The text was valued not for itself but as an image of the victorious performance.[4]

In some cities, however, it happened that even these poetry contests died out once a text, having been definitively fixed, became the object of a solemn recitation, or even a reading. They turned into contests of diction. It comes as no surprise to find that it was a tyrant, Hipparchus of Athens, who was eventually the first to sanction the state's confiscation of epic, by having the *Iliad* and the *Odyssey* set down in writing and recited annually on the occasion of the Panathenaea by a string of "poets" who performed in relay.

The Festival Culture

From then on, there were two poetic cultures in Greece, the one traditional and shifting, epitomized by the culture of banquets, the other modern and institutional, the culture of festivals. The latter was a characteristic feature of individual city-states as well as of panhellenic Greece. This festival culture remained a culture of festivity and events, even though it was not fitted to be a culture of musical or Dionysiac intoxication. But it also represented a decisive stage in the process of fixing canonical texts definitively and inventing authors. It was in this way that the song for Cleobulus came to be preserved under the name of a certain Anacreon.

The Author as a Cultural Guarantor

Performances in a poetry or singing competition had nothing to do with the pleasures of a banquet. The Muses were absent and so, also, was the irresistible seduction of their *kharis*. When the public listened to an epic poem or a banquet song in a competition, it did not respond to it as a banqueter in Ithaca or as one of Cleobulus's drinking companions. It judged it from afar. Even if it derived pleasure from it, that pleasure was not the same: there was no intoxication. Instead of this being a chance for him to escape from himself and experience otherness, a spectator at a competition listening to the song for Cleobulus constructed for himself an identity as an Athenian or a Greek, or both at once. But who could stand as guarantor for the poem's beauty and power, for its *kharis?* Only an author.

Poetic models were elaborated as traditional performances of popular Greek culture went under. It is not hard to reconstruct the phenomenon if one studies the changes that epic underwent. The former banquet singer, familiar to us as the Homeric bard, literally fell apart. The priest of the Muses who used to be "author-composer-interpreter," all at once, performing his triple function in the singing of his song, at the center of the banquet, was now replaced by a number of separate speech and music technicians. Some were purely performers, operating for the duration of the performance: these were the rhapsodes. Others operated separately, in advance of the performance, preparing for it by either producing a text or composing some music—that is to say, either as poets or as musicians. (For the lyric genre, the rhapsode would be replaced by a cithara player or a flute player. These would sing and play either a recorder [*aulos*], or else a stringed instrument, a lyre, cithara, or *barbitos*.)

The point is that all the actors in these new kinds of performances in competitions distanced themselves from the song or poem that they presented to the audience, making no claims to be anything but performers. They effaced themselves before whoever had been the first actor in this process, an inventor-hero whom they traced back to the very earliest days of the city, claiming for themselves no poetic or musical skill. All they themselves did was find a way to sing a text by some mythical author, Homer, Archilochus, or Anacreon, the inventor of whatever genre it happened to be. It was the authority of this mythical "author" that underpinned the performances of his disciples.

Consequently, the author, the one to whom a poem was attributed, was not the poet. The same applied for music: the composer hid behind a mythical musician such as Terpander or Olympus, the inventors of the flute and the seven-stringed lyre respectively.

The way in which epic was presented in these competitions is particularly revealing of this change that implied the invention of an author. Epic was no longer sung but was recited. Those who recited it were called rhapsodes; the literal meaning of the Greek word was "stitchers of songs." That, at least, was what they claimed to be: the interpreters of poems that they themselves had not composed, even though they certainly had recomposed them. Those poems were now said to be the work of some divine and untouchable poet. The Homeridae, for example, all attributed the poems that they recited to a founding ancestor by the name of Homer. So it was the poem that became the center of the performance, rather than the man who was reciting it and was an integral part of it and inseparable from it. The guarantor of the poem was thus no longer its singer but the one whom we would call its "author," or rather the one with the authority to defend the poem who, without being its author in the modern sense, was the person at the origin of new speech that was a part of him. Homer was, by definition, the greatest of absentees.

More generally, whether he was called Homer or Anacreon, this invariably absent author was a theoretical Greek whom it was necessary to identify with his poems just as it was necessary to identify his poems with Hellenism. For that reason, the works entered in the panhellenic competitions tended increasingly, with each performance, to eliminate anything that could tie them to any particular time or place, until eventually the language would sometimes become an incredible patchwork of dialects. Every Greek city yearned to win, through its victories, the right to represent the very acme of a particular genre. To that end, its poets would deliberately censor themselves in order to offer to all Greeks works that the latter would be able to adopt, and thereby to establish their own monopoly over those works.

Thanks to the efforts of the Homeridae, the Homeric epic of the people of Chios was more successful than any other and became the only version in which Greeks would eventually recognize themselves. Some schools of rhapsodes resisted this imperialism for a long time, committing their destiny to one particular city. Thus the Creophyleians of Samos produced the only version of the Trojan epic officially recognized by Sparta, while the rhapsodes of Boeotia put together a panhellenic theogony for Greece, that is to say a theological epic, under the name Hesiod, in which no individual city could find its own particular mythology but with which every city could identify.

In this way, an imaginary Greece, ideal and abstract, was constructed, with its own mythical authors, a Greece that served as a collective image of Hellas as a whole and the epitome of which each city, town, and family could consider itself to be, in that it constituted a contextual variant or a localized version of it. It is this trompe l'oeil representation of Greece that the historians bring us, a cultural fiction that the Greeks themselves constructed. In fairness to those historians, it should be added that they could hardly have done otherwise since for the most part the "literary" documents that had been preserved were theoretical models, even if it is sometimes possible for us to set real bodies in place of those abstract models, thanks to the analysis of archaeological remains and epigraphical inscriptions.

But that is not to suggest that the Athenians, Spartans, Thebans, and Milesians who attended the poetic festivals of Delphi or Olympia did not truly consider themselves as Greeks. They really did regard these as consensual festivals and did identify with the image presented, confident that to do so was to demonstrate how cultured they were. They believed in Homer, Hesiod, and Anacreon as they believed in their gods, for both groups vouched for their culture.

Real Speech Acts and Fictitious Speech Acts

We must imagine a passive public that expressed no opinion on either the choice or the length of the poems that were recited. It was just a public at a spectacle. It attended but did nothing else: its members neither ate nor drank nor courted those seated next to them. Each spectator sat there in the position of a citizen at an assembly. The places where these spectacles were held reproduced the symbolic form of a circle, which symbolized political equality. All the citizens were positioned at an equal distance from the center, where the speech on which they were required to pass judgment was pronounced: in political life, that speech would consist of laws; in a competition, it would be a poem or a song. That is why odeons, like theaters, were circular. The poem or song to which the audience listened already existed before it was performed publicly, for the competition was not an occasion for inspiration, rather a place where theoretical works were put to the test. There was a distinction between the statement and the speech act. The real speech act—the competition—accommodated a statement that had been produced earlier, outside this speech act. But that statement bore the marks of another speech act, a fictitious one, namely—in the case of an epic—a Homeric banquet. And that speech act was doubly fictitious: for one thing, the public at the competition had to imagine it; for another, the statement, even if it had been generated in a real banquet, had since then been revised and reworked by a number of poets, until it acquired the requisite degree of neutrality, shedding the marks of the event that had produced it. From this point of view, the poets were creating statements as fictitious as the texts of the *Iliad* and the *Odyssey* that have come down to us.

The alternative between real speech acts and fictitious ones was from this point on to be a constant feature of ancient cultures. And it is that dichotomy that, for ourselves, will mark the boundary between hot culture and cold culture, between popular culture and institutional culture. In short, if we are looking for a historical origin for literature that is rooted in the way that texts were received, it could be that that origin lies not in writing, but in the switch from real speech acts that produced statements to fictitious ones.

This dislocation of the speech-act process, as defined from the point of view of its reception, is inseparable from a particular type of production. The separation introduced between the production of a statement and its speech act implied a disjunction between poetry and music and also the elaboration of a technique of poetic composition that enabled the poets, however much they declared themselves to be mere rhapsodes, to recompose the text of memorized songs. They had to imitate the creative act of the bard in the absence of the Muses, to produce poetry in vitro rather than in vivo. That is why they elaborated poetics that divided their songs into parts, allowing them to rework each of these in isolation from the rest. The art of metrics developed in this way. One can see how this process was eventually to lead to Aristotle's *Poetics*. Concurrently, the art of musical composition was developing. Although the earliest rhapsodes seem to have merely recited the epic, soon the general tendency was to reintroduce music to accompany the recomposed texts. This musical art, about which little is known today, appears to have been considerably more complex than Greek poetics.[5]

Transcription and Inscription: Poetry That Evolved and Poetry with Variants

The selection operated by successive contests maintained the reductionist process initiated by the festival culture and ended up by determining for each genre *one* mythical poet founder—that is, model works supposed to have been composed by him but of course improved upon year by year by the competitors. The poet and the poems became indistinguishable. Thus Homer became the official epic of Greece, thanks to the Homeridae, the rhapsodes who specialized in Homer, and despite the desperate efforts of their rivals who sang the songs of Arctinus of Miletus or Creophylus of Samos. Initially, Homer had probably been the cultural hero of a college of priests of the Muses on the island of Chios, known by the emblematic title of "he who gathers together," a semantic doublet of an epithet used for the Muses, *arteipeiai* 'those who assemble words'. Later, the Homeridae, that is to say a particular school of rhapsodes, made this Homerus their mythical ancestor, the inventor of the "Homeric" epic that sang of the Trojan War and the return of the victorious Achaeans. Eventually Homer became the author of the *Iliad* and the *Odyssey* and people would say "Homer" when they wished to refer to those two poems. Finally, the poems were fixed in writing at the command of the tyrant of Athens, which thus became the proprietor of Homer. How should this fixing of poetry in writing be understood, in the context of Greek culture?

More generally, it has been established that there existed, in the historical period, sanctuaries consecrated to the mythical heroes of oral poetry. One such was the Archilocheion on Paros,[6] where, from the sixth century B.C. on, the Parians maintained a cult of the poet Archilochus. The cult involved ritual readings of the poet's work written on his funerary monument.[7] These works were inscriptions, read out loud word by word. It was a way of making the poet live again, breathing new life into his words, just as traditional libations restored strength to the poor, parched dead. But, as Aesop's fable and the epigrams of the *Palatine Anthology* repeatedly point out, the written characters "killed" the voice, a written poem entombed its poet. The singing man was forgotten, while the words that he had sung were memorized and a statue was raised to the dead poet. The function of writing on stones was always to allow mute material, or someone absent, to speak. In this instance it served to bring the past back to life, to repeat words now extinguished and preserved like a corpse mummified within the writing. Here, to read was to commemorate. But these written songs would be read, not sung, repeated but in isolation from the event that had prompted them. The music and the body had been lost; and the tomb and the lines inscribed upon it spoke only of absence and death, even if they proclaimed the fame of the dead man. To recite or read the verse written on the stone was a way of prolonging the *kleos* of the poet so that his name and words should still resound among men;[8] but it was not a way of getting a work known.

Transcription in books was quite a different matter from inscription on a tombstone or the walls of a sanctuary. For festivals were themselves events. The written words would be recontextualized, probably with a number of variations introduced. In fact, it seems doubtful whether these written poems constituted a single definite text. In view of the large number of variants that have come down to us in manuscripts, in all probability, for the ancients, a poem fixed in writing was not a recorded poem but represented a number of potential performances, all considered to be equivalent.[9] The use of writing did not automatically imply textualization in the modern sense of the term, a fixing of the poem, word by word. Instead, a recorded performance would suggest a whole series of different readings, and each of those "readings," in its own particular context, would shift the statement slightly in one direction or another. However, that hypothesis of variation relates only to written transcriptions; it could hardly apply in the case of written inscriptions or tomb poems. The reading of such an inscription made the reader subservient to the signifier; he had to speak words engraved by the dead poet. In contrast, the reader of a transcription voiced a different signifier, for he had appropriated the words of the dead man and made them his own, altering them if necessary.

The difference between transcription and inscription is an important one, for each implies a different kind of reading. A reading of an inscribed poem, which scrupulously respected the terms of the statement, made the dead poet the subject of the speech act, using the reader to perpetuate his fame by making his (the poet's) voice and name resound. The signifier was textualized, even if the meaning was of little importance. Poems spoken again and again in this fashion corresponded to the exhibition of the discus used by a victor in the discus-throwing contest. People would look at it each time they passed; they did not repeat the exploit themselves, but celebrated it. Transcription, which gave rise to variable readings, did not turn written words into a text that imposed its discourse upon the reader, for the variations that the latter introduced would change its semantic meaning in order to obtain the same pragmatic meaning. Traditional epic was constantly evolving, for it belonged totally to orality, and each performance involved a recomposition. The festival culture, which created models with guarantors, namely mythical authors, at the same time introduced a new form of memorization that allowed for the use of writing and that introduced a shift from poetry that was constantly evolving to poetry with variants.

The Cleobulus Theorem

The history of lyric poetry is rather different from that of epic, for it is, as it were, out of step with it. Like all the traditional genres, erotic, lyric monody was certainly affected by panhellenism and the festival culture, but somewhat later than other poetic performances. That may have been partly because, unlike epic and choral songs, it did not lend itself to the creation of a common mythology, because the symposion did not admit epic and the glorification of warrior heroes; perhaps also because it celebrated a Dionysus of intoxication, who was absent from many Dorian cities.

First the Dionysiac symposion had to become a cultural practice with which most Greeks identified. Only then did the poetry characteristic of it likewise come to be exhibited in panhellenic or civic contests. But at the same time, the banquet song continued to be something that anyone could sing, transmitted in banquets through direct participation in the ritual—at least, that was certainly the case in aristocratic cities. This kind of poetry was not separated from its music, nor was lyric meter formalized. That only happened later, in the Hellenistic period. To be sure, lyric in festivals was singing in vitro. Cithara and flute players played lyric monodies before a public and judges. But, unlike the performances of the rhapsodes, which would have been most unlikely to take place at a banquet, given their length and the absence of music, the lyric songs selected for festivals were not recompositions but potential performances, albeit cold ones. The speech act was fictitious, but not the statement.

The cities of Asia that chose erotic lyric in order to give themselves a particular identity within panhellenism now laid claim to the paternity of these songs and set up models under the names of three mythical poets: Alcaeus and Sappho of Lesbos, and Anacreon of Teos. It is certainly thanks to panhellenism and state culture that the song for Cleobulus has come down to us, yet the song for Cleobulus was not an abstract model, an ideal of a song. For, in contrast to the Homeric epics, in the text that we possess of it there is nothing to suggest that it is a recomposition. We do not know whether bards still existed at the time of Pisistratus, when the rhapsodes produced a fixed Homeric text; but the symposion, for its part, certainly was still very much alive in the years when the Ionians invented Anacreon and his works. The spectators at festivals were also Dionysiac drinkers. They may never have heard a real bard singing, but they did know about intoxicated singers and were familiar with the ritual that ruled a symposion. So they recognized the song for Cleobulus as a possible symposion song.

The reason why the song for Cleobulus came to be preserved was that it was considered a model song for a proposis, and so could be used, give or take a few contextual variations, as the starting point for other songs for other Cleobuluses. At the same time, it also became a monument to the fame of Anacreon and may well have appeared, in one form or another, as an inscription on the mythical poet's tomb in Teos.

A theoretical song it may have been, but it was nevertheless also still a real one—as it were, a Cleobulus theorem. For it remained an integral part of the fictitious speech act of an authentic symposion, as did all the songs that went to make up Anacreon. In fact that is why he is always represented as a banqueter.

The Novel of a Drinker

"I am a drinker of wine," declares one of the many funerary epigrams for Anacreon produced by the Alexandrians.[10] His imaginary life presents him as an Ionian Greek, a professional symposion-goer, the guest of a succession of tyrants.[11] The life attributed to him is derived from a biographical interpretation of the canonical texts of banquet songs preserved under his name. The reason why he was presented as a drinker, lover, and singer was that the "I" of his songs did nothing else, and the author is confused with the subject of those statements, the linguistic traces left by the subject of the speech act of the song, the banqueter in situ. "His life was devoted to love and song," declares one anonymous ancient.[12] If he is depicted as moving from one tyrant to another, that is because tyrannies existed at the time when the Greek cities were elaborating poetic models. Wherever he traveled, the banquet song would have acquired its credentials and become a superior form of culture. Finally, if Anacreon is said to be an Ionian from Asia Minor, that is because it was Ionia that claimed paternity of the banquet lyric: this was *its* contribution to the common, ideal Greek culture: Ionia was where Anacreon evolved, where he influenced other Ionians, and the place that he left to go off and produce other followers elsewhere.

Anacreon is supposed to have been born in Teos, in Ionia, in 570 B.C. The threat of Persian invasion (Cyrus seized Lydia and took Sardis from Croesus in 546) explains why he left in about 540. Already well known as a singer in his native town, he was invited to Samos by its tyrant, Polycrates, and was thus spared exile. It is in Samos that the first part of his autobiographical novel takes place. Before his arrival there, the Samians are said to have known nothing of the delights of the symposion. His presence softened the harshness of the tyranny, by "mingling"[13] with it (the Greek term *kerasas* is that used for mixing wine and water in a krater) the gentle sweetness of love, "that is to say, the locks of Smerdies and Cleobulus, the beauty of Bathyllus, and Ionian song." Banqueting with the tyrant, he would fall in love with boys and girls whom he seduced not through his own beauty—he was not as young as he used to be—but through his art, singing their praises in his songs. Sometimes he was the tyrant's rival, but he knew how to efface himself when necessary. The "sweet" Anacreon was neither a revolutionary nor a romantic lover. When the jealous Polycrates had the head of the young Smerdies shaved, to discourage Anacreon's love for him (for the ancients, a cropped head was always ugly, denuded of its *kharis*, since the erotic seduction of boys and girls lay in their flowing locks), the poet pretended to believe the boy himself had taken that initiative.[14] During the long years spent in Samos, he taught Polycrates' son lyric poetry, making the young man a model of virtue and culture and thereby proving that erotic lyric was an essential part of a liberal education, what the Greeks called a *paideia*: this was another way in which the banquet song was integrated into the panhellenic culture.

When Polycrates died in 522, a victim of the Persians, Anacreon moved to Athens, to the court of another tyrant, Hipparchus, the eldest son of Pisistratus. According to Plato, this tyrant was the very epitome of city culture:

> The eldest and wisest of Pisistratus's sons, and who . . . first brought the poems of Homer into this country of ours, and compelled the rhapsodes at the Panathenaea to recite them in relay, one man following on another. . . . He dispatched a fifty-oared galley for Anacreon of Teos, and brought him into our city. Simonides of Ceos he always had about him, prevailing on him by plenteous fees and gifts. All this he did from a wish to educate [*paideuein*] the citizens in order that he might have subjects of the highest excellence: for he thought it not right to grudge wisdom to any, so noble and good was he.[15]

By importing forms of poetry foreign to Athenian traditions, he gave his city a panhellenic dimension, which, he thought, would reinforce the civic spirit and political identity of the Athenians. However, it was perhaps somewhat premature to forget the traditions that characterized the Attic aristocracy and its taste for liberty; and Hipparchus was assassinated by two young and handsome liberators, Harmodius and Aristogiton, when Hippias, Hipparchus's younger brother, tried to abuse his tyrannical power and force his love upon one of the young men.

According to some biographers, after the downfall of Hippias, in 510, Anacreon left for Thessaly. But the Athenians claimed that he soon returned to live with them. His return was indispensable to the image that the Athenian democracy wished to present of itself, for it was keen to keep the symposion as a self-defining practice, linked with the Ionian origins of its aristocracy. This eternal lover, by now close on sixty, thus returned to Athens, lured there by a boy, of course, the handsome Critias, the forebear of Socrates' pupil. According to Anacreon's biographical novel, he lived long enough to witness Aeschylus's tragedies, the lyrical parts of which he is supposed to have appreciated greatly:[16] an Athenian way of claiming the cultural standing of the Dionysiac symposion songs for its own tragic choruses.

Despite his white hair, Anacreon also continued to pursue young girls, who eluded him and poked fun at him. Eventually he died, aged eighty-four. His end was a fitting one for a drinker, for he choked on a grape pip as he downed his last cup of wine. Athens erected a statue to him on the Acropolis;[17] it represented him drinking and singing.

This biographical outline was subsequently much embroidered, and Anacreon's life was turned into a sentimental serial. Moderns, overinterpreting a number of his songs, have been prone to add psychological depth to the aging lover. The ancients, for their part, were more given to exemplary anecdotes that imparted a fatalistic dimension to Anacreon's life:

> Anacreon, the Poet of Teos, is said to have been punished by Love in the following way. One day, at the Pan-Ionian festival on Mount Mycale (in honour of Poseidon), a nurse was carrying a baby across the agora when Anacreon came along, tipsy and shouting, with a wreath on his head, and stumbling against the woman and her charge let fall some words of abuse. The indignant nurse contented herself with expressing a pious wish that the very scoundrel who now cursed the child should live to praise him in still stronger terms—which indeed came to pass; for the god heard her prayer and, the child growing to be the lovely Cleobulus, Anacreon expiated a little curse with manifold praise.[18]

The invention of Anacreon the author was complete, serving to close his poems upon themselves by dint of creating an imaginary referent. His songs were him and he was his songs. The subject of the statement was embodied. The statement was now self-sufficient, for it was independent of both time and the space of a speech act. The song for Cleobulus was in grave danger of ending its life in a book.

The Anacreontics

As indeed it would have, had Anacreon simply been reduced to an anthropomorphic statue and embalmed in letters. But he remained alive elsewhere, so to speak, eluding that poet's fate in his own distinctive manner by giving his name to two Dionysiac forms of intoxication: he now struck attitudes on Athenian vases and sang in new banquets as far away as the shores of Alexandria. It was in vain that attempts were made to shut him away deep inside the closed corpus of Anacreontian poems; he was now reborn in Anacreontic speech acts.

Anacreontic Vases

One series of Attic vases, carefully dated to between 510 and 460,[19] is decorated with painted images depicting men dancing round a krater, drunk on Dionysus and playing lyres,[20] and led by a flutist. They are engaged upon what the Greeks called a *kōmos*: an unruly procession of drinkers that would sometimes precede, sometimes follow a symposion. The *kōmos*, unlike the symposion, was not an Aphroditean event; each komast danced for his own personal delight, without forming a couple. Furthermore, these men were dressed as women, but were not really disguised. They displayed plenty of marks of their virility at the same time as wearing feminine clothes. They were bearded men sporting long dresses and feminine headgear, and carrying sunshades.

On some of these vases the inscription ANACREON can be read or pieced together. Of course, the painter had not painted a portrait of the poet, labeled by his name. For him, this was just a way of representing an "Anacreontic" way of being possessed, in a particular kind of Dionysiac *kōmos* in which music was present. This Anacreontic *kōmos* may have corresponded to a greater, more dangerous stage of intoxication than that of the symposion, or at any rate to intoxication of a different kind. For in a *kōmos* the intoxication of wine was compounded by that of dancing: a Dionysiac liberation for both men and women. Men in a *kōmos* thus defied any strict sexual definition, for in their case the sexual distinction was neutralized—only in their case, however, for the flute players who got them to dance remained, for their part, altogether feminine.

In this way they moved as close as was possible to Dionysus, by immersing themselves in song, wine, music, and dance, all at the same time. This allowed them to "advance a little in his direction, but never the whole way, never as far as his divinity itself, never as far as pure wine, and never as far as womanhood or barbarity. For had they tipped over into such a state, they would have been in danger of becoming satyrs, half human, half beasts, and losing their identity."[21] The patronage afforded by Anacreon provided a cultural legitimation of this drugged experience. It is not surprising to learn that these vases are all dated to after Anacreon's supposed arrival in Athens. The vase painters represent him as the cultural hero of the songs of the *kōmos* and hence also of the particular kind of intoxication that characterized him and gave him his panhellenic standing. The *kōmos* seems to have been recognized as providing the speech-act context for Ionian lyric, as a fragment of an Anacreontic song seems to confirm: "He performs a *kōmos* just like Dionysus";[22] as does an epigram from Alexandria: "Anacreon, beloved by the Muses, . . . master of the *kōmos*."[23]

Anacreontic Songs

These days, no Greek scholar would fail to make a distinction between the works of a real Anacreon and songs that are labeled as "Anacreontic." For literary history, that is an article of faith. However, it is all a matter of the point of view that you adopt. If you stick to a strict chronology, it is quite true that the style of the Anacreontic songs often reflects a different aesthetic context. The Alexandria of the Ptolemys was indeed not the Athens of Pisistratus, nor that of Aristophanes. But if you forget about classical literary history, with its cult of "the man and his work," and instead adopt a religious perspective, what matters is no longer the author of these songs but rather the context in which they were produced. Given that the Dionysiac symposion continued to be celebrated, continued to afford an experience of intoxication through wine, love, and song, there was no reason why Anacreontism should disappear.

That was how the ancients saw it. They made no distinction between what was false and what was true when they assembled under the general name of Anacreon a whole mass of banquet songs, which, one day, would fall into the hands of Henri Estienne. He published them just as they were, in 1554. Ronsard went into ecstasies over them:

> I drink to Henri Estienne
> Who from Hades has restored to us
> That sweet lyre of Teos
> Of long-lost old Anacreon.

There were others at this time who challenged the authenticity of the texts, suggesting that the whole collection was a sham fabricated by the man who claimed to be its editor. Scholars clashed over this issue. From the nineteenth century on, philology, an exact discipline, set about separating the grain from the chaff: on the right, the true Anacreon and his archaic splendors; on the left, the Anacreontic affectations, no better than pale imitations. It would be pointless to do battle with the philologists: they are always right in their own domain. Where they can be challenged, however, is the point at which they start speaking of imitation, that is to say, of a technical process of rewriting in such a way that a new statement is produced on the basis of an earlier one.

But it could quite well be that this is a series of banquet songs of the Anacreontic type dating from the Alexandrian period, the preservation of which presents no mystery at all. As we shall see,[24] the Alexandrians were prone to preserve everything, in archives. In which case, moving from the statement to the speech act, we can abandon all remarks on style, tone, and language, and all research into the literary sources, and instead examine how these texts functioned within the context of a symposion, on the basis of what we already know about Anacreontic intoxication.

This point of view would not have surprised a Roman of the second century A.D. any more than it would his Greek masters.[25] For them, there was no doubt about it. In the course of a recital of Greek lyric songs given at the end of a banquet in the Rome neighborhood, young slaves would come in to sing *Anacreonteia*, *Sapphica*, and other erotic poems. Our source adds that, for the pure pleasure of it, he will add a few lines of the old Anacreon (*Anacreontis Senis*):

Τὸν ἄργυρον τορεύσας,
῞Ηφαιστέ, μοι ποίησον
Ηανοπλίαν μὲν οὐχί,
Τί γαρ μάχαισι κἀμοί;
Ποτήριον δε κοῖλον,
῞Οσον δύνῃ, βάθυνον.
Καὶ μὴ ποίει κατ' αὐτὸ
Μήτ' ἄστρα μήθ' 'Αμάξασ,
Τί Πλειάδων μέλει μοι,
Τί δ'ἀστέρος βοώτεω;
Ποίησον ἀμπέλουσ μοι
Καὶ βότρυας κατ' αὐτῶν,
Καὶ χρυσέους πατοῦντας
῾Ομοῦ καλῷ Λυαίω
῎Ερωτα καὶ Βάθυλλον.

Shaping the silver, Hephaestus,
Make me no panoply, pray;
What do I care for war's combats?
Make me a drinking cup rather,
Deep as you ever can make it;
Carve on it no stars and no wains;
What care I, pray, for the Pleiads,
What for the star of Bootes?
Make vines, and clusters upon them,
Treading them Love and Bathyllus,
Made of pure gold, with Lyaeus.

In contrast to the ancients, who in such cases classified the songs according to the circumstances in which they were sung, attributing them to

Anacreon, the moderns, who look no further than the statement, place such a song among the Anacreontic works, thereby denying Anacreon's authorship. But it was the ancients who were right, for from a religious point of view this song can be interpreted on the model of "the song for Cleobulus." That is why I shall call it "the song for Bathyllus," since the boy named at the end of it is, like Cleobulus, the person for whom a proposis is intended. The proposis is, furthermore, as in the song for Cleobulus and others in the same series, ritually linked with the introduction of the gods of the symposion.

The first god to be invoked is not Dionysus but Hephaestus, who arrives, bringing with him the expected deities, Eros and Lyaeus (Dionysus), and with them is Bathyllus. There is nothing surprising about the presence of Hephaestus. He is there as the goldsmith-god who fashions the cups and jars made from precious metals that are used in the banquet. He has supervised the fashioning of the cup from which those assembled are about to drink and which will be first of all presented to Bathyllus. Thanks to its decorative motifs, it will bring Eros and Dionysus into the banquet, for that decoration echoes the meaning of the gesture of the proposis, the first sharing of wine and desire. The drinkers can contemplate the images of Eros and Dionysus on the cup in just the same way as they listen to their names pronounced by the poet. The golden image on the cup that the singer raises to catch the light and shows to all present is the song's double. The song and the image are analogous means of invoking the gods and bringing them into the symposion. Similarly, Bathyllus is both to be seen with the gods on the cup and mentioned by name by the singer. The three golden silhouettes shine out from the silver cup, rendered more visible and more divine by the overlay of gold. What the image on the cup depicts is the effect wrought by the proposis: the gods are present among the men, rendering the latter similar to themselves, while they, the gods, become civilized by using human techniques, for the dance of the three figures imitates grape harvesters treading the grapes (*patountes*). Dionysus is in the wine, Eros is in the desire, and Bathyllus is Bathyllus, the child who is desired and who accepts the cup.

This demonstrates the functional equivalence between the image on the cup and the song of the poet: both are means of setting the ritual scene.[26] The cultural interplay between them is very much part of the implicit poeticoreligious tradition according to which a banquet always excluded war and epic. That is why half the poem is devoted to rejecting the warlike Hephaestus, who makes arms and adorns shields with images connected with epic, such as the constellations. The lines expressing that rejection constitute a quasi citation from a passage in Homer that describes Hephaestus forging the arms of Achilles.[27] They use the well-known metaphor that assimilates the drinking cup to "the shield of Dionysus." In this way the singer distinguishes between two Hephaestuses, one who is excluded from the banquet, namely the god of weapons, fighting, and epic, the other, the Hephaestus of the banquet, the god of wine cups and the art of the goldsmith.

This song has been preserved in various forms in the *Palatine Anthology*, and philologists strive pointlessly to reconstruct the "true" text, seeking for the truth of the song in the statement that it makes, whereas that truth really lies in its speech act.[28] Some versions omit the rejection of epic so that the poem starts immediately with "Make vines." In these, what follows varies from one to another. After the "vines," they may mention "Maenad grape harvesters" or "laughing Satyrs" or a "wine press," but all these elements in the picture are carved in silver. Only the gods are carved in gold. They vary too from one version to another: Dionysus is sometimes alone, sometimes accompanied by Aphrodite. What we have here is a phenomenon of evolving poetry, implying that recomposition has taken place.

These Anacreontic songs all use the same ritual setup as the one analyzed here, in the song for Cleobulus, a setup that serves to link the invocation to the gods with the proposis. The name Anacreon here indicates the choice of a particular speech act, which is a ritual variant for acceding to the twofold invocation to Dionysus and Eros (not that Anacreon's name invariably indicates that choice, for sometimes it is used to give access to the ambivalent intoxication of the *kōmos*). Disparities may follow, according to whether the god first invoked in the song is Dionysus or Hephaestus, or some other one. Thanks to the ritual scene setting, the song has a performative force. The cup "ordered" from Dionysus is already in the hands of the singer, but the invocation to the god reactivates the god's presence in the cup and actualizes his divinity through its dazzling metallic ornamentation. Present in the shining gold, Hephaestus displays the gods of the symposion to its dazzled members, as the metal flashes suddenly in the lamplight. The "laughter of the clusters of grapes" and the "laughter of Aphrodite" burst through in the flash of the wrought metal and comprise, at the same time, the laughter of the happy drinkers.

Reformulated, as they were, rather than rewritten, these Anacreontic songs were contextual compositions. The drinker was not a writer finding his place in a genealogy of texts. The latest performance was worth as much as the earliest one and was listened to for its own sake, not in relation to any other. These songs had nothing to do with any memory bank of words. To sing Anacreon was not to sing the poems of Anacreon, to produce a citation or to put on a textual drama as the rhapsodes and cithara players or the young slaves at a Roman banquet did.[29]

The drinkers would hear a song that was pragmatically always the same, even if it was semantically different, since it always played the same role at this particular moment in the banquet and always boiled down to making the same contextual choice. They knew what to expect, maybe even as soon as they heard the particular rhythm of Anacreontic music starting up.

From the Hellenistic period on, by which time the song for Cleobulus had been committed to a book, there were to be two Anacreons, one living, the other dead. The latter, the only one that historians of literature choose to recognize, was an invention of panhellenism; the other was a particular way of drinking, loving, and singing.

The Ups and Downs of Dionysus in Athens

While traditional forms of Greek oral culture—epic and the banquet song—were being unified and confiscated first by the cities and then by panhellenism, to end up, later on, embalmed in the library of Alexandria, other forms were being generated, created by the city culture, which established different links with writing and orality. Of these new forms, the best known to us is Athenian drama. This, albeit only for a few dozen years, was to avoid the choice between, on the one hand, traditional, evolving, one-off orality, exploding into a thousand and one idiosyncratic forms—along with the variance that followed on from this—and, on the other, being confined within books, there to constitute exemplary and definitive models.

Although it was a pure creation of the city culture, Athenian drama was remarkable in that it did constitute an event, since it took place in the context of a festival. Each theatrical representation constituted a unique, oral performance, despite the fact that the text pronounced by the actors had earlier been written down, then learned by heart, so was in a sense "read"—but only read once. In this respect it differed from, for instance, the theatrical festivals constituted by the rhapsodes' contest in the Panathenaea.

In Athenian theater, Dionysus and the Muses once again were present, for a tragedy was performed within the ritual framework of a Dionysiac festival and these tragic stories all derived from the epic tradition. But here, neither the Muses nor Dionysus took possession of either the tragic poet or the actors or the public. In this respect theater marked a break with the traditional culture of both kinds of banquet, since it was a festival art.

The Tyrannical Origins of Theater

The creation of theater in Greece was everywhere due to tyrants, whether in Athens or in Sicyon; nowhere did it precede the introduction of festivals.[30] Without entering into an erudite discussion of sources and their interpretations,[31] let me sketch in a brief account of how tragedy was created in Athens, under the Pisistratidae.

It all began when Pisistratus moved the Dionysia, the festival of Dionysus, traditionally celebrated in the countryside, into the town. These urban Dionysia then developed into the Great Dionysia. This event incorporated a festival of dithyrambs, choral songs in honor of Dionysus. A form of traditional, religious song thus became a form of official poetry. An "inventor" was attributed to these dithyrambs, namely Lasus of Hermione, a native of the Peloponnese who was the master of Pindar, so that dithyrambs were presented, fictitiously, as a form of Dorian poetry. But a different patronage for it suggested that it was an Ionian form, claiming that its inventor was Arion of Lesbos, who was supposed to have arrived in Corinth during the reign of Periander. For the Athenians, attributing a foreign origin to a poetic form that was the object of a contest was a way of declaring that it also concerned Greeks from other Dorian or Ionian cities and that it could claim panhellenic status. The more origins were postulated, the greater were the potential audiences.

Next, the Great Dionysia became the occasion for a tragic contest. Although tragedy did not really emerge from dithyrambs, for the latter continued to be sung at the festival each year, the former absorbed them, presenting choruses along with a recited dialogue on the model of the epic of the rhapsodes. Furthermore, tragic poets took their subjects from the epic tradition. According to some accounts, Arion the Ionian, having introduced the dithyramb in Corinth, went on to Athens, where he organized the first tragic contest in 534, in the reign of Pisistratus. The contest was won by Thespis.

Athenian tragedy was thus a pure product of the abstract Hellenism promoted with a view to unifying the city. Times, places, and texts were all exploited to create a form of art identified with the Hellenism that was to enfold all Greeks. The Great Dionysia was organized at the end of March, when winter was coming to an end and it again became possible to travel by sea, and the events were open to all Greeks. Their audience was thus assured. Tragedy was very much a panhellenic setup, a poetic patchwork that became increasingly complex. Gradually, it was to absorb all other forms of song, including drinking songs and funerary lamentations. Each spectator would find something in it to remind him of his own city, whether he was an Ionian from the islands, a Dorian from Sicily, Crete, or the Peloponnese, a Boeotian, or a Cypriot. Hymns, paeans, dithyrambs, pantomimes, odes—Athens combined in tragedy all the forms of song that were practiced in the various cities. Soon (in 486), ancient tragedy split into three new forms: tragedy in the strict sense of the term, satyr plays, and comedy. The theater thus came to exercise a veritable imperialism over the culture of the city of Athens; and Plato was to protest at this "theatrocracy" through which the state managed to confiscate the culture of the Athenians, even if it did so for the greater glory of Athens. What the Athenians set out to do was indeed to present their own theater to all the Greeks, as a synthesis of all Greek poetry, and they thereby made their tragic theater the best in the world. In doing so, however, they certainly made considerable sacrifices where traditional Dionysism was concerned.

Masks and Writing

What had been the nature of the festivals of Dionysus before Pisistratus? What we know of them is enough to prove that, between the Dionysiac trance and the cold institution of the theater, a definite cultural break did take place. There were two ritual aspects to the Greek Dionysus. One was solely masculine: the wine that brought intoxication; the other was more particularly connected with women, but was also present in the *kōmos* and the dithyramb. It was this second Dionysus who, in Athens, became the Dionysus of the theater, once he had been civilized and divested of his magical powers. The cultural manipulation of this Dionysus of women, who became the Dionysus of the theater is reflected, in the form of a myth, in Euripides' *Bacchae*.

All over Greece there is evidence to show that in the historical period, as late as the time of the Roman Empire, women would gather together in the wintertime, under the patronage of Dionysus, to go off running, virtually naked, in the mountains. They would be in the grip of a collective possession (*synenthousiazein*), believing they could see springs of honey and rivers of milk flowing.[32] The same ritual sometimes served as a rite of passage for young girls entering the class of married women.

Women possessed by this "enthusiasm" or rapture would roam through a paradisiacal wilderness that existed solely for them, in which they were neither civilized women nor bestial females. Dionysus turned them into women "gone wild," creatures with no existence outside Dionysism. For them honey and milk, the most civilized forms of nourishment, obtained by the two civilized techniques of herd raising and beekeeping, were produced naturally by the wilderness; and, conversely, these women gave suck to wolf cubs and fawns. Dancing in the mountains, they experienced an otherness similar to that experienced by men in the symposion and the *kōmos*. But the otherness discovered by the women was different from that of the men. Since, as women, they were already excluded from the extreme civilization of the men, they became Maenads, the companions of Dionysus.[33] The domain of women gripped by rapture was a natural and paradisiacal wilderness in which love and singing had no place. The domain of men in the grip of rapture was love, song, music, and sexual neutralization.

The tragedy of the *Bacchae* turned drama into the cultural equivalent of that ritual of feminine possession. Briefly summarized, the subject of the play is a confrontation between Dionysus, who has come to establish his cult among the women of Thebes, and the king, Pentheus, who refuses to allow the women, his mother Agave included, to go off into the mountains. Dionysus is never seen but manifests himself through theater masks and demonstrates his power by creating deceptive visions that lead Pentheus to his doom. While up in the mountains, Agave mistakes her own son for a young fawn, which she kills and tears to pieces with her bare hands. The Dionysus of the *Bacchae* and of Athenian tragedy generally is the god of women in trance, the god of masks, and the god of illusion.

In one essential way, the Dionysus of the theater differed from the god of Dionysism in all its other forms: tragedy was not a place for "enthusiasm" (rapture) and visionary illusions. In the *Bacchae*, the feminine experience of possession was converted into a theatrical convention and thereby became as accessible to men as it was to women. Bacchae truly did see another world; what the spectators in the theater saw, as they watched the masked actor playing the role, was a conventional representation of Pentheus, the mythical king of Thebes. The reason why Athenian drama was performed in the sanctuary of Dionysus and on the occasion of the festivities held for him, was that he was the god-in-a-mask.[34] The actor—*hypokritēs*, the original meaning of which was interpreter—was created on the model of the rhapsode reciting a poem attributed to someone else. To get the spectator to forget that the man speaking was a well-known artiste, or possibly his own next-door neighbor, the actor wore a Dionysiac mask. That was why a Greek theater was known as a *theatron*, which meant "a place for looking": the spectator needed to see the face of the masked character so that the role that he heard declaimed by the actor meshed in with the mask, and all the indications of real personality, time, and place came to refer to an invisible elsewhere, the world of epic that was conventionally present in all Athenian tragedy. A mask, known in Greek as "a face" (*prosōpon*), had no existence unless it was looked at by the public in a theater: it was a virtual image of heroes and gods.

Not only was the Dionysus of the theater the god of masks, he was also the god of the dithyramb.[35] The distance between the two coincided with the distance between ritual and the theater and, in this instance, between a real possession and a technique that imitated the musical effects of that possession. Traditionally, the dithyramb was a song of orgiastic possession, the forms of which varied from one city to another. The schema of the ritual may be reconstructed as follows: the *exarkhon*, the singer leading the celebration, would strike up with a prologue improvised under the spell of Dionysiac possession, itself a result of the intoxication produced by wine and flute music. The chorus would encourage him with ritual cries of acclamation; then its members would themselves be swept into the dance and the singing, copying the *exarkhon*, as they formed a circle around the altar of Dionysus (this was known as a cyclical chorus). As the dancing and the music speeded up, the members of the chorus also fell into trance, possessed by the god.

In dithyrambic competitions, the ritual of possession disappeared. The song had been composed in advance by a poet such as Pindar or Simonides, then learned by the singers in the course of rehearsals, so as eventually to be performed at a festival in Athens or elsewhere. Later, in similar speech-act conditions, tragic poets returned to the poetics of the dithyramb, when composing their own tragic choruses.

Athenian drama was thus a combination of a number of rituals involving singing and dancing, all derived from the hot culture of the Greeks, but subsequently frozen into techniques of writing and musical composition and theatricality. Furthermore, theater split those taking part in the spectacle into two separate groups, with the actors and the poet on one side, the spectators on the other. It was a separation that reflected the fact that spectators did not communicate with the actors in a sacred rapture or ardor, but instead passed judgment on them at the end of the competition. The writing of a text for the theater and its recitation on the stage stemmed from the technique of inscription, for it subjected the actor to a text that he had to repeat word for word, and the true subject of the speech act was the tragic character, that great mute to whom the actor lent his voice. Without writing of the inscription variety, there would have been no Athenian theater.

Tragic Myth

Yet, despite being derived from poetry festivals, Athenian theater seems to have had the power to open onto an otherness, to make visible what had been invisible, to continue the mythical exploration that had been the speciality of living epic. How was that possible? The Muses were banished from the theater. A dramatic poet had written the words of the tragedy or comedy in advance, a musician had composed the music for the choruses, and the actors had rehearsed all this, as had the members of the chorus who were invariably amateurs.[36] No trace remained here of Dionysiac "ardor."

However, in the first place, the popular success of theater in Athens made it a consensual art, as the song of the bard had been. More importantly, each tragedy was also—as was each performance of epic—always a "one-off," always the same, always for the first time. In Aeschylus, Sophocles, and Euripides, Electra urges her brother Orestes to kill their mother Clytemnestra, along with the latter's lover, Aegisthus, to avenge their father Agamemnon, whom the couple had murdered upon his return from Troy.[37] The story is the same, but each of the three tragedies concerns a different myth. In Aeschylus, Orestes, defiled by the worst of crimes, human sacrifice, is pursued by the Erinyes, whom he has allowed to drink his mother's blood. In Sophocles, Orestes and his sister remain in the palace of Argos, where the son will succeed his father without difficulty, since he has wrought his vengeance within the set limits of the period of mourning, when the living dead can kill each other without defiling the living. In Euripides, Orestes and his sister both have to leave Argos, to found new families elsewhere, because the murder of their mother—who, as mistress of the family house (*oikos*), had brought it water drawn from the springs of the Nymphs, thereby establishing a genealogical link with the land—has cut them off from the city territory. Tragedy thus presents us with the same kind of mythical exploration as we have found to characterize ancient epic:[38] in Aeschylus, the exploration is of libation; in Sophocles, it is of mourning; in Euripides, it is of a woman's place in the *oikos*. This mythical dimension made a tragic performance part of the world of orality. To be sure, Athenian theater connived in many ways with writing, for the text was composed coldly by a poet who did not perform the speech act for it. However, that did not make it a transcription of a fictitious speech act, because the operation had more in common with inscription writing. Furthermore, it also allowed for a live production of myth that it then proceeded to explore for itself: Euripides' *Bacchae*.

An Example of Cultural Entropy

How did a tragic poet compose? How were the poetic forms synthesized in tragedy transmitted? The answer to these questions is probably connected with the fact that these poets attended festivals and listened to other tragedies. There is no need to postulate the existence of any formulated poetics that could be taught. None of the great tragic poets were professionals of language. They did not belong to any schools of rhapsodes or cithara players. Nor were they professors of eloquence or sophists. They were ordinary citizens who had sung in the choruses and seen dramas performed in the theater. They were still operating within a system of transmission through immersion that was perfectly suited to the democratic ideology but, at the same time, corresponded to a hot culture. To that extent, Athenian theater was Dionysiac. The poet was simply one of many spectators, one of the amateurs with whom the city was swarming. He was himself a meeting point for the poetic forms that tragedy would synthesize. He, personally, embodied the panhellenic culture that his city wished to offer as a model to all the other Greeks.

At the beginning of its existence, a tragedy was thus a one-off performance, the written text for which was generally destined to disappear once the event had taken place—except that it was not long before Athenian imperialism set up the plays of some poets as models, fixing the text once and for all. This marked the end of popular theater: culture as an event gave way to culture as a monument. Once the "classics" began to be reperformed, Athenian tragedy was mummified, just as the text of Homer had been.

The history of Athenian theater, both tragedy and the dithyramb, is that of a politically organized cultural degradation. In the interests of integration into the city culture, the Dionysiac trance, which had taken ritual forms that varied from men to women and from one city to another, was effaced in favor of a theatrical illusion that was no more than a social convention. It is true that the public saw what was invisible, but the spectators did not feel the presence of the god within their individual selves, did not take the risk of losing themselves, driven to the limits of their humanity. The Dionysus of Athenian theater was colorless and domesticated. Dionysism lost its orgiastic power once Dionysiac illusion was no longer an effect of rapture, but instead resulted from a carefully organized spectacle. Nevertheless, Athenian theater did remain part of a culture of events, a celebration of Dionysus-the-mask. If the dividing line passes between a fictitious speech act and a real one, theater is on the side of hot culture, for what is said in the theater is only meaningful and effective when said in the theater, even if the theater was not the place where it was composed. All the same, theater was an event that the gods of intoxication and song did not visit any more than they inspired the composition of the dramatic poet, for he was one of the new breed of writing hacks, the artisans of panhellenic culture and city cultures.

Athens can be used as a yardstick for reflection upon today's theater. Its undeniable renaissance, at a time when cinema is being swept aside in the audiovisual debacle, is clearly connected with the fact that it constitutes an event. Each theatrical enaction is a performance, in which there is always a risk of the public failing to engage with the actors. To be sure, by presenting the same play many times over, day after day, so that anyone can see it (all you have to do is buy a ticket), it does lose much of its force as an event. But events are what the public wants: hence the success of the marathon spectacles put on for festivals—at Avignon, for example, where *Le soulier de satin* has been played in its entirety, lasting all night. It is no bad thing if attention sometimes gives way to exhaustion, if the brilliance of the stage fades, to reappear in hallucinations brought on by fatigue, and if both actors and public are stretched to the limit. Culture burns more brightly when it ceases to be economical, ceases to be a reasonable distraction or an educational spectacle.

In our own culture, which has forgotten how to make good use of collective drugs and is wary of excessive festivity (quite rightly, given that it recognizes its inability to control it), only the theater still has the power to draw crowds from all sides. In these annual pilgrimages, theater is no longer simply one leisure activity among others, but becomes the goal of a journey. And the efforts required from the spectators, what with the cold, the darkness, and the length of the spectacle, make it possible to experience the drama physically. The only kinds of intoxication acceptable in our culture are those brought on by fatigue or much effort.

Unfortunately, the theater is threatened by a literary backwash. Too many directors, these days, opt out of creating a spectacular event, of presenting the public with new images and making it see what is invisible—that is to say, what is visible only in the theater. Instead, they turn themselves into "readers," claiming to efface themselves modestly behind the text, as if that text has an autonomous existence, as if it could take over the actors and itself become embodied in the spectacle. The end result is overwhelming boredom and nontheater. Those directors are on the side of monumental culture, tomb visiting. In contrast, those who create spectacles out of texts are more like symposion or flamenco singers. The text in question, more or less known to the spectators, makes it possible for the latter to recognize themselves in the spectacle while at the same time providing the framework for an improvisation, a one-off performance. The spectators are familiar with *The Tempest* and the *Oresteia*, but what they have watched, the event in which they have taken part, was not the play by Shakespeare or Aeschylus: it was Peter Brook's *Tempest*, Ariane Mnouchkine's *Oresteia*. The directors recontextualized the written words, giving them their pragmatic meaning on that particular day.

The history of Athenian theater outlined here will serve as an example to introduce the idea of cultural entropy. It is intended simply as a suggestion to stimulate the imagination, not as a proposed method of analysis elaborated on the basis of some kind of thermodynamics.[39] If we agree that any tendency toward homogeneity and resemblance is a form of entropy, that is to say a degradation of the social system as a result of the introduction of disorder and a tendency toward immobility, then culture that reintroduces complexity, dissymmetry, and distinctiveness into society, considered as an open-ended system, strikes a blow against social entropy, is antientropic. That is why it uses up so much external energy, only being successful at great economic cost. So oral culture, by reason of its evolving nature and the constant diversification that it brings about, possesses a greater antientropic power than theater. Any culture that becomes generalized and static simultaneously becomes less and less able to resist social entropy or, in other words, to reaffirm the order of the society in which it operates.

Banquet versus Theater: Anacreon Goes to School

In Athens, the Dionysiac symposion seems to have constituted an aristocratic means of resisting the theatrocracy, but unfortunately with the paradoxical and perverse result of forcing it toward writing, and thereby sapping the culture of intoxication[40] and eventually producing the book banquet that was to flourish in Rome. However, in fifth-century Athens, all that was still a long way off.

The banquet song was one of the rare minority cultural practices to survive the high tide of civic poetry and Athenian centralism. All the same, it is worth noting one curious feature of those Athenian banquets: in them, it was considered normal to complete one's duty as singer by citing the greatest authors. This practice was credited with the patronage of the famous musician Terpander and the citing operation was known as a *skolion*. The association of Terpander, believed to have evolved musical techniques, once the music of a song had been separated from its words, proves that the *skolion* was a musical form, not a type of text. But when the heading *skolion* is used to assemble texts, it in fact covers more or less anything and everything: citations sometimes from the works of great masters of the banquet lyric (Alcaeus, Archilochus, Anacreon); sometimes from choral lyric (Pindar and Stesichorus); sometimes from tragic choruses. Alternatively, the citations could be from a whole variety of texts of unknown origin, which have come down to us under the generic heading of "Attic scholia."[41] Among this mixed bag is to be found a patriotic celebration of Hipparchus's two assassins:

> Forever shall their fame survive on earth
> Dear Harmodius and Aristogiton
> Because they killed the tyrant
> And installed liberty in Athens;

an invocation to Athena, the town's patron:

> Pallas, born of Triton, Athena, queen,
> Guide our city and its citizens
> Spare us from suffering and civil wars
> And premature deaths, you and your father.

There is even a funereal piece in praise of soldiers who died defending the fort of Leipsydrion, on the Parnes, against the troops of the tyrant Hippias:

> Alas Leipsydrion, you sacrified our friends!
> What men they were who died for you!
> Magnificent in combat, well-born men
> On that day they certainly showed who their fathers were.

There are snatches of Homeric epic too:

> Son of Telamon, mighty Ajax, they say that
> You, with Achilles, were the best of the Greeks who left for Troy;

and a genuine banquet song:

> Drink with me, come with me, love with me . . .[42]

We know that this practice of quoting to music was part of the education of well brought up children from good families. An educated man was supposed to be able to sing of Stesichorus and Anacreon, at a banquet.[43] Not that this stopped other drinkers from embarking upon their own Dionysiac improvisations: the two kinds of singing both existed in an Athenian symposion. How should we interpret this custom of citation, which was altogether new to Ionian tradition and one of whose ultimate consequences was to fix Anacreon's model works, in writing, for educational purposes?

Gregory Nagy suggests the following interpretation: in reaction against the state theatrocracy culture, the Greek aristocracy organized a poetic resistance, defending all the—extremely diverse—traditional forms of lyric. The symposion, the place where the Greek nobility of most cities could meet sociably, was used as a scene of speech acts that existed alongside the civic festivals, one where poetic forms in danger of disappearing could continue to be heard, and so be preserved.

This involved a measure of manipulation: the use of *skolion* certainly made it possible to include all forms of lyric, but at the same time the musical specificity of each genre disappeared: choruses were changed into melodies and epic was sung to the music of the lyre. As so frequently happens, the desire to preserve cultural forms by fixing them resulted in changing their very nature. In this case, the defense of lyric resulted in the dismemberment of song. Musical banquet speech acts proved ill-suited to many of the lyric statements that the drinkers cited. This resulted in developments similar to those that we have noted taking place in festivals: statements and speech acts were separated, as were music and poetry. The transmission of this type of banquet poetry that did not consist of banquet songs became impossible within the symposion itself. So young men had to go elsewhere, to school in fact, to learn both the poetry texts and the lyre music to go with them.

To fight against the oral instruction that all young Athenians received through participation in civic festivities and singing in tragic choruses, dithyrambs, and other festival concerts, the Athenian nobility sent their sons to private schools, to learn how to hold their own in a symposion. Fifth-century Attic cups thus display scenes of young boys receiving a musical and poetic education, the purpose of which is clearly to render them capable of singing in a symposion.[44] This education separated the teaching of poems, through reading, from the purely instrumental teaching of the lyre. One cup shows a boy learning the written text of a choral song; another shows an epic text, also written down, which looks like Hesiod or Homer. In both cases a powerful contrast is suggested between, on the one hand, the text of a song that invokes the Muses and thereby presupposes a traditional speech act and, on the other, the writing down of these texts so that they can be learned.

Banquet culture was in danger of cooling. To be sure, Dionysism was not dead, nor was poetic intoxication, but a crack was developing, separating two cultures: the singing of banquet songs eventually became regarded as a trivial practice, perpetuated by, for example, Anacreontic songs; meanwhile school learning took over from enraptured improvisation and cultural prestige came to be credited to this alone. No longer was trust placed in the first drinker to hand. No longer could such a one be counted on to ensure the survival of Greek culture; instead, he was replaced by pedagogic books. Anacreon now became an educational course author. To be sure, young Athenian aristocrats did still practice a culture of variants, for on each occasion they recontextualized their quotations, even if only musically. However, it was no longer simply a matter of transmission from one man to another, for transmission became partly dependent on writing, used as a depository of memory.

To return to the parallel drawn earlier with flamenco, it is worth noting that, in both cases, the desire to preserve a minority culture by fixing it and teaching it had the effect of killing and mummifying it. The movement that Antonio Mairena launched to restore flamenco's purity imposed a straitjacket of rules upon it, confining it to fixed models that prevented it from evolving and, by the same token, from being transmitted orally and flexibly, risking all the hazards of improvisation. It cut flamenco off from life, demonizing modernity and turning it into an art of the conservatory.[45] This kind of flamenco was cut off from its popular roots and essentially flourished only in competitions and festivals. Where real flamenco did continue to live, in villages or families, it did so totally unaffected by that movement of intellectual purists. For a popular culture cannot be decreed or subjected to rules; it lives and dies thanks to the life of the group that it expresses. An ecological kind of relationship exists between it and that group: a symbiosis. Whenever a new element appears or an existing one dies in the cultural niche inhabited by the group, one form of its culture may be wiped out. This can happen if people are moved from their gypsy quarter and are dispersed in some other urban structure, if excessive poverty demoralizes a clan, or if modern economic prosperity dislocates family solidarities, or if the rock music of transistors brutalizes the rising generations. Ghettos and marginalization are not necessarily the worst of evils.

This persistent comparison drawn between the ragged gypsies of the suburbs of Seville and the Dionysiac songs of the aristocrats of Athens may be found somewhat surprising. But both cases feature minority cultures surviving despite being marginalized by history and the state, cultures that serve to bind their members together socially. In each case the culture is in danger of dying if it leaves its ghetto and is taken over by the majority. Once it is modelized, theorized, historicized, and given claims to universality, it loses its savor and its soul, and also its ability to communicate intoxication.

Theories on a Monument Culture

The switch from human memory to object-dependent memory elicited contradictory theories from the two greatest opponents of the democratic culture: Socrates and Aristotle. Socrates was implacably hostile to transcription, to writing that presumed to take the place of orality, to speech that was decontextualized. Aristotle, in contrast, proposed a technique for constructing decontextualized speech: he elaborated a doctrine of writing without reading, writing that dispensed with the protocol of speech acts.

Ion, *or the Materiality of the Text*

Plato's dialogue entitled *Ion*, elaborates a strange theory that centers poetry on a text, in the manner of the rhapsodes, rather than on a singer-poet. It is hard to tell whether Socrates, the hero of the dialogue, is elaborating this theory with a view to promoting the new Athenian culture or with the intention of undermining it. Whatever the case may be, it clearly reveals a changed point of view when it declares that the transmission of poetry is no longer effected by the passing of a skill from one poet to another; now, it depends solely upon a text that is recited.

Ion, the character after whom the dialogue is named, is an Ionian from Ephesus, a rhapsode by profession, specializing in Homer. He has come to Athens for the Panathenaea, straight from Epidaurus where he has just taken part in the festival of the Asclepeia, which every four years organized "musical" competitions, that is to say competitions in the various poetic genres. Ion has won the prize for epic. Socrates proceeds to manipulate him by putting to him questions designed to get him to confess that he possesses no particular knowledge of the Homeric poems, but is simply a divine man, a kind of "priest of Homer," possessed by his master.[46] He begins by putting forward a theory on poetic speech with which Ion agrees, without realizing where this will lead. Socrates' starting point is a belief shared by all Greeks, namely that poets are not artisans of poetry; they sing inspired by the Muses, with no composition technique of their own. (It should at the outset be noted that Socrates assimilates poetry and song, "forgetting" that although a bard certainly possessed no technique for composing poetry, he nevertheless had to have been initiated into the musical art. A bard was not a drinker at a banquet, but a priest of the Muses.)

Next, Socrates points out that each poet practices one particular genre, as decided by the Muses. Without suggesting an explanation for the origin of the musical impulse that launches the poet into action, he adds that once he "starts on the melody and rhythm"[47]—the two terms used to describe lyric poetry, not epic—the song comes to him spontaneously. The voice that is heard is not his, but that of the Muses. So it is that the most mediocre of men are sometimes capable of producing the most beautiful of songs. He cites the example of a certain Tynnichus of Chalcis, a nonentity in other respects, who one day produced the most beautiful of paeans, "a paean that today is sung by everybody." Although not necessarily fixed word for word, Tynnichus's performance was somehow memorized—in other words, was considered as a model.

Socrates, for his part, objectivizes that performance: the paean now exists materially, independent of Tynnichus, and the object that it constitutes itself possesses the musical and sacred power that presided over its creation. That inspiration has left Tynnichus but has been crystallized in his song. Whoever sings it will resuscitate the inspiration. Socrates has merged the model of the bard with that of the banquet singer, the lyric poet with no particular skill of his own, in no way specially prepared for the Muse's choice that alights upon him.

Returning to the rhapsode, Socrates then explains that as he recites the poems of Homer (it is worth noting that music has by now disappeared), Ion is seized by rapture and is, in his turn, possessed by the text, whose surrogate voice he becomes, just as the bard was the surrogate voice of the Muse. He will then communicate that rapture to those listening to him, both in the religious ceremonies in which he takes part, such as certain sacrifices, and also in the competitions in which tens of thousands of listeners may be assembled. Those listeners will weep, be frightened or become impassioned, just as if they were really present at the frightening or moving scenes described by the rhapsode: the death of Hector, the grief of Achilles at the death of Patroclus, the farewells of Andromache, or the threats of the Cyclops.

Socrates likens the rapture transmitted from Homer's Muse to the spectator at the Panathenaea, his own contemporary, as he listens to Ion reciting, to the power of a magnet that draws to it a first iron link to which other links then become attached because each magnetized link has the power to attract others. But a comparison is not a reason, and it would be easy to reverse that image: a link loses its magnetic power once the magnet is removed; in the absence of the Muse, outside the time of performance, the communicated rapture also disappears. However, there is no point in arguing with a man who has been dead for two thousand years, so let us simply note that the three kinds of rapture—that of the poet, that of the rhapsode, and that of the spectator—are not all of the same nature. The first is a ravishing, similar to the possession of the *Bacchae*:

> Lyric poets do not indite those fine songs in their senses, but when they have started on the melody and rhythm they begin to be frantic, and it is under possession—as the bacchants are possessed and not in their senses when they draw honey and milk from the rivers—that the soul of the lyric poet does the same thing, by their own report. For the poets tell us, I believe, that the songs they bring us are the sweets they cull from honey-dripping founts in certain gardens and glades of the Muses—like the bees, and winging the air as these do.[48]

The rapture of the rhapsode and the spectators, on the other hand, is purely affective. They are seized by emotions that imitate those that they would experience faced with the same scene actually taking place. The statement acts upon the rhapsode and his listeners through an effect of recognition. They weep over the death of Patroclus as they would over that of a close relative or dear friend. Plato replaces the ethics of possession by the aesthetics of imitation of reality. Instead of using fiction and otherness to explore culture and its limits, poetry is reduced to a self-referential representation, a mirror held up to men by poets who resemble them.

The only remaining link between men and the Muses is constituted by a number of scattered texts, monuments left to men by mythical poets, which can now only be repeated indefinitely. Those great inventors have become the new Muses, and rhapsodes have become the new poets. Homer, Hesiod, or whoever (it is suggested) offer men of the present the spectacle of a world of gods and heroes that is now lost, conjuring up an illusory vision of that epic world for them. In this dialogue it is possible to detect the seed of the theory of *mimēsis*, which Plato later uses to banish poets from the city and which Aristotle uses to justify a renewal of poetic activity. With poets fashioning new poems, new epic deprived of inspiration since the speech-act context for it (the Homeric banquet, in which the bard was inspired) has disappeared from the official culture, only the texts—in other words, Homer—are left to "inspire" the producers of epic. The imitating poet will multiply *mimēsis*, producing an image of an image of an image. Imitation operates like Socrates' magnetic chain. But there is one difference: Socrates was speaking of a world in which Homer was still recited, whereas Aristotle was to set out rules for a world of books in which the living culture would take no interest in the imitative epics produced by the new poets, whether these were Alexandrians such as Apollonius or Romans such as Virgil.

Mimēsis produced a two-headed monster: textual materiality along with on the one hand hermeneutics, on the other papyrology. As Socrates concluded in the *Ion*, a rhapsode understood nothing about what he was reciting and, anyway, nobody understood anything about Homer except by dint of applying himself to semiological, interpretative research.[49] A rhapsode was no more than a reader of Homer, which was why he had to be his commentator—in other words, speak his language; in other words, also possess his professional skill: in a word, be Homer. The Greeks were confronted by the fact that a pure statement either never meant anything or else meant anything you liked. It was at the time of Socrates that allegorical readings of epic were flourishing. All our own contemporary contortions—textology, narratology, semiology—the purpose of which is to extract confessions under torture from all the texts classified in our various literary categories, stem from those readings. But it has never been possible to extract a confession from a corpse. Meaning only emerges from a speech act, and when that does happen, it cannot be mistaken.

The other effect of the materialization of texts was a fanatical cult of word-for-word accuracy. The philologists of Alexandria were the first professional critics. As they corrected, cut, and reconstituted manuscripts, they were in pursuit of the true version, so as to be able to read the authentic, original, actual Homer. But why, given that in any case they would read into it whatever they wanted to? Besides, restored to the context of its original speech act, Homer would have liberated the philologists from all their worries, for the text would have recovered its original uncertainty, its live variations, and these alone could produce the meaning that, though self-evident to those listening to the bard, was bound to elude those reading it.

Imitation and Memory: Aristotle's Poetics

In contrast to the Socrates of the *Ion*, who condemned the decontextualization of epic in competitions for rhapsodes, Aristotle claimed to believe that separation between a statement and its speech act was in the nature of all things to do with poetry. He deliberately ignored all forms of oral composition, presupposed that all poetry was initially written down, and decided that reading provided an adequate reception that made it possible to evaluate any form of public, poetic, or rhetorical speech. Was it, perhaps, Aristotle who invented literature?

The opening pages of his *Poetics* contain a curious passage in which the author expresses surprise that Greek provides no generic term to designate

> the art which employs words either in bare prose or in metres. . . . [This] happens up to the present day to have no name. For we can find no common term to apply to the mimes of Sophron and Xenarchus and to the Socratic dialogues: nor again supposing a poet were to make his representation in iambics or elegiacs or any other such meter.[50]

Aristotle therefore proposes introducing a new term, the "poetic art," but it is to cover only representations in verse, or in meters, not those expressed in prose: the poetic art is thus a subdivision of the general art of speech, which, it seems, remains unnameable. However, without naming it, Aristotle does provide a definition for it: it is the art of representing through speech, and he includes this art within a general "mimetic" concept of all the arts.[51] Music represents through melody and rhythm, painting represents through color and design, dance represents through rhythm, and so on.

In introducing this category of representation, *mimēsis*, Aristotle ignores speech as an act and concentrates solely on the production of statements. What he does is make this representation the final cause of poetic activity rather than the means of completing a religious or social ritual, such as a sacrificial offering or a dramatic spectacle. In consequence, Aristotle systematically ignores the pragmatic meaning of tragedy, epic, and lyric songs. He thus makes a tragedy, for example, into a self-sufficient text that ideally does not need to be performed on stage. That kind of spectacle provides a supplementary pleasure, which, however, it is not necessary to take into account when evaluating the worth of a play: "Spectacle [*opsis*], while highly effective, is yet quite foreign to the art and has nothing to do with poetry. Indeed the effect of tragedy does not depend on its performance by actors, and, moreover, for achieving the spectacular effects the art of the costumier is more authoritative than that of the poet."[52] As some contemporary editors of Aristotle cheerfully point out, he "never desists from attacking stagecraft," which is a terrible thorn in his flesh. But, in truth, the same problem arises with lyric poetry and epic, even if this Aristotelian treatise does not mention those two genres.

Aristotle thus arrives at the following paradoxical conclusion: theater, etymologically "a place for seeing," has no need of spectacle (*opsis*, another term etymologically connected with seeing) to be effective. Indeed, for Aristotle, everything to do with the spectacle of bodies, unless it be in a representation by means of dance, is "vulgar" (*phortikon*).[53] To savor the effects of tragedy to the full, all you need do is read it: "Tragedy fulfils its function even without acting, just as much as epic, and its quality can be gauged by reading [*dia tou anaginōskein*]."[54] This is a theater of words but also a theater of stories, for Aristotle rejects the music of verse: "It is clear then, from what we have said, that the poet must be a 'maker' not of verses but of stories [*mython*] since he is a poet in virtue of his 'representation' and what he represents is action."[55] That certainly constitutes a radically realistic view of language and its uses: words represent things—*mimēsis*—

and are valid in themselves as they act on the public. It is the story of Oedipus that arouses "terror and pity" in the audience—and this, according to Aristotle, is the true purpose of the tragic genre—not tragedy as a particular kind of speech act. This is borne out by the fact that he does not really know what to do with the chorus, which initially was a part of, not the story, but the tragic spectacle, so he reduces it to the status of merely another character, just like the rest.[56] Just as, ideally, rhetoric fights not by means of words, but by means of "things themselves,"[57] ideally theater should represent actions. What will make good tragedy will be a good story that mingles the probable with the magical, thereby arousing "terror and pity."

To relate Aristotle's theory of epic and tragic poetry to my own suggestions regarding what I have called "mythical exploration," we should note that all that Aristotle has retained from the mythical performance that Athenian tragedy and the song of the bard constituted is a mythical fiction: hence his idea that tragedy is a mixture of the probable and the magical, which is another way of saying that mythical fiction is created out of the common culture (what Aristotle deems probable—war, for example) with an admixture of an element that is culturally impossible (what Aristotle deems magical, like a ten-year war). But by eliminating speech acts and performance, Aristotle at the same time removes any possibility of a pragmatic meaning, the possibility of a tragedy or epic having an exploratory, mythical function. Now, mythical fictions are empty forms without the mythical performances that they make possible. Once artificially isolated, they derive from language, not from speech. For Aristotle, tragedies and epics can become timeless stories, transcribed statements, since they possess no referential meaning.

It is not hard to see that, in such circumstances, lyric poetry was in danger of disappearing. Since music was separate from speech according to Aristotelian classification, a poetic genre could not be defined by a musical instrument; instead, it was classified according to its meter and the subject of which it produced a representation. Aristotle thus defined satirical poets as iambic poets, going on to explain that they took as their subject one particular individual who was the target of their invectives. Then came a brief mention of elegiacs. But what could he possibly do with banquet songs?

It would have been difficult to fit the songs of Anacreon into the classificatory system of Aristotle, who was interested only in statements that could be read; and, in any case, his theory of representation could only have reduced them to narratives told in the first person and interpreted in biographical terms.

Aristotelian poetics did not develop in a vacuum, simply bursting forth from the perverse imagination of Alexander's tutor. What we find elaborated here is a theoretical blueprint for a self-referential Greek culture, the end product of the panhellenism sketched out in the culture of festivals. Aristotle's *Poetics* is above all a political manifesto, a program for the cultural unification of Greece under the Macedonian monarchy, an announcement of the death of the liberty of Greek city-states.

The obliteration of all individual particularities effected by the obliteration of particular speech-act conditions was, as might be guessed, brought about through writing-reading. At the same time, Aristotle's theory focused solely on the object produced, not on its reception, so, clearly, from the point of view of his theory there was no need for those works to be heard, seen, or even read. All that mattered was that they should exist, even if they remained buried in some cupboard beneath layers of dust. From this time on their purpose was essentially educational, but only in the case of a few of them: only the canonical works of this unified Greek culture known as Hellenistic would be preserved so that they could be droned and recited by schoolboys under threat from their teacher's ruler, should their memories fail. All the children of the peoples conquered by Alexander would thus know what to think of the tears that Achilles shed at the death of Patroclus, the fury of Atreus, and the pride of Oedipus. No; Aristotle did not invent literature, but he did make schoolteachers responsible for the transmission of poetic forms, and he also elaborated a premonitory theory of realism.

When an everyday culture dies, and along with it the events that used to celebrate it, it frequently happens that an aesthetics of realism comes to be developed. For instance, in nineteenth- and twentieth-century France, the development of the novel accompanied the distress caused by the death of traditional rural societies. Even as folklorists were collecting the fragments of a dying memory and George Sand was at some length recounting the customs of a Berry that she sensed was forgetting itself, Balzac was trying to represent modernity, and Zola took over where he left off. When one is not in control of one's culture, that is to say no longer or not yet in control, because one has been born either too early or too late into a world that is either too old or too young, exploratory fiction becomes impossible. The

Hellenistic period likewise experienced a frenetic bout of archivism that reflected a similar distress, a symptom of the loss of a living memory that had been transmitted through social life and its ordinary rituals. A glut of museums and libraries is indicative of a culture sick in its daily life. But the remedy is worse than the sickness, for those are the very worst places for memories. Having failed to preserve a cultural genre, society delegates to such places the responsibility for preserving its past masterpieces. These come to resemble the fetishes of dead magicians in ethnographic museums, reduced to handfuls of dusty feathers or faded, painted masks, now that men have forgotten how their ancestors used to make the gods come to them. The "artists" who copy them will pass on nothing but the sickness of death and the plague of oblivion.

Anacreon in the "Cage of the Muses"

When Alexander united the Greek cities under his authority and the Macedonian victories extended Hellenism as far as the limits of the inhabited world, the break initiated by panhellenism between monument culture and events culture, official culture and popular culture, self-referential culture and exploratory culture, was completed once and for all. The symbol and instrument of this change was the library associated with the Museum of Alexandria. Greek culture now became confused with an encyclopedic knowledge enshrined in writing and an ability to imitate its canonical works, also preserved in books.

The Hellenistic period invented the culture of books, but that does not mean that it invented literary culture. For the numerous libraries set up on the model of the library of Alexandria never attracted many readers and most of those who did use them were seeking no more than knowledge that was immediately usable or a stylistic model to help them to become authors themselves. The book-lined Museum was the sanctuary of a dead memory.

The Museum was one of the institutions created by the Macedonian kings of Egypt, with the aim of making Alexandria the capital of Hellenism.[58] Museum—*Mouseion*, in Greek—means "temple of the Muses." The name on its own suggests simply one more of the sanctuaries that, as we have noted earlier, were devoted to the Muses in many Greek cities, most of them associated with a local poet-hero, Homer in Chios, Hesiod in Thespis, Archilochus in Paros, Mimnermus in Smyrna, and so on. These museums had played their part in the elaboration of the poetic models of panhellenism, by fixing in writing the songs attributed to their heroes and inventing a biography for them. But now they were to make room for a far more ambitious enterprise, for what the Museum of Alexandria was designed to amass, as if it were as war booty, was the whole of the world's knowledge: all its songs, all its philosophical works, all its scientific treaties.

The Museum of Alexandria was created by Ptolemy Soter, the first Macedonian sovereign of Egypt, on the advice of Demetrius of Phalerus, who had taken refuge at his court after being ejected by the Athenians.[59] This disciple of Aristotle turned Peripatetic philosophy into the kingdom's official doctrine. The Museum was founded on the model of the Lyceum, but was on a quite different scale. It was situated inside the precinct of the royal palace and comprised, as well as the temple of the Muses, a series of buildings designed to house intellectuals on the prince's payroll. These boasted many rooms, a peristyle, a portico, and banquet halls. But, above all, it included a vast library. And, truly, the only memory to be celebrated in the sanctuary of the Muses of Alexandria was the memory of books, without the latter even being used for ritual recitations designed to bring a particular hero back to life.

The scope of the plan behind the foundation of this library was worthy of the conquests of Alexander, for it was an imperialist and universalist project, namely to assemble in one place and in book form the entire knowledge of the world, from its earliest beginnings. The Ptolemys ordered all existing books in Greek, in Athens, Rhodes, and elsewhere to be seized. Under Ptolemy Evergetes, all ships putting into the port of Alexandria were searched and any scrolls discovered were copied: the copies were then returned to the owners while the originals were preserved in the library. Books written in foreign languages were transcribed in Greek. It was in this way that the Septuagint or Alexandrian Bible came to be translated, as did the two million lines of verse attributed to Zoroaster.

To be serviceable, such a library needed a classification system: librarians threw themselves into producing catalogs and elaborated a wealth of bibliographical knowledge. Works were classified by "genres" and each was attributed to an author. These authors were listed chronologically, succeeding one another in, as it were, genealogies of masters and pupils. Each author was attributed a biography. Each work was supposed to consist of a single text, a requirement that occasioned intense activity of an editorial nature, to the end of unifying all its different versions by dint of pruning, correcting, and reordering them. Each work also had to conform to certain rules that defined its textual nature—it had to be coherent, not repetitive, and so on. Meanwhile, philologists were turning out streams of commentaries in the form of questions and answers. They would assess the value of each author and pick out the best of them, as Callimachus did, for example, when he produced his *Catalogs of Authors Who Shone in Each Discipline*. And as they worked, they were torn by two contradictory desires: both to preserve everything and to keep only the best.

Anacreon was edited by Aristophanes of Byzantium. It was he who classified the lyrics according to genre (banquet odes, epinicians, and so on) and had the idea of setting out the odes in lines. His successor Aristarchus was to introduce a new classification, according to musical genres (Dorian, Phrygian, Lydian . . .).

The library of Alexandria and its cult of books for their own sake represents the very epitome of a cold culture of concern only to a handful of intellectuals shut away in the royal palace, slaving away over a few lines of Homer. Timon the philosopher called them "bookish scribblers constantly pecking at one another in the cage of the Muses." Unfortunately, this Alexandrian culture confiscated Hellenism, and those who considered themselves its heirs, the Romans, were to find themselves having to manage a monstrous quantity of books, preserving it, extending it, and reproducing it.

From this point on, knowledge was a matter of accumulation, and poetic culture was a matter of citation; and for both, books were necessary. But does that mean that this was the beginning of the age of literature? As we shall see, books, for the ancients, always remained dead letters and writing always spoke of an absent body and would only recover life and warmth when it gave birth to a new orality.

However, all this was still a far cry from our own libraries, places where culture is transmitted through the reading of literary works. The fact is that there were only three roles for these Alexandrian books. In the first place, they were archives of knowledge, what we would call "data banks"; and in this respect the writing used was conceived in the same way as that of the storekeepers of Cnossos: it was transparent to its object; to read was to learn. Second, these books were funerary monuments to the great men of Greek culture. To read them was not to communicate with the dead, but to celebrate their fame by getting the words that they had written down to resound in the air. Only in this respect was the signifier important: to read was to cite. For the ultimate form taken by that celebration was citation, an act of mutual recognition between the "educated" men of Greco-Roman antiquity, who would exchange educational memories when they gathered together. Third, a few scholars would imitate those books, produce, as it were, up-to-date versions of them, to prove that in their own day and age it was still possible for a "child of Alexandria"[60] to write an epic or a tragedy. This kind of writing was addressed solely to a restricted circle of scholars, who would either approve or reject the imitation and, if they approved it, would provide it with a fictitious speech act, thereby interpreting the rules of composition in the spirit of Aristotle. To read was to write.

So this was not the birth of literature, but rather the birth of the ideology of a literary culture, that is, a culture transmitted by written letters. For from this point on, in the Hellenistic world, a cultivated man, although still described, in Greek, as a *mousikos anēr*, a "musical man," was in fact a man of letters, *litteratus*, as the Romans put it, "lettered" or "literate." This adjective, derived from the noun *litterae*, implied not only knowing how to read and write, being literate, but also being familiar with the monuments of culture that were written in the Greek and Latin languages and that redounded to their credit. The wide diversity of the uses of the term *litterae*, in Cicero, speaks volumes: it could mean a "missive," "official records," "documents" used in evidence in legal trials; *litterae* and *monumentae* were the literary monuments of a city; and Cicero also speaks of a man's *litterae* when he wishes to refer to his culture, his learning, or the education he has received. So from now on, in cities that recognized or wished to be part of the Hellenistic culture, books were systematically produced, to be used as the city's memory; and this culture of books became the basis of its children's education. It was a culture made up by compilations of knowledge that could be accumulated and masterpieces fixed word for word, which could therefore only ever be used for citing.

But this "literature" has nothing to do with our modern kind of literature, for it implied a kind of reading that separated the form from the content and that produced neither pleasure nor oblivion of the surrounding world. This Alexandrian literature was addressed solely to book professionals, men who were also commentators, philologists, professors, poets, librarians, and editors, all rolled into one. They were the official managers of a Greek memory that was totally isolated from collective social practices.

Anacreon in Autun: Greco-Roman Letters

Relatively recently, in 1965, a Roman mosaic was discovered in Autun, the ancient Augustodunum of Lyonese Gaul. The mosaic was dated by archaeologists to the second century, possibly the late second century, and it shows that by this time Anacreon had become a monument to letters: he was no longer a way of drinking or even of singing. Anacreon had become a way of writing or something even dryer, a collection of lyric meters.[61]

The poet is depicted perched on the edge of a high-backed chair, like Virgil in the famous first-century Sousse mosaic, in Tunisia. This way of depicting poets who had become the emblematic representatives of a particular literary genre fixed in some monumentalized work, ornaments of the libraries in which they served to identify particular book stacks, dated from the Alexandrian period. The most ancient example was probably the Pindar in the Sarapeon of Memphis, dating from the third century B.C. A similar statue of Archilochus is known to have stood in its second-century B.C. museum of carvings.

The portrayal of Anacreon in the guise of a writer contrasts sharply with the representations of him as a drunken singer, such as his statue on the Acropolis, which presented an image that continued to be transmitted by the Anacreontic tradition in the *Palatine Anthology*. In the Autun mosaic, Anacreon is no longer even the subject of a romantic statement, let alone the cultural hero of ritual intoxication. Instead, he is one of the great masters of a culture of schoolteachers, who has become an end in himself. He represents a chapter of literary history, the lyric poetry defined by two particular metric structures. Anacreon is here identified with the Anacreontic meters. His name is not even inscribed in the mosaic; instead, two easily identified fragments are cited: they turn out to be two examples used by the teachers of antiquity to illustrate the two meters peculiar to Anacreontic verse.

As has already been mentioned, meter was an invention of the Alexandrian philologists, for the purpose of classifying poetry that had been reduced to a text, without its music. Anacreon without wine, without a lyre, and without love became an Aristotelian category, a decreed sequence of short and long beats that nobody could hear: he had reached the ultimate stage of scholastic abstraction and cold culture.

Archaeologists have pondered at length on the nature of the edifice in which this mosaic was found, and have tried to imagine who its proprietor might have been. It is very tempting to postulate a link between the archaeological discoveries and the speech by Eumenes entitled *For the Restoration of the Schools of Autun* (298), for from the latter we learn that Autun was then one of the university centers of Lyonese Gaul that used to attract professors of Greek from Greece. Although the idea that this building was itself used as one of these schools seems ruled out for topographical reasons, it remains nevertheless possible that it may have served as a dwelling for one of those professors and that this mosaic of Anacreon may have adorned its atrium. It is known that Romans without glorious ancestors of their own were prone to place in their homes busts or portraits of great representatives of the official culture, either poets or philosophers, particularly if they were themselves scholarly men. By so doing they acquired a spiritual family and rooted themselves in a language, generally Greek, even if it was not possible for them to do so in the families and memories of the locality. In this case, one imagines a professor of anaclastic Ionic or catalectic iambic dimeters, since by this time that was all that Anacreon stood for.

II

THE CULTURE OF THE KISS: SPEAKING WITH NOTHING TO SAY

Roman Lands

THE GREEKS HAD COMMITTED a few songs to writing—that is, a few sung events—and had thereby turned them into monuments, because they believed in the poetic, or rather exemplary, value of these songs and had at the same time lost confidence in the survival of their living culture. They had created a mythology of great poets, great inventors, and had conferred fame upon imaginary heroic figures such as Homer and Anacreon, who were confused with those monumentalized events.

Rome went through neither that self-glorification nor that fear of the future. In general, it kept its live practices separate from its monumental policies. It made no record of oral performances within the framework of banquets but did commit to writing an artificial poetry whose only purpose was to constitute monuments, without ever having been a part of events. On the one hand there were the diversions of banquets, essentially lost forever, and on the other written works such as Virgil's *Aeneid* and Horace's *Odes*, designed to preserve continuity between Rome and Greece, in the Alexandrian manner and on a genealogical model: Greek texts were reproduced in the form of Latin texts that resembled them and appeared beside them on library shelves, works of scholars destined for other scholars. The men of the Renaissance continued to behave in this way, anchoring their period in a culture from elsewhere, in order to accede to eternity by wresting the birth of their own society from history and making it coincide with what they called civilization.

Some people favor a Promethean exercise of this kind, which constructs an abstract, universal, eternal man, both author and addressee of works preserved in museums and libraries—that is to say, a "humanist" way of proceeding. It offers a historical and social asceticism which, to some, seems the only possible remedy for the despair engendered by the ravages of time and history.

But others prefer a different type of human adventure, the kind by which anthropologists are attracted. Michel Serres has succinctly summed up the fundamental choice imposed by the adoption of any cultural attitude: it is a choice between being rooted in the earth and being rooted in books. If you choose the earth—the idiosyncratic, day-to-day, live, vulnerable, shifting culture of a group of people here and now—you swap literature for exploration and set off to discover new words and new customs.

Opting for the earth in Rome means embarking on a necessary but difficult expedition. Where banquet speech is concerned, it may even seem a doomed endeavor, given that the diversions of Roman banquets, by their very nature, defied monumentalization. However, it sometimes is possible to catch a handful of Romans on their banquet couches, and, as we shall see, the games that they play, though different, are just as strange as those of the Greek drinkers possessed by Eros, Dionysus, and the Muses. The kinds of intoxication developed in Rome involved no religious rites and developed on the margins of traditional conviviality.

The Dangers of the Mediterranean

Some readers might now like to be presented with a history of the Mediterranean banquet, reconstructed on the basis of archaeology, except that the very idea of such a unique, model banquet turns out to be an artifact of a by now discredited historical theory. However, if one does assume there to have been a common Mediterranean civilization that later became diversified, much of the evidence available—the tableware found in tombs, the funerary frescoes, the positioning of the beds, as reconstructed from the excavation of private homes—might indeed seem to suggest that the peoples of Italy, Greece, and the Middle East all banqueted in the same manner. The Homeric *dais* might even seem to justify the idea of a general model: free men of the same high social rank, gathered in the home of one of their number, sharing bread, meat from a sacrifice, and wine: a Mediterranean banquet that was both a means of offering hospitality and an act of prestige, an opportunity to demonstrate one's wealth and generosity and to negotiate alliances.[1] An archaeologist might even add the information that the reclining position, although unknown in Homeric banquets, first appeared in that period in Greece, is attested in Italy by the second half of the seventh century B.C., and also appears to have been extremely ancient in the East.

Resemblances and affiliations constitute one of the great temptations of history. And a historian of antiquity is furthermore faced by another diabolical tempter, comparative philology. But the latter may equally well operate as a safety device. To reflect upon the etymology of the word "wine," for example, is enough to make one's head spin.[2] The Latin word *uinum* certainly has the same root as the Greek *oinos* and the Mycenaean *wono*, but it cannot have derived from it since this *uinum* is to be found as early as the seventh century B.C. in various forms in all Italic languages, Faliscan, Umbrian, Siculan, even Etruscan. In the East, it is present in both Hittite and Armenian. It is known that the term is not Indo-European and it might have been supposed to be of Semitic origin, except that in a number of major ancient Semitic languages there is no such root to designate wine: although present in Hebrew and Arabic, it is absent from Akkadian and Phoenician. Nor is it to be found in Sumerian or Egyptian, from which it might have been supposed to come. The languages of these peoples certainly have a word for wine, but one formed on the basis of a different etymology. In the end, philological exertions such as these teach us historical prudence and can lead only to the following, negative, conclusion: on the basis of the words used to designate wine, it is not possible to maintain that the use of it spread throughout the Mediterranean from a single original point, nor—a fortiori—can one make a similar claim for the banquet. So it is not possible to postulate a common Mediterranean banquet.

In any case, even if legitimate, an imaginary history of the banquet from its origins on would simply establish a framework for shared conviviality and would grind to a halt at the precise point where real history, the kind in which we are interested, begins: namely, the history of how, in different places and in different periods, banquets in reality developed from different experiences, as a result of the effects of wine, the physical closeness of the drinkers, and the pleasurable sensuality of the mouth. The advantage of diversity is that it produces live, day-to-day cultures, and the beauty of traditional cultures lies in their ability to recognize and cultivate that diversity,[3] as the Greek cities did when they were still free.

For as soon as we come to deal with historical periods, we find a whole range of different practices that may have been developed out of that primordial theoretical banquet but about which that banquet, even if reconstructed, could tell us nothing. We have already seen how the aristocrats of some Greek cities developed the symposion culture—the culture of a banquet devoted exclusively to "drinking together," in which men shared no food, just wine, and made this a self-reflexive leisure pastime with which they identified. The important, if not essential feature of that kind of banquet was the presence of a god of possession, Dionysus, for this turned the symposion into a sacred, drugged experience that led to speech-song in which the event reached its fulfillment.

That is why to dream up a common origin for all Mediterranean banquets is more dangerous than it is useful. To be sure, it would help us to connect Rome with Greece, on the grounds of a more or less similar protohistory in which Greek, Etruscan, Campanian, and Latin clan chieftains were all banqueting at the same time, reclining on similar couches, and drinking from cups imported from Greece, painted with the same orientalizing motifs, the same wine that ships were delivering to all four corners of the sea. But this is where the danger begins, the temptation to attribute what is known of some to others too, to maintain, for example, that bards were singing all over the place, celebrating the exploits of those present at the feast, or that intoxicated singers were everywhere lifting their voices in drinking songs. The Greek example itself should serve to warn us. In Greece, the same applied to banquets as to gods: the cities all developed different forms of conviviality, and it would be rash, to put it mildly, to assume that they all stemmed from a single model.[4] It could well be, for instance, that the reason for the disappearance of the *dais*, or sacrificial banquet, was that elsewhere symposia were being held, while in Sparta, where wine was forbidden, free men were organizing communal meals (*syssitia*) in public places.

So I, like others, reject the idea of too direct a thread linking Anacreon to Horace.[5] For it would lead to a loss of Rome's own soul, which is precisely what I should like to rediscover.

Eating or Drinking: Two Different Kinds of Roman Banquet

Does all this mean that no comparisons can be made between one shore of Mare nostrum and another? It would be as pointless to set out to draw a systematic opposition between Greece and Rome, as if they were irreducibly different, like black and white, as to confuse the two together. The real difficulty is to maintain just the right distance between the three: Rome, Greece, and ourselves.

Seen from Greece, nothing could be more disorienting than the Roman banquet. At first, there is a strange and misleading sense of familiarity about the Roman *cena*, the very name of which is, so to speak, a translation of the Greek *dais*.[6] All present partake of sacrificed meats and other delicacies. The *cena* is a place of conviviality, a welcoming place of pleasure where the reclining guests eat and drink wine. As in Homer, that wine has nothing to do with Dionysus or any intoxicatory techniques. In one essential respect, however, the Roman *cena* does differ from the Homeric banquet: it is not a place where memories of the past are celebrated or where a common culture is consolidated through the sharing of sacred stories and songs presided over by one or more deities, such as the Muses.[7]

The *cena* played a particularly important role in the Roman civilization. The shared partaking of delicious foods—meats, fish, seafood, wines, cakes, and fruits—was a central element in the symbolic network of gestures that organized and maintained the social scale. Friendships, hospitality, clientship, and social duties (*officia*) all made use of the *cena*, at every level in the hierarchy—hence, in Rome, the development of a sumptuous gastronomic culture of both recipes and products and also of a social code of politeness for banquets and table manners based on an anthropology of sensual pleasures involving the faculty of taste and, more generally, physical repose. The Romans are inexhaustible on the subject of good and bad hosts and guests. For a *cena* implied not only that one "forgot" one's worries as a public figure, something which, in antiquity, had been taken for granted ever since Homer's day, but also that both body and soul relaxed, softened, opened up to others. This "openness" of a Roman banquet host could take many forms: he would be generous, loosening his purse strings to pay, without counting the cost, for the delicacies intended for his guests. At table, his relaxed features would expand in a permanent smile and his good humor (*hilaritas*) would be unfailing. He would be appreciative of everything offered him, listen to the chatter of each and every guest, be ready with a laugh for every jest or joke, and, if young enough, would even go so far as to dance or sing for the amusement of his guests. This was known as *benignitas, comitas*, a tolerant complicity that bound drinking companions together but did not necessarily amount to mutual loyalty or affection, being more a kind of moral inertia, a "going with the flow." The worst of sins would have been to offend, to be boorish or a bad host.

The only limitation to this temporary license was the self-respect and respect for others that dictated each individual's place in the social hierarchy and his sense of what was seemly. It was all a far cry from the

Homeric kings seated upon silver-studded thrones, listening to a bard in the great *megaron* of Odysseus.

The *cena* was not the only form of Roman hospitality, although it was probably the principal one. There was also another kind of banquet, known by a Greek name, the *comissatio*, from the Greek *kōmazein* 'to be festive'. As always with Roman practices known by Greek names, it would be mistaken to think that this was a Greek festivity imported to Rome virtually unchanged. The comissatio may have had a Greek origin, but even if it did it was an altogether Roman practice and had nothing in common with the Dionysiac *kōmos*, the bands of revelers who would rampage drunkenly through the streets of Athens and burst in upon other people's banquets, as happens in Plato's *Symposium*.

The Roman comissatio was a banquet for reclining guests that either preceded or followed a *cena*: those present simply drank and chatted. Admittedly, we know very little of the customs of the comissatio, for it seems to have been less popular than the *cena* and certainly never held a strategic position in the symbolism of Roman pleasures since, unlike the *cena*, it by no means constituted a common form of leisure pastime. To put that another way, whereas gluttony and greed were certainly capital sins in Rome, sins that presented a threat to the moral and physical health of the community, drunkenness was never censured in the same way. On that account, the comissatio was not a subject for normative discourse and escaped reprobation, usually our best source of information.

The comissatio, possibly practiced only by the town's young nobility, may have been one of the forms of life in the Greek style that a section of the Roman aristocracy had, since the Punic Wars at least, been cultivating as a distinguishing mark of their identity. Not only was the Roman nobility consistently bilingual (bilingualism frequently extended even into the daily life of the urban plebs), but, for Romans right across the board, Greek culture represented the highest form of urban refinement. The elite was inevitably, as they say, "philhellenic." Everything sophisticated, different, oriental, or sensually gratifying was, a priori, Greek.

As less documentation exists for the comissatio than for the *cena*, so that, unlike in the case of the *cena*, it is not possible to elaborate a model of it, perhaps the best representation of one may be provided by a specific example.[8] Under the Roman Empire, in the second century, a young man, clearly from the nobility, since he belonged to a family of knights, invited his friends round to celebrate his birthday, and offered them a *cena* in a small country house not far from Rome. After the eating (*ubi eduliis finis*) came the time for wine and words, *poculis mox sermonibusque*: the Latin terms suggest the wine circulating and a conversational interchange. A comissatio was not a Roman symposion and never acquired the literary and philosophical prestige of a Greek symposion.

As compared with Greek customs, the situation in Rome was thus rather curious, for two kinds of banquets were held there, the *cena* and the *commissatio* and, as in Greece, the one was devoted to wine, the other to food. Yet from the point of view of their symbolical importance, their positions were reversed.

The Blood of the Earth

Roman wine was not Greek wine; it was not a drug that led to a mystical intoxication. Dionysism and Dionysiac trance never became acclimatized to Rome. But nor was Roman wine simply nourishment or a drink like any other. To discover the particular nature of a Roman item of nourishment and reconstruct its place in the Roman culture, it is often helpful to examine the rituals in which it played a part and to set one's findings alongside the techniques used by agriculturists.[9] Wine that was pure (*temetum*) was, in certain conditions, offered as a libation to the gods, in the course of sacrifices. This wine had to have been produced from pruned vines, not from wild ones.[10] It was also important that it should not be adulterated. This pure wine was reserved for the gods and for men and was forbidden to women who, on the other hand, were allowed to drink wines that the gods spurned.[11]

These precise religious recommendations make it possible to reconstruct an image of Roman wine: when pure, it was to some extent an antimeat, an antidote to the poison of death and old age, a drink forever young. Spontaneously "hot," with time it became more concentrated through a kind of self-cooking, sometimes becoming as thick as honey.[12] So instead of rotting as does dead flesh or other foodstuffs that contain water or are prepared with water, instead of dissolving into a cold, stinking liquid, it grew younger and more and more compact. Honey, to which it drew closer, was the very epitome of a stable and incorruptible product. That is why pure wine was the liquor of Jupiter, the god who, more than any other, held death and rotting corpses in horror; and it is also why it was the drink of civilized men, for it was, so to speak, naturally "cooked." Wine possessed a vigor that made it "boil" in the vats, and it was a vigor that kept the wine alive but also that any man who drank wine had to be prepared to cope with.

The addition of water, cooking over heat, and cooling were all means that were employed to "break" (*frangere*) the strength of the wine and produce a drink that was less potent. When the must (*mustum*) obtained by pressing grapes was not of the highest quality, it went off as did any other form of nourishment (*uitiatum*) and produced vinegar (*acetum*). To avoid this happening, the Romans devised countless methods of preserving wine, the most frequently used being an addition of fermented wine.

Pliny the Elder, contrasting wine to hemlock, the drink of death that freezes the drinker, remarked that wine is the blood of the earth, apparently borrowing a Greek expression.[13]

> Vinum poterus, rex, memento bibere te sanguinem terrae.

> Remember, o king, that the wine you are about to drink is the blood of the earth.

The Latin term *sanguis* designated not blood that was spilled, *cruor*, but the blood that gave life to human bodies; it was connected with life and vitality, was the seat of the *anima*, the "vital breath," the hottest and lightest element that man possessed. Blood also designated agnatic transmission: father and son are of the same blood in Latin, as in French and English. Blood was thus on the side of life; it had no connection with death.

Roman wine animated the drinker, imparting its warmth and life to him and associating him with Jupiter, the god of festivity and games (*ludi*). The comissatio, a leisure occupation "in the Greek manner," exploited the Roman potentials of wine, distinctly separating itself from the *cena*, the place of "the corrupt," old age and death, in order itself to be the place of "the cooked," youth and immortality.

THREE

The Games of Catullus

Two Charming Boys: Comissatio Words

THIS IS HOW ONE spoke of the secret pleasures of the comissatio at the end of the Roman Republic:

> Hesterno, Licini, die otiosi
> Multum lusimus in meis tabellis
> Ut conuenerat esse delicatos
> Scribens uersiculos uterque nostrum
> Ludebat numero modo hoc modo illoc
> Reddens mutua per iocum atque uinum.

> Yesterday, Licinius, in the leisure hour
> For a long time we played on my tablets
> A game of charming boys
> Writing each other flirtatious verses
> Now in one metre, now in another,
> Answering each other, while we laughed and drank our wine.[1]

"Yesterday," Catullus says. He reminds his play fellow, Licinius, how they drank and played word games together. "In the leisure hour": it was during the *otium*, the Roman space of time that constituted a parenthesis in civilized, "normal" life, a period in which cares both public and private were suspended, "forgotten," so to speak, from midday to midnight. Bodies, and principles too, relaxed, faces lost their tenseness, it was the time for banquets. Reclining, even langorous, men gave themselves up to pleasures that were frowned upon at other times, savoring their laziness and passivity (*inertia, mollitia*).

For in general the Roman civilization cultivated an ethic of effort and action, of striving to surpass oneself, of self-control, of resistance to cold, hunger, thirst, and pain both physical and moral—all of which was summed up by the term *labor*. But it also allowed its heroes interludes of relaxation (*otium*), in which they were refreshed and rested. During these periods of repose, pleasures helped to comfort a man, and they were always passive pleasures that tended to counteract the tensions of *labor*. In *otium*, a Roman allowed himself to be invaded by sweet sensations, he partook of soft nourishment, smooth wines, breathed in fragrances, was lulled by soothing voices and the calming music of the flute.

These two contradictory poles of the Roman culture were indissociable, for they were complementary. Every individual had to be capable of striking a balance between the part of his life that he devoted to the one pole and the part that he devoted to the other. Achievement of that harmony within one's character was the mark of a sage or a great man such as Scipio, Sylla, or Caesar. Public opinion was critical of those who fell into excess on one side or the other: Cato was too hard, too severe; Lucullus and Maecenas too soft, too sensual.

To return to Catullus and his friend, the poet Licinius: they had given themselves up to the pleasures of an afternoon of *otium*, as sophisticated men of the world who knew how to relax with wine and words. For the duration of this little interlude, they had agreed (*ut conuenerat*), he and Licinius,[2] to be "charming boys" (*delicati*), expert at the pleasures of the comissatio. Although the game brought them close together, socially they were divided: the one was noble, the other not. Unlike Licinius, Catullus did not belong to the political class. Whereas Calvus was a "notable," an orator allowing himself some time off in the *otium*, Catullus was a professional, an entertainer only invited to banquets of the high and mighty because he could amuse them. Catullus was in tune with the values of the *otium* through and through. Now a jester, now a troubadour, he was a past master of speech designed solely to please. He was the antithesis of Licinius the orator, also a master of speech, but of the kind that seeks to move in order to convince, serious speech loaded with concrete implications: about war, famine, justice.[3] Nevertheless, they were bound by a common taste for words and appreciation of their power. Jokes and wordplay were part of Catullus's profession. Licinius resorted to them for refreshment from his *labor* as an orator, as a soldier eases his muscles amid the soothing pleasures of a banquet.[4]

Assuming the roles of "charming boys" (*delicati*), Catullus and Licinius, relaxed and perfumed, deliberately entered this domain of pleasure, systematically making use of wine and wordplay (*per uinum et iocum*). This other world had a language of its own, through which one sense aroused another, just as one pleasure led to another. Play (*lusus*), the key word for these charming boys, suggests both the fun of nonserious activities and the fantasy of imitation: wordplay, role play, and erotic play were indissociable. This playful aspect of the comissatio was typically Roman, for Roman games, whether collective, as in the theater or the circus, or private—even intimate—as in banquets, were all, by right, part of *otium*, during which they magnified the values of pleasure, gratuitousness, and fantasy. Above all, this playfulness produced an atmosphere of derision innocent of any malice, in which serious activities of every kind could be imitated and stripped of their solemnity. The playfulness of *otium* flourished on formalism, gestures made for their own sake, dance.[5]

A Fusional Eroticism

But what kind of games were played by Catullus and Licinius and in what sense were they erotic? Each jotted down amorous verses (*uersiculi*) on wax tablets.[6] The tablets were then passed from one to the other, each in turn responding to the poem addressed to him by the other. The partners took it in turn to address each other and be addressed. No distinction was made between the two of them. The game was also a kind of contest in the manner of two-part songs in which one singer embarked upon a rhythm (*numerus*) and the other had to respond in the same rhythm, then start up another of his own, and so on. But the "rhythm" was not really a meter—in the usual sense of *numerus*—but rather a particular syntactical and semantic composition. Some idea of this technique is conveyed by Virgil's *Eclogues*.[7] Two shepherds engage in a poetic contest:

> *Damoetas*
> Triste lupus stabulis maturis frugibus imbres
> Arboribus uenti nobis Amaryllidis.
>
> *Menalcas*
> Dulce satis unor, depulsis arbutus haedis
> Lenta salix feto pecori, mihi solus Amyntas.

> *Damoetas*
> Baneful to the folds is the wolf, to the ripe crop the rains, to trees the gales, and to me the anger of Amaryllis!
>
> *Menalcas*
> Sweet to the corn is the shower, to the new-weaned kids the arbute, to the breeding flock the bending willow, and to me Amyntas alone!

The rhythm (*numerus*), set by Damoetas, is constructed on the basis of four similar sequences, each composed of a subject and an object and all linked within a common pattern consisting of "a copula + an adjective with either a good or a bad connotation." Furthermore, the first three sequences refer to the rural economy, a combination of herding and agriculture, while the fourth refers to the subject's love for someone, either a girl or a boy, whose name soon rings out. The rhythm clearly provides a framework that is at once syntactical, rhetorical, and semantic. The first distich is pronounced by Damoetas, who sets the rhythmic pattern. On the model of this, Menalcas immediately constructs his response. He makes use of a number of simple figures of rhetoric, starting with an antithesis: what was ominous becomes sweet and welcome. Then he uses a chiasmus: the seedlings (agriculture) take the place of the stables, reversing the earlier order, and the young goats then take the place of the ripe wheat. The kids and the stables, and the ripe wheat and the seedlings stand in a metonymic relationship to one another, in the widest sense. In the second verse, there is a reversal between the nature of the subject and that of the object: the trees, earlier the victims of the wind, become beneficent to the pregnant ewes, and the anger of Amaryllis, whose name suggests a girl, is balanced by the love of a boy called Amyntas. The last line in Damoetas's poem was expressed entirely in the plural; Menalcas's last line is expressed entirely in the singular. It is not too hard to see that the point of the game is to apply rhetorical rules of reversal that preserve the *numerus* but at the same time transform the text. The greater the semantic distance from the initial text, the better pleased the listeners. A complete change of tone produces the most satisfactory result.

These twinned verses did not themselves produce erotic effects, despite their subject matter. It was the game itself that would arouse the two boys. Who would read out the table once it was written? The one who received it or the one who had written it? Probably the former. That, at least, is what is suggested by the text if, as some commentators believe, the participle *reddens* also has the sense of "read."[8] For in that case "uterque nostrum . . . reddens mutua" means, literally, "each of us reading to the other the words that become our shared delight." The interest of this interpretation lies in the fact that the interplay with the tablets contributes to the fusion between the two friends that is suggested by the text, since it eliminates any possible differentiation between the two. For the "I" of the words written by the one becomes the "I" of the same words read out by the other, so that the two of them become one. To write, to read—each of those speech acts produces the same statement, namely the *uersiculi* that pass from one hand to another like a cup of shared wine. Curiously enough, the text indicates that the tablets that are used belong to Catullus, who is presumably the host and who accordingly provides the writing materials, just as he does the drinking cups, the wine, and the couches. The implication is that the two drinkers use the same tablets, which are passed to and fro from the one to the other, now written upon, now read, now rubbed out, now rewritten upon. That seems very likely since, in Rome, these tablets would be covered by a coating of wax on which letters could be written, then effaced by a sweep of the thumb. The writing materials used in this instance were designed for words inscribed just for a moment, then consigned to oblivion. The final point to make is that, in Rome, words had a stronger effect on whoever pronounced them than on those who heard them.[9]

In this game, then, each participant seems to have submitted himself to his companion's text, which made him say its words, and then responded by imposing upon his partner a similar text with a similar constraint. The ideology here is that of inscriptions whose written words subject the reader to their signifier. An erotic fusion binds them together since each word is the loving speech of the reader's companion, who possesses him through his reading. But at the same time, this is only a game in which each of them is playing a role under the direction of the other, and laughter (*iocus*) is interjected as a reminder of the distance that each of them should maintain in this fleeting amorous interlude, laughter that is provoked in each by the skill with which his companion responds within this same framework, thereby forcing his partner, in turn, into further unexpected linguistic postures. It is not hard to see why these words were never intended for posterity. They were only meaningful at that particular moment and could not be detached from the imaginary scenario that linked them together in this improvised intoxication.

There was usually no winner or loser in such games as these, no judge to award the prize to one or the other player, for each was the sole judge of speech addressed solely to himself. Yet on that particular day something happened to upset the proper outcome of the comissatio. Catullus was seduced by Licinius more than the game allowed for and lost the distance introduced by laughter that should have enabled him to emerge unscathed from the party.

Catullus's Mistake

Atque illinc abiei lepore
Incensus, Licini, facetiisque
Ut nec me miserum cibus iuvaret
Nec somnus tegeret quiete ocellos
Sed toto indomitus furore lecto
versarer cupiens uidere lucem
Ut tecum loquerer simulque ut essem.

Since I left that place, Licinius, aroused
by your charm and your joyful inventions
I find myself unhappy, with no pleasure in dining
Unable to find rest in sleep, to close my eyes
Maddened, I tossed ceaselessly in my bed
Watching for the light of day
When I could once more be with you and talk with you.

The charm exercised by Licinius was only that of the role he had assumed, as a delightful (*lepos*), witty (*facetiis*) drinking companion. That kind of social charm affected the attitudes of the guests in all the Roman banquets already described. It was a charm that stemmed from a man putting himself totally at the disposal of his fellow guests, in particular the one placed alongside him.[10] A comissatio would magnify the open sociability of a *cena* to the point of converting it into a temporary eroticism. The ardor that united Catullus and Licinius was not supposed to last. It was a controlled, accidental result of the wordplay and the wine and the roles that they had adopted. Once the banquet was over and the excitement of the party had died down, those roles committed them to nothing.[11] Unfortunately though, Licinius's banter (*facetiis*) had created a joyful, imaginary world in which Catullus had allowed himself to be trapped. When he should have returned to the ordinary world and recovered his civic identity there, he was unable to do so.

The comissatio, a banquet of wine and words, should have ended at this point, with each of the participants going off to enjoy himself elsewhere, in a *cena*, with good food and other pleasures. But Catullus failed to switch to that other kind of conviviality that owed nothing to any imaginary world. He could not snap out of the earlier time of the comissatio and found it impossible to readapt to a different social phase. Committed to the delight of words of love, his mouth was not available for the pleasures of the gullet (*gula*).

In the right order of things, sleep ought then to have carried him through from the time of *otium* to the following morning, the time for serious matters, *negotium* and *labores*. But Catullus could no more sleep than he could eat; he remained trapped in yesterday's time. He was impatient for the sunrise not because he was keen to start a new day, but in order to repeat the last one. He was maddened, a prey to *furore*, which in Rome meant that he was out of his mind, lacking the judgment and will that he should have possessed. In this *furor*, I was Another. He had not recovered his autonomy, but had remained merged with Licinius and his whole being was taken over by the pain of an "us" deprived of its other half.

This "other" person whom Catullus misses so much is not the citizen Caius Licinius Macer Calvus, but his charming comissatio partner who played so delightfully with words. Catullus was not madly in love with the respectable married orator. The desire by which he was tormented was simply to repeat yesterday's delight, "to be with you and talk with you." They had played with words, swapping tablets and breathing words of love at each other, and the love in those words and that breath was utterly self-sufficient.

All the same, however verbal that love had been, it required the physical presence of his partner, for such oral pleasures could not be written down.

The Letter to Licinius

Writing was now used to express the absence of the Other's body. The shift from orality to writing implied the loss of words of love since it also implied the loss of the speaking, loving body. The letter, whose very existence implied a distance, was resorted to only because of the pain of separation.

At defessa labore membra postquam
Semimortua lectulo iacebant
Hoc, iucunde, tibi poema feci
Ex quo perspiceres meum dolorem.

But with my body exhausted by pain
I was lying, half-dead, on my little bed
When, my darling, I made you these lines
So that you should see my suffering.

This text is presented as a letter, which explains both what kind of a written text it is and, by the same token, justifies its existence. The past, the time of the writing, *feci*, is opposed to the present of the object that has been composed, *hoc*, which is now in the hands of the reader: a common ploy in the epistolatory style of the Romans. For in Rome the time of a letter's speech act was when it was read, not when it was composed. This suggests that the letter was not a passage of orality caught in writing and recovered through reading; rather, it was from the outset a piece of writing designed to be made oral just once, when it was read. Seen in this light, the letter did not represent a deferred dialogue. That is why Catullus wrote "so that you should see" (*ex quo perpiceres*): the seeing is not simply a metaphor, but refers explicitly to the reading of the letter. One further point of interest: it is not through the letter's contents that Catullus's pain is expressed, but through its very existence.

The letter signifies the absence of a dialogue, the absence of those twinned banquet songs, which cannot be reproduced in an epistolatory communication. But the letter also has a healing effect, for it establishes a separation. Licinius ceases to be the absent half of the double, fused being that only a comissatio can produce and becomes, instead, the distant recipient of these written words. The "us" is disentangled, "I" and "you" become separate in space and time, thanks to the role each now assumes in the use of the tablets. "I wrote, there, yesterday; you read, here, today." Catullus has reintegrated the organized space of ordinary life and the normal succession of days. The tablets that were used in the comissatio for bonding games are reused in a different manner to effect a separation and a return to normality. The writing-reading sequence now fits into the context of letter writing. A letter was a message that could be interpreted without equivocacy by the recipient, for the speech-act situation was defined by the type of relationship that existed between the two actors in the deferred dialogue that a letter constituted for the Romans. A letter belonged to the category of the *sermo*, communicatory language with no poetic function.

A Constructed Object: The Trophy of a Defeat

The Letter and the Vase

"I made you these lines." The letter form was merely a means of transmission, for what Catullus sends Licinius is a constructed object, *poiēma*, whose Greek etymological meaning he recalls to mind through his Latin translation, *feci*, *epoiēsa* in Greek. The term *poiēma* initially meant "a constructed object," before Aristotle used it to signify "poem." Furthermore, in apposition to an object, the word *epoiēse* could be used to sign a work, a painted vase for example, and to indicate to whom it was dedicated. The *iucunde*, "my darling," seems like a transcription of an adjective used, in Greece, to designate the handsome ephebe who was the intended recipient of an erotic present and who would often be described as *kalos*.[12] The poem constructed in this case is thus in a sense reminiscent of the Greek painted cups bearing an inscription, designed on the model of the cups used in symposia. The object speaks to indicate the name of the artist: "X made me," and also celebrates the beauty of the beloved ephebe: "Y is beautiful." The words written on the tablets bearing the letter, which reproduced the tablets used in the game, proclaim the author of the poem and also the seductive charm of some young man.

So this is not really a letter and, true enough, proper letters were not written in verse, nor were they published in books. A letter was not designed to become a monument or to exist outside the intimacy of the two actors in the communication that it effected. Besides, the kind of speech used in letters, namely *sermo*, was not "constructed"; the mere gesture of sending it turned it into a gift. In this case, Catullus's letter-poem is a fine object dedicated to Licinius, a gift sent to him by Catullus. This poem presented to Licinius constitutes homage paid by the vanquished to the victor in what did, after all, turn into a poetic contest. In it, Licinius's victory is celebrated with an epigram that is a trophy.

The Aesthetics of the Graffito: The Epigram

Epigrammatic writing, which took the form of a public inscription, justified the publication of a poem, since epigrams were originally graffiti written on walls in the town, for all the neighborhood to read. This epigram placed between the two men establishes a dissymmetry in the distance already suggested by the use of the letter form, a dissymmetry that befitted the social inequality between them: the reader is now no longer Licinius but, instead, the passersby in general. Licinius, for his part, is the object of this speech, a part of the statement, and is no longer an actor in the speech act. He is exhibited in a social relationship that links him with Catullus and that is subjected to the normative gaze of the group. The egalitarian camaraderie of the comissatio has been superseded by a hierarchy that sets up a clientship, or what the Romans called *amicitia* 'friendship'. It is within the framework of this *amicitia* that the epigram-letter concludes:

> Nunc audax caue sis precesque nostras
> Oramus caue despuas ocelle
> Ne poenas Nemesis reposcat a te
> Est uehemens dea laedere hanc caueto.
>
> Now take care, do not go too far, the pleas that we address to you
> Please do not trample upon them, light of my eyes
> For fear that Nemesis punish you
> She is a terrible goddess, take care not to offend her.

The epigram has turned into a retaliatory graffito[13] in which Catullus implicates the Greek goddess of vengeance, Nemesis. Catullus is reminding Licinius of the laws that protect the vanquished from the excesses of their conqueror and he does so using Greek terminology, in the Hellenistic tradition of erotic poetry. Nemesis will avenge Catullus by wounding Licinius in his turn, thereby restoring equilibrium and justice. That wounding can only be of an amorous nature; Licinius will succumb to the seductive attraction of some other "charming boy." What is the nature of the pleas that Catullus is begging him to gratify? Without doubt, that he should agree to more playful interludes, more time for games (*lusus*). The Latin *inuidia, livor* means not so much the jealousy of the gods, such as the Greek Nemesis, but rather the secret resentment of fellow citizens, which targets a man who is excessively fortunate and who uses his good luck to bad effect—the kind of jealousy that often found expression in epigraphic insults: precisely the kind in which Catullus is indulging. If Calvus treats Catullus badly, he will unleash public *invidia*. The apostrophe, "light of my eyes" (*ocelle*), may be an insulting sexual innuendo, given that Calvus, like so many others, is accused of *mollitia*. The epigram thus turns into a plea addressed to an unfaithful "mistress."

The last part of the text establishes as great a distance as possible between Catullus and Licinius by using a "we/us" that designates only Catullus: *nostras preces, oramus,* which stands in opposition to the "you" who is the epigram's addressee, ironically called "light of my eyes." This "we," often interpreted as a "royal we," in truth has the effect of reinforcing the individual by associating him with a whole group, which, it is suggested, is also involved in the situation. This is thus a social and collective "we," constituted by Catullus along with other Romans, all arrayed against poor Calvus, the solitary object of these sarcasms. This "we" of the end of the poem stands in opposition to the dual "we" of the beginning of the text, the "we" of the fused couple.

In adopting the form of the epigram, that is to say a graffito written on an exterior wall, Catullus was making use of one of the Roman civilization's traditional techniques. In the same way as a funerary epigram, a recriminatory graffito could be read by anyone passing. The individuals against whom these epigrams were targeted, in other words their victims, belonged to the neighborhood community, as did the other passersby who could read them, the rumor-mongering representatives of public opinion, who would echo the words of blame written there, exaggerating them all the more when they had been amused or surprised by them. That is how it was that epigrams, which mobilized public opinion against or in favor of individuals, always appealed to the norm in their attacks on hidden vice or eccentricity. The use of epigrams conveys some inkling of what life must have been like in an ancient city, where one was always exposed to the gaze of others; and it conveys a sense of the extent to which the community regulated the behavior of individuals. Graffiti would appeal to other citizens as to witnesses of injustice or scandal. It was thus that Catullus addressed the inhabitants of Verona, appointing himself their spokesman, on the subject of a bridge that was poorly maintained:

Colony, you would love to make merry on the bridge
And are ready to launch into dances there
But beware, the supports of the bridge are not solid,
The arches are built with secondhand materials
And you could end up with all four limbs in the air.[14]

And he attacked the governor of Cisalpine Gaul, Piso, and his advisers in similar fashion:

Porcius and Socration, the two left hands
Of Piso, the pestilence and cholera of the earth,
You are the ones that he has preferred to my little Veranius and
  Fabullus
That circumcised Priapus that he is![15]

A graffiti poet might even go so far as to write his avenging words on the facade of the house belonging to his victim.[16] So the threats of a composer of epigrams truly were to be feared: if he was in good form, a few words daubed in black or red paint on a wall would be enough to set the whole town laughing the next day, at the expense of some great lady or politician. The content of such attacks seldom varied. They were usually of a coarsely sexual nature.

As we have seen, however, this particular text amounted to rather more than the transcription of an epigram, for that epigram simply constituted the poem's conclusion, bestowing upon it a particular status in day-to-day life before it came to be consigned to a book. Earlier on, it had been a letter and the sole purpose of that letter had been to signify nostalgia for the absent poetic and erotic games of a comissatio now over.

The transition from orality to writing was a lengthy one, passing through grief and social violence on the way from games played on tablets instantly erased to a papyrus on sale in a bookshop. The poem that has eventually come down to us has preserved nothing of the joyful, emotive culture that found expression amid games and wine—nothing, except the memory of an event reduced to its simplest expression: oblivion.

Catullus and Anacreon: A Culture of the Present Moment and Oblivion

Speaking or singing with nothing to say: Catullus and Anacreon provide comparable examples of this. They are examples of a poetic culture that can only pass into writing at the cost of disappearing, for it is a culture of ephemerality, of the day-to-day, of the present moment, which has nothing to say or to pass on. The poetry is exhausted in an instant, as the statement is in the speech act. For what is said is simply what there is now and what there will be tomorrow, a shared knowledge that implicitly organizes the lives of one and all.

Books or banquets: the alternative was unavoidable. Writing had nothing to do with the pleasures of speech experienced at a banquet. A monument did not preserve the memory of an event; it abolished it. This idea of writing-as-a-tomb resurfaces in action in the allegory of the cicada and the ant.[17] The poet, Archias, a contemporary of Catullus and a friend and client of Cicero, was at the time writing a funerary epigram, what was known as a "tomb," for the cicada who fell victim to the ants.

> Once, seated on the green tips of the luxuriant pine
> or the umbrella pine casting its thick shade,
> Clapping your feet on your sides, you used to sing a resounding song,
> Cicada, sweeter than the lyre to lonely shepherds.
> But now the marching ants have killed you
> And you are caught in the recesses of Hades that suddenly seized you.
> You are certainly not to blame for perishing, for even the Meonid,
> the prince of poetry,
> perished in the enigmatic nets of the fishermen.[18]

As Jesper Svenbro has shown both fully and clearly, the cicada slain by the marching columns of ants is Homer (the Meonid), killed by the letters set out in lines of writing resembling tangled fishing nets that transcribed his voice. The poet Archias, himself a native of Asia Minor, could also claim to be a Meonid, that is to say a Lydian by metonymy. He too, writing monuments for his new masters, the Romans, had killed his song, enfolding it in a shroud of enigmatic words, the cryptic figures of the epigram.

Grief at the passing of *lusus* thus associates the loss of the pleasures of love, through the epistolatory form, and the pleasures of the poet's voice, following in the direct line of Hellenistic epigrams; but the "tomb" of

Table 2. Catullus

	Event	*Object 1*	*Object 2*	*Object 3*
Style	Poetic and erotic games	Letter	Epigram	Book monument
Means	Voice and tablets	Tablets	Wall	Papyrus scroll
Social framework	Comissatio	Correspondence	Rumors	Literature
Time	The present of the banquet	The time of epistolatory correspondence	Present result of a past action: a constructed object	Future eternity
Sentiment	Love	Pain	Hatred	Nothingness
Persons	Presence of the "other": confusion of person addressing and person addressed	Absence of the "other"	The "other" is the object of discourse destined for passersby who know him	The "other" is the object of a statement without a referent
Senses	Hearing and seeing the "other"	Seeing the inscription	Seeing the papyrus	
Reading	Oralization	Epistolarity	Inscription	Citation
Writer	Me and you	The signatory of the letter	Anonymous	Author of the book
Reader	Me and you	You, the addressee of the letter	They (passing by)	They (the readers)

Table 3. Anacreon

	Event	*Monument*
Style	Poetic and erotic games	Book
Means	Song and cup	Papyrus scroll
Social framework	Dionysiac banquet	Intimate reading
Time	The present of the ritual	Future eternity
Sentiment	Love	Nothingness
Persons	Presence of the "other": the addressee of the ritual gesture	The "other" is the object of discourse intended for an anonymous reader who does not know him
Senses	Hearing and seeing the "other"	Seeing
Subject of the speech act	A drinker	Author of the book
Recipient	A drinker	They (the readers)

Catullus, a funerary epigram, is transformed into an avenging epigram written on the walls of Rome, as a result of a shift from a Greek type of writing to a Roman type, a kind of cultural translation from one type of publicity into another.

Tables 2 and 3 show how the one was wiped out by the other, as a result of Catullus substituting one kind of writing for another. The philologists of Alexandria, who took over from the priests of the sanctuaries of heroized poets, thus for their part pass directly from column 1 to column 4 in Table 2, from an event to a monument, simply by dint of recording statements, which thereby become texts. The statement is not altered by the change of speech act, the switch from being sung at a banquet to being read in a book. However, the same cannot be said of texts produced for festivals. The latter certainly belong to an ideology of citation in which the signifier is preserved word for word. In contrast, Catullus's contemporaries generally expected a book to be presented as such and to involve the fiction of one or several real scriptural practices, in this case a letter and an epigram. In other instances, it might be an ex-voto, a dinner invitation, a note attached to a gift, and the like.

That is how it is that the words of the banquet are preserved in Anacreon's poems, whereas they have disappeared from Catullus's text: with

Catullus, the written speech act has eliminated the oral statement. That is the only difference between the two poems, for the semantic content of both is empty; both are monuments to unmemorable events about which there is nothing to be said except that they happened and that the poetic performances that took place made it possible for everything to pass off as it should—that is, as it was normal for it to pass off. Even if, in respect of its quality, the event was exceptional, nothing can be preserved of that quality. To sing or speak the same words again, at a different moment, among other men, with other moods, under different stars, would not produce at all the same effect.

A comparison between these two poems thus shows us that preserving banquet songs in writing did not enable the ancients to transmit the banquet culture. Reduced to the state of written words, these songs no longer exist as songs, nor do they even have an existence as texts: they say nothing, for they never have said anything, never have possessed any informative content. As a result only their signifier is preserved by the words. That signifier may be the object of a citation. But it may also be read without its context, in which case the semantic significance becomes the text's raison d'être. As we have seen, a poem by Anacreon underwent a metamorphosis and became a biographical document on the poet's love affairs. As we shall see later, there are other possible readings, which may turn erotic poems into a form of pornographic literature.

The poem that we possess here and have now read was from the start intended to be preserved in a book, published under the name of Catullus, and the book was itself presented as what it was: *libellus* or, to be still more precise, a papyrus scroll both of whose ends had been polished with pumice stone before being put on sale.[19] This object would be seized upon by readers and would thereafter be read in privacy.[20] The readers would have bought, or been given by the author, a collection of texts of various kinds.

It is true that some of these were epigrams, that is to say inscriptions of an avenging nature intended for walls in the town. This is the closest a book seems to get to a traditional use of writing, for in both cases what was written was intended to tell as many people as possible some piece of damaging gossip about somebody or other. When a book was a libel, it was as public as graffiti. But both the book and the graffiti were bound to be ephemeral. Once the shame of the victim had been forgotten, once the event had been covered over by another, the graffiti were wiped off the wall and the book lost its topicality and meaning.

On that account, from the point of view of its reception, Catullus's book cannot be assimilated to the inscriptions on walls or tombs; it is also why it contains texts in plenty of other forms. In truth it was not intended to be read as epigrams were, not intended for the kind of reading that presupposed readers who were briefly contemporary with the inscriptions and belonged to a group that was likewise limited, such as that of the inhabitants of Verona, or those acquainted with the great families of Rome. Catullus's book is a compilation in the Alexandrian manner, a book that was intended, among other things, to testify to the epigrammatic productivity of the Romans, nothing more. It was a museum piece and was expected to be received as such.

FOUR

Kisses in the Greek Manner and Roman Cuisine

WHAT WRITING DID away with, removing all raison d'être from those games of the Roman banquet as it made them available for a decontextualized reading—whether in the form of a letter or as an epigram—was not so much the music of the voice, which played no part in the comissatio, but rather the presence of the "other" 's eloquent body and the physical relationship that that presence made it possible to establish during the time for games.

The poetic games of the comissatio take on their full meaning if they are reintegrated into the complex Roman system constituted by the pleasures of the banquet, in particular the eroticism engendered between the banqueters. Kissing held a place of central importance. A kiss was a breath of love passing from one person to another and setting fire to their bodies. In fact, it may well have provided the model for the game played with the tablets in which Catullus and Calvus indulged, just as the giving and circulation of wine provided the model for the love and singing of the symposion.

Plato, a Master of Kisses

In Rome the only possible provenance for the "fathers" of the loving kiss of the comissatio had to be Athens. The most famous of those fathers was the recognized master of Greek love, Plato. Thanks to his patronage, the kiss became a practice of sophisticated life, a form of elegance in the Greek manner. Cultivated Romans were prone to quote the following two lines about a kiss given to a boy, which is attributed to Socrates' disciple in his youth:

> Τὴν ψυχὴν Ἀγάθωνα φιλῶν ἐπὶ χείλεσιν ἔσχον
> Ἦλθε γὰρ ἡ τλήμων ὡς διχβησομένη.
>
> My soul, when I kissed Agathon, did pass
> My lips; as though, poor soul, 'twould leap across.[1]

The setting provided for these lines by the scholar of the Roman Empire through whom they have come down to us is particularly revelatory of his own extremely Roman view of Plato and his games of love. For it to be acceptable for Roman kisses to claim this Greek patronage, it was necessary for Plato, in fourth-century B.C. Athens, even then to have been the kind of *adulescens* who would be found at a comissatio, an adolescent with leisure and from a good family who busied himself with letters (*litterae*) until such time as he could enter upon his real career. While still a young man and before becoming the grave philosopher about whom everyone knows, he is thus represented as having amused himself by composing erotic poetry, at a time when he was also writing tragedies. To refer to this youthful activity, which the Romans would have regarded as somewhat frivolous, the Latin text twice uses the verb *ludere*. It implies that Plato was still at the age for playing and learning: he was writing for the theater (*ludi scaenici*) and indulging in love play (*lusus*).

The Romans never for a moment doubted that these lines were *uersiculi* similar to those of the Roman banquets.[2] They possessed all the required qualities: Aulus Gellius delighted in "their charm and graceful [erotic] terseness" (*lepidissimae et uenustissimae brevitatis*). We are plunged back into the pleasures of the comissatio by the use of those conventional terms, charm (*lepos*) and seduction (*venus*). The reason why this distich has been remembered, Aulus Gellius tells us, is that it provides such a good example of *brevitas*: a succinct concentration of meaning within the sounds, which is a quality particularly sought after by poets. These two lines of poetry attributed to Plato were thus, as it were, a Greek paradigm of the games of the comissatio. And the great man, Plato, provided a reference for all the enamored drinkers who would endlessly reuse these lines by translating them. Aulus Gellius cites one such translation, without naming its author (which suggests that it was one of many remakes of the distich, rather than the expression of a desire to produce a new poem). Actually, this particular translation fails to recapture the *brevitas* of the original. The Greek text must have been the starting point for many improvised translations written down in the course of Roman *comissationes*, later to be read aloud at the banquet by their authors.[3]

Kisses, Breath, and Wine

A Roman friend of Aulus Gellius, also an *adulescens* and, like the young Plato, a poet, had translated those two lines of Greek into a light, erotic poem. He was an educated young man (*doctus*), but also appears to have been a "charming boy" (*delicatus*), able to combine a knowledge of Greek books with the sophisticated culture of the comissatio. Aulus Gellius judges this Latin "remake" to be even better than Plato's two lines of verse. He declares them to be more "free" and "less conventional." In other words, they are more in conformity with the idea that Aulus Gellius, along with other Romans, had of *uersiculi*. That is altogether to be expected, for otherwise what would have been the point of producing a Roman interpretation? The aesthetics that governed the "remake" consisted of treating the speech act as more important than the statement and never judging the latter in isolation. The *uersiculi* of Aulus Gellius's young friend were thus considered more suitable for a comissatio than Plato's distich was.

Cum semihiulco sauio
Meum puellum sauior
Dulcem florem spiritus
Duco ex aperto tramite

When with my parted lips I kiss,
And quaff the breath's sweet balm from open mouth, . . .

This beginning of the text may strike us as somewhat strange. With its "parted lips" and "open mouth"—the Latin has "passage"—it seems to place a heavy emphasis on the breathy aspect of the whole operation. But we should not regard this as clumsiness on the author's part. He has simply transcribed the Roman way of life and its manner of representing a kiss at a banquet: as a communication between two bodies, effected by an exchange of their respective vital breaths. The model for the image was wine being poured into a mouth and this Roman interpretation of Plato's lines plays upon Latin words that can refer to drinking as well as to kissing. Thus, the verb *s(u)auior* 'to kiss' and the noun *s(u)auius* are derived from the adjective *suauis*, which means "sweet, agreeable, delicious" and is essentially used to qualify a perfume or a wine.[4] An erotic kiss[5] thus gives a pleasure that is not that of flesh pressed to other flesh, but stems from the transfer of a light, living fluid, the active principles of which are referred to as a "bouquet" (or "sweet balm"): the bouquet of a wine, a perfume, a breath. The one who takes it in absorbs it—*duco*—draws it into him.[6]

This wine drunk in like breath and this breath savored like wine suggest pleasures that clearly have nothing to do with the drinking and eating of the *cena*. The comissatio belongs to a world of perfumed pleasures, a world of aromas, of what is cooked and can be digested—a far cry from all that is raw or rotten.

The lover's mouth comes to rest upon the mouth of the child, whether girl or boy (*puellum*), whose vital breath (*spiritus*) is fragrant and intoxicating. Like a pure wine, it exhales a "bouquet" (*flos*), its smell and quintessence. The boy's mouth is "ajar," "open," there is a passage (*trames*) through which his breath escapes. The double opening, like the mouth of a flask or amphora from which pure wine flows into a cup or a krater, conveys the very essence of a Roman kiss:

> Animula aegra et saucia
> Cucurrit ad labias mihi
> Rictumque in oris peruium
> Et labra pueri mollia
> Rimata itineri transitus
> Vt transiliret nititur

> Smitten with love, my soul mounts to my lips,
> And through my love's soft mouth its way would take,
> Passing the open gateway of [smiling] lips

The breaths of the two friends flow into one another. This kiss constitutes a fusing, symmetrical, asexual union. In ordinary Roman kissing, known to us mostly through the lovers of comedy, it was more common for lips to have a sex, for Latin distinguished between the slight, delicate lips of women and children (*labella*) and the mouths of men (*labra, labia*).[7]

Here, however, the terms used to designate the lips of the two partners are indistinguishable. The sweetness of this kiss really stems not from the delicacy of the mouths, but from the breath that they exchange, the *spiritus* or *anima*, which is the very life that animates each of them.

The breath in the kiss has the same burning quality as Roman wine:[8] it is the quintessence of the blood that carries it through every part of the body, from which it departs at the moment of death, thereby consigning the muscles and viscera to humidity, coldness, and putrescence. This vital breath, which has nothing to do with a divine soul or any principle of immortality, is all the more active and ready to take wing when a man is himself inflamed by wine and love. For pure wine, like love, brings to the lips things that the heart dissembles. Intoxication (*uis caloris*) boils up within the body, just as wine does in a vat, and is converted into vapors that seek to escape.[9]

So there seems to be a coherent system that links together love, kissing, and wine in the eroticism of the comissatio, and, as we can see, it owes nothing to Greek Dionysism. It is part and parcel of the Roman symbolism according to which a comissatio was opposed to a *cena*, just as pure wine was to oysters, as a Roman might put it, or as herbs and spices are to putrefaction, as Lévi-Strauss would say. The pleasures of the *cena* were those of the *gula* and consisted, essentially, in the consumption of meats, that is to say carrion, which brought the body no nourishment but putrefied within it without being digested. The wine that was adulterated or diluted with water that was drunk in the *cena* itself contributed to the internal putrefaction, the striking effects of which made themselves felt the following day in what the Romans called the *crapula*, the fetid odor of drains or the bilges of ships. The flaccid, cold body of the *cena*, which was evacuated from both top and bottom, in disgusting liquids, was contrasted to the evanescent body of a lover, drunk on pure wine and the breath of his friend to the point of collapse. Banquet kissing was a dangerous game to play:

Tum si morae quid plusculae
Fuisset in coetu osculi
Amoris igni percita
Transisset et me linqueret
Et mira prorsum res foret
Vt fierem ad me mortuus
Ad puerulum intus uiuerem.

> But if our kiss, delayed, had been prolonged,
> [That kiss that made us one],
> By love's fire swayed my soul that way had ta'en,
> And left me. Faith, a wondrous thing it were,
> If I should die, but live within my love.

What should we make of this wandering of the soul, this transfer of vital breath into the body of the other? We are faced here with the ancients' famous concept of love experienced as servitude, often represented as the soul's captivity in the body of another:

> Aufugit mi anumus, credo ut solet, ad Theotimum
> Deuenit. Sic est perfugium illud habet
> Quid si non interdixem ne illunc fugitiuum
> Mitteret ad se intro sed magis eiiceret?
> Ibimus quaesitum. Verum ne ipsi teneamur
> Formido. Quid ago? Da Venus consilium.

> My soul has fled; as usual, I expect
> It has gone to Theotimus, its refuge,
> As if I had not forbidden him to welcome
> This fugitive, he should have ejected it!
> We shall go in search of it. But what if we remain there
> Captives? I am afraid. Venus, counsel me![10]

The soul of the poet (the term "poet" is here used to designate the author's role for the duration of this particular speech act, not his social identity or function) has passed into the body of one Theotimus, whom he loves. The final reference to Venus makes the erotic character of the poem altogether unambiguous. The context is probably the following: in the course of a comissatio, a first kiss has made the poet "fall in love," that is to say become thirsty for kisses that do nothing to assuage his thirst. The trouble is that a kiss, far from satisfying desire, calls for more kisses. Just as wine acts as both fire and water and is a drink that brings on more thirst, the kiss brings pleasure-desire. Drained of his soul, the poet aspires to recover it in another kiss, but one in which he risks becoming totally absorbed—becoming once and for all dependent upon this love-desire-pleasure.

This text uses the term *animus* 'will', not *anima* 'vital breath', making the most of the phonetic proximity of the two. When he loses his vital breath, the lover also loses his will and becomes Theotimus's slave. By moving from "breath" to "will," Catullus's verse to some extent conveys the alienating power of a kiss.

Kisses, Wine, and Poetry

A Roman kiss courted and only narrowly avoided the social death that hovered, like a warning, in the wings of a banquet, an emotional death that made one a prisoner. After too long, too open a kiss, the scales of life could tip and sensuality, extended into sentiment, could spill over from the time of the comissatio, as we have seen from our reading of Catullus. Roman kissing required you to exercise self-control even as you let yourself go, lest the breath of the loved one should become a drug without which you could not live.

The dangers of kissing are the same as those encountered by Catullus in the course of his poetic games with Licinius. The pleasure engendered by reading those tablets is similar in kind to that of an exchange of breaths in a kiss. Each of the two involved is filled by the breath that comes to him from his partner as he reads out the words of the writer, who thereby becomes present in the body of the reader and fires and inspires him, turning him too, in his turn, into a poet and a writer. The game with the tablets produces the same fusion and erotic symmetry as the kiss does. In Rome, the eroticism of words, which in Greece was conveyed by song and Dionysism, can only be conveyed by writing-followed-by-reading. But the only purpose of that writing is to produce the orality that alone can bring to life the words written on the tablet. Writing is used in a strategy designed to draw out the breath of the loved one, rather than in a process of poetic creation. This erotic use of writing, in which the lover gets what he has written read by him or her whom he loves, in order to possess him or her through his words, may be compared with the way in which writing was represented in Greece, where the reader was shown to be physically possessed by the writer.[11] But unlike in Greece, where it was a matter of a brutal subjection, plain sodomization that was humiliating to the one subjected to it, this Roman eroticism of writing is, like the kiss, symmetrical, asexual, and playful.

In Rome, a loving kiss, in the context of a banquet, could lead into an experience that revealed one's own limitations, an experience not unlike the effects of Dionysiac intoxication: to lose oneself in another, to suffer a self-inflicted death through fusion in a *coetus* that had nothing to do with a sexed, sexual union between a man and a woman, a man and a boy, or two men, was dangerous, for it could tip the balance over into something short of humanity, with all psychological and social sanctions lifted. It is true that, in Rome, such an experience was neither sacred nor ritualized. Nevertheless, only with some kind of technique for coping with pleasures could these develop simultaneously without provoking a catastrophe. In banquet Dionysism, it was the ritual of the symposion that usually saved the drinkers from being left stranded. In Rome, maintaining control over the *lusus* depended on a personal asceticism that consisted in not allowing yourself to get carried away by the love play, and in exercising lucid control over your body and its intoxications. You had to know when to stop. "And you can never have enough of kissing a boy; the more you drink, the more thirsty you are for more kisses and you can never tear your mouth away until the moment when, in the culmination of delight, kisses are refused."[12]

It is well known how important the Romans considered it to devote the right amount of time to each of a man's occupations in life: it was correct to begin a *cena* no earlier than midafternoon and to finish it before nightfall, to sleep during the night, not the day, and so on. This temporal discipline was central to each individual's morality, allowing one to live at ease with oneself and to indulge in pleasures without becoming a slave to them. There was a time and a place for dangerous intoxications in Rome. Particular spaces were deliberately left free in daily life, which the urban aristocracy then filled with the sophisticated delights of kisses and wordplay. The wine that accompanied these pleasures suspended the judgment of one's fellows. In this civilization of shame, which, however, had no sense of guilt, only the gaze of other free men exercised censure and a check on an individual's behavior. Away from that gaze, anything and everything was allowed. That is how it was that the effect of intoxication temporarily isolated a liberated society:

> Omne uitium ebrietas et incendit et detegit. Obstantem malis conatibus uerecundiam remouet; plures enim pudore peccandi quam bona uoluntate prohibitis abstinent. Non facit uitia ebrietas sed protrahit; tunc libidinosus ne cubiculum quidem expectat sed cupiditatibus suis quantum petiuerunt sine dilatione permittit.

> Drunkenness kindles and discloses every kind of vice, and removes the sense of shame that veils our evil undertakings. For more men abstain from forbidden actions because they are ashamed of sinning than because their

> inclinations are good. When the strength of wine has become too great and has gained control over the mind, every lurking evil comes forth from its hiding place. Drunkenness does not create vice, it merely brings it into view; at such times the lustful man does not wait even for the privacy of a bedroom, but without postponement gives free play to the demands of his passions.[13]

There is no need to dwell on the moralizing tone of this text of Seneca. It certainly does censure Roman drunkenness, but it also reveals its symbolic basis. An archaeologist of Roman *mores* frequently needs to resort to this kind of document, for it is harder for a Roman historian to rediscover the cultural controls set upon daily life than it is for a historian of Greece. Unlike the latter, the former does not have a profusion of myths at his or her disposal, enabling him or her to study the whole system of cultural categories.[14] Yet the culture of daily life was just as central, just as much of a constraint in the life of a Roman as it was in the life of a Greek, and it was equally formative for his personality and identity as a civilized man, even if it often found expression through moral norms. But in Rome, morality and traditional culture were inseparable. The *mores were* the habits and customs of Rome.

Pleasure without Shame and without Effort

The comissatio did not invent the kiss, but it converted into an end in itself what, in most love affairs, was only a preliminary, as can be seen from, for example, Roman comedy. One scene in the *Satyricon* shows clearly that a thousand kisses, instead of constituting an end in themselves,[15] were sometimes no more than a preamble. The scene takes place between a young man and a very young woman:

> In hoc gramine pariter compositi, mille osculis lusimus quaerentes voluptatem robustam.

> We lay there together on this grass and exchanged a thousand light kisses, but we looked for sterner pleasure.[16]

The boy's problem—this is Encolpius, the narrator of the *Satyricon*—is precisely that he cannot get beyond the stage of preambles, since Priapus, the god who reigns over virile erections, has condemned him to impotence, so he never can move on to "sterner pleasure." The preliminaries of love are not subject to the authority of Priapus, however; and these kisses exchanged with the ravishing Circe resemble the pleasures of the comissatio. The lovers are locked in each other's embrace, with nothing to distinguish between them: they are *paritur compositi*, and their kisses are games (*lusimus*).

Compared with priapic pleasures, these kisses retain a modest, controlled quality, as Circe ironically remarks to the wretched Encolpius:

> Si libidinosa essem, quererer decepta; nunc etiam languori tuo gratias ago, in umbra uoluptati diutius lusi.

> If I were a passionate woman, I should feel betrayed and hurt. As it is, I can be thankful even for your coldness. I have amused myself long with the shadow of pleasure.[17]

The young woman's sarcasm is not just a joke. Given that an erotic kiss is a game, a *ludus*, it has nothing serious about it, no moral or physiological consequences: it creates no child, no shame. In Rome, play (*ludus*) was a way of pretending, of imitating reality. Kissing was an imitation of the loving union of sexed bodies, just a shadow of the real thing. A union of souls-breaths was playing at real, sexual union. No serious immorality was attached to kisses, but at the same time they could not produce real satisfaction.

There were thus some who limited themselves to banquet kisses and the infinite pleasure that went with these, yet could never satisfy their lovers' desire; and there were others who sought satiation in more substantial pleasures.

The hero of the *Satyricon* is caught between two kinds of eroticism. Although some people, and society in general, demand priapic exploits from him, he himself does not seem particularly keen: for him, real pleasure lies in the fusion of breaths; the rest is simply a matter of duty. In his relationship with Giton, that is the only pleasure that he praises, sometimes using the *uersiculi* of a comissatio to do so, as in the following example:

> Qualis nox fuit illa, di deaeque
> Quam mollis toruus! Haesimus calentes
> Et transfudimus hinc et hinc labellis
> Errantes animas Valete curae
> Mortales! Ego sic perire coepi.

> Ah! gods and goddesses, what a night that was, how soft was the bed. We lay in a warm embrace and with kisses everywhere made exchange of our wandering spirits. Farewell, all earthly troubles. And so [I was on the point of death].[18]

A night of *mollitia* meant a night of the "soft" pleasures that, in Rome, were the only real kind. The two lovers fused into one another, in each other's arms, clinging together as closely as possible (*haesimus*). Their respective breaths (*animas*) were somehow poured into each other (the exact meaning of the Latin verb *transfundere* is "to pour a liquid from one vessel into another") through their symmetrical kisses, *hinc et hinc*, on equally delicate lips (*labellis*). In these embraces, our hero comes close to death. Pleasures that liberate men from their humanity, making them forget the "troubles" that make them mortal and distinguish men from gods are risky, for they may tip them over into death. In this respect banquet kisses test one's limits.

Fortunately, the pure wine that inflames a lover also sends him to sleep, thereby saving him from these deadly pleasures of fusion by detaching him from his partner's body: "Cum solutus mero remisissem ebrias manus . . ." (I was overcome with drink and let my shaking hands fall . . .).

Encolpius makes these kisses the climax of his infinite desire for Giton and says nothing further about the nights that he is commemorating,[19] even though something "more" still remains possible.

> Soculisque tandem bona fide exactis alligo artissimis complexibus puerum fruorque uotis usque ad inuidiam felicibus. Nec adhuc quidem omnia erant facta, cum. . . .

> At last I could ask for kisses openly. I hugged the boy close in my arms and had my fill of a happiness that might be envied. All was not over. . . .

With another boy, Endymion, he engages in the same embraces. The text here becomes even more explicit, for he represents the fusion of the two breaths as the goal of the pleasure, all other gestures being simply means to reach that end:

> Iam pluribus osculis labra crepitabant, iam implicitae manus omne genus amoris inuenerant, iam alligata mutuo ambitu corpora animarum quoque mixturam fecerant.

> There was the sound of a rain of kisses as our lips met, our hands were clasped and discovered all the ways of love, then our bodies were held and bound by our embrace until even our souls were made as one soul.[20]

The *Satyricon* can be read as the story of a boy, Encolpius, who desires nothing more than Giton's kisses and would be perfectly content with the loves of a *delicatus*, but who becomes the victim of Priapus who, like any god scorned, demands his due and takes his revenge. As a result, Encolpius becomes impotent and is obsessed by this affliction that puts him beyond the pale of a society in which Priapus is the unchallenged god. For the very existence of Priapus is threatened by lovers who seek no more than kisses.

A fragment of a text that is also attributed to Petronius clearly explains the opposition between love's two kinds of pleasures, kissing and ordinary copulation.[21] It is easy to see which the poet prefers:

> Foeda est in coitu et breuis uoluptas
> Et taedet Veneris statim peractae
> Non ergo ut pecudes libidinosae[22]
> Caeci protinus irruamus illuc
> Nam languescit amor peritque flamma
> Sed sic, sic fine feriati
> Et tecum iaceamus osculantes
> Hic nullus labor est ruborque nullus
> Hoc iuuit, iuuat et diu iuuabit
> Hoc non defecit incipitque semper.

> The pleasure of the act of love is gross and brief, and love once consummated brings loathing after it. Let us then not rush blindly thither straightway like lustful beasts, for love sickens and the flame dies down; but even so, even so, let us keep eternal holiday, and lie with thy lips to mine. No toil is here and no shame: in this, delight has been, and is, and long shall be; in this there is no diminution but a beginning everlastingly.

This short comissatio poem tells of reclining lovers engaged in kissing each other. One of them praises this pleasure, contrasting it to ordinary sexuality. Kissing is represented as possessing all the virtues of civilization, copulation as possessing all the ugliness of animality. Man ought to learn to master his bestial desire and eschew a brief, dishonoring union that separates the two who love each other, since desire satisfied in this way provokes a *taedium* 'satiety and disgust' (*taedium* belongs to the register of the pleasures of eating). Kissing, in contrast, prolongs a desire that is never satisfied but is ever born anew, uniting the friends forever amid timeless joy. There are other very Roman reasons for preferring kisses. First, they demand no *labor*—"no toil." Ideally, pleasure in Rome is always *mollis* 'passive', which certainly cannot be said of copulation in the case of the man, and frequently not in that of the woman either.[23] Second, kisses are not dishonoring to the lovers, since they do not imply any submission on the part of either of them. Petronius, or whoever the author of this fragment was, thus produced a theory for the lovemaking of the *Satyricon*, setting up a clear opposition between kissing and priapic copulation: the former was beautiful, the latter ugly.

To conclude this sketch of the symbolic network that situated the comissatio kiss in Roman culture as the common ideal of erotic pleasure, here is one last, rather curious text. It consists of a description of coitus between a man and a woman and is part of a speech defending marriage and heterosexual love. It puts forward an argument that is particularly important. The orator claims that in the course of the sexual act a woman is capable of kisses far superior to those of a boy:

> At Aphrodite's supreme moment, she lets herself go, under the effect of pleasure, her mouth opens for a kiss, she holds nothing back. . . . When the moment comes for Aphrodite's climax, the woman breathes with difficulty, so much does the pleasure burn her, and her breathing, in a breath of love, rises to her lips and mingles with the wandering kiss seeking to penetrate to the depths of the loved one. This breath, ejected by her respiration, becomes one with the kiss and strikes the heart. And the heart, disturbed by the kiss, begins to quiver. And were it not attached to the entrails, it would be carried away and would allow itself to be drawn upward by those kisses.[24]

These speculations on the subject of breaths were in all likelihood intended as a parody designed to caricature the by then conventional discourse employed by supporters of the love of women in arguments against supporters of the love of boys. From our point of view, what is interesting is that the argument depends on a representation of kissing that never varies: a kiss, a mingling and exchange of breaths, constitutes the supreme pleasure peculiar to human love. To enhance the value of heterosexual copulation, it was necessary to show that it brought pleasures equal or even superior to those of the kisses of boys. The text thus restores sexuality to these kisses and attributes to women in the throes of copulation kisses that are more intense than those exchanged during the preliminaries of love. It argues that their breath, rendered more ardent by pleasure, flows into the man and plunges all the more powerfully into his heart, threatening to wrest it from him.

In ordinary lovemaking the usual place of kissing was confined to the preliminaries. Its function was to whet desire and impart a cultivated dimension to the pleasures of love, preventing them from becoming a bestial copulation that would disgust most people. But the effects of the kisses would subsequently be wiped out by those of copulation, and fragrant desire would be extinguished in stinking disgust. Desire linked lovers together in an embrace that desperately sought for fusion; then disgust pushed them apart, setting them free.

When kissing ceased to be a means and became an end, the lovers remained linked in eternal embraces that neither disgust nor lassitude would ever loosen. If their will did not bring them to a halt, wine would do this for them. Here, in the comissatio, its double function is clearly revealed, as befits its double nature:[25] to excite or else to stultify to the point of sleep.

Kissing was at once a game, a hint of sensuality, and also the climax of that sensuality. Just as play was the activity cultivated par excellence in Rome, and one of the most delicious too, stemming purely from aesthetics, kissing likewise bestowed a cultivated dimension upon human love. But these games (*ludi*) were dangerous, because one could never have enough of them, as could be seen by observing the spectators at a Roman circus: they would never tire of feasting their eyes on the spectacle of an endless succession of identical chariot races round the track, willing them to go on forever.

Kisses That Stink, or Pornography to the Rescue of Eroticism

In preliminary love play, the kisses intended to ignite the lovers' desire might, if they stank, have the opposite effect. Instead of belonging to the perfumed world of the comissatio, such kisses returned a lover to the ignoble world of physical humors into which he should not have been replunged until after copulation. That is why Circe, humiliated by the priapic coldness of Encolpius, ironically asks him:

> Numquid te osculum meum offendit? Numquid spiritus ieiunio marcet? Numquid alarum negligens sudor?
>
> Do you find some offence in my kiss? In my breath that faints with hunger? Am I careless about my armpits?[26]

The upper part of the body, which is what is involved in kissing, the mouth that opens and the arms that enfold and in doing so are lifted away from the body, was supposed to be perfectly civilized. Such a cultivated body was characterized by its fragrance or, basically, by its lack of unpleasant odors.[27] Such odors were associated with uncivilized, "natural" bodies: the smell of sweat, for example, or the smell of ill-nourished bodies, that is to say bodies deprived of civilized nourishment. In Rome, both those kinds of odors were associated with mourning, during which men and women temporarily ceased to cultivate their bodies. They became physically unbearable (*sordidi*), repugnant to their fellow citizens. In short, unsurprisingly, uncivilized bodies were considered incapable of kisses.

While the upper part of the body could accede to the perfumed charms of culture, the lower part remained forever excluded from them. It was irremediably ugly and smelly, "shameful," particularly its sexual organs. So the worst infamy imaginable was to confuse and bring together mouths and sexual parts, with kisses that stank. To do so was shameful both because of the act itself and because it presupposed submission on the part of the partner, who was forced into this action despite the disgust that it provoked. Culture and servitude were incompatible. A slave stank.

Stinking kisses of this kind recur time and again in satirical epigrams. The worst of all insults was to liken the smell of one's enemy's mouth to that of his bottom:

Non ita me di ament quicquam referre putaui
Vtrum os an culum olfacerem Aemilio
Nilo mundius hoc, nihiloque immundius
Verum etiam culus mundior et melior.

Nam sine dentibus est dentis os sesquipedalis
Giungivas uero ploxeni habet ueteris
Praeterea rictum qualem diffissus in aestu
Meientis mulae cunnus habere solet.

I didn't—God help me—think it made any difference whether I sniffed at Aemilius' mouth or his arse. That's not cleaner than this, nor this dirtier than that, in fact, his arse is cleaner and better, for it has no teeth. His mouth has teeth a foot and a half long, gums like a worn-out cart-frame and, on top of all, a gaping jaw like the open slit of a pissing mule in summer.[28]

Disgusting mouths such as these, in bodies totally sunk in bestiality, were associated primarily with prostitutes, whose saliva was repugnant. Saliva, absent from perfumed kisses that are nothing but breath, is elsewhere again associated with all that is ignoble. One boy whom Catullus kissed insulted him by wiping his mouth, thereby indicating his revulsion, his nondesire.

> Nam simul factum est, multis diluta labella
> Guttis abstersi omnibus articulis
> Ne quicquam nostro contractum ex ore maneret
> Tamquam commictae spurca saliua lupae.

> No sooner was it done than you washed your lips clean with plenty of water, and wiped them with your dainty fingers, that no contagion from my mouth might remain, as though it were the foul spit of some filthy whore.[29]

The saliva of a whore was like urine. And conversely, the arse of a homosexual was said to be as avid as a mouth: this was a way of classifying passive sodomy among the repugnant pleasures.[30]

Moral turpitude was confused with behavior that was barbarous. For instance, it was believed in Rome that Spaniards cleaned their teeth with urine.

> Nunc Celtiber es Celtiberia in terra
> Quod quisque minxit hoc sibi solet mane
> Dentem atque russam defricare guingiuam
> Vt quo iste ueater expolitior dens
> Hoc te amplius bibisse pradedicet loti.

> As it is, you are a Celtiberian; now in the Celtiberian country everyone regularly brushes his teeth and ruddy gums in the morning with his piddle; so that the more highly polished your teeth are, the more urine they will prove to have passed your lips.[31]

The shift from simply rubbing with urine to actually drinking it shows clearly how a mouth came to be ignominious: first it came into contact with what had to do solely with the lower part of the body, and then it went on to absorb something that ought to repel it.

The horror of fellatio stemmed from the same representation. In the morning Gellius's lips are white,[32] defiled by a repugnant white foam as a result of his having spent the night "devouring the shameful parts of an adult man."

All these practices were the exact opposite of the fragrant, modest comissatio kiss, but at the same time, whoever overindulged in such kissing was suspected of also enjoying the shameful kind; for fragrant kisses and stinking kisses all belonged to the sphere of *mollitia*, pleasures unadulterated by the slightest effort of priapic *labor*.

That is why it was not socially acceptable for a man to stop at perfumed kisses: he needed regularly to demonstrate his "virility." Encolpius is told by women, and even by small boys, to prove that he is up to it—which is something that the anger of the god Priapus prevents him from doing. Meanwhile Catullus, for his part, wrote obscene couplets, threatening to force his sex upon those who poked fun at his *uersiculi*:

> Vos quei milia multa basiorum
> Legistis, male me marem putatis?
> Pedicabo uos et irrumabo.

> Because you've read of my many thousand kisses, do you think that I'm less virile on that account? Yes, I'll bugger you and stuff you alright![33]

The culprits in question were two men, Aurelius and Furius, whom Catullus, using Greek insults, calls respectively *cinaedus* 'dancer' and *pathicus* 'pervert'. They would, he threatened, fall victim to the aggressive virility of Catullus, who would thereby prove that he was not a man for stinking kisses. To be sure, he says, his *uersiculi* are *molliculi*, his "love poetry" is "languid"—and he launches into a brief defense of erotic poetry, justifying it, amusingly enough, on the grounds of its pornographic uses:

> [uersiculi]
> Qui tum denique habent salem ac leporem
> Si sunt molliculi ac parum pudici
> Et quod pruriat incitare possunt
> Non dico pueris sed his pilosis
> Qui duros nequeunt mouere lumbos.

> Why, they acquire wit and spice if they are rather naughty and immodest, and can rouse with their ticklings. I don't mean boys, but those hairy old'uns unable to stir their arthritic loins.[34]

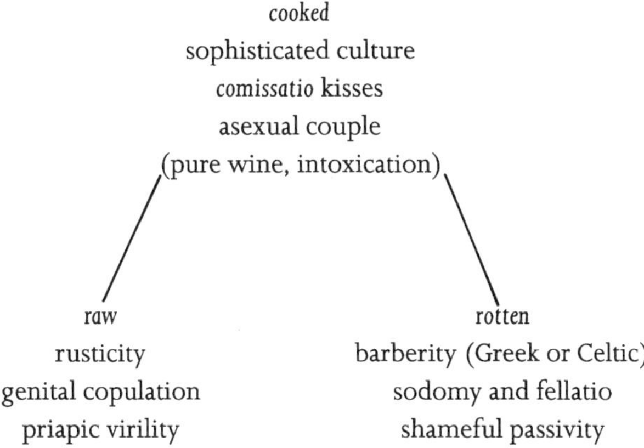

His reasoning is instructive: the eroticism of a kiss is linked with its function in amorous foreplay; his *uersiculi* have the power to enflame just as loving breath does; and the languor that they convey certainly brings a softening, but that softening is indispensable to leathery toughs whose excessive *labores* have made them resistant to desire. Their *duritia* is incompatible with even the most elementary form of love, for they lack the first indispensable spurt of desire. His *uersiculi* will communicate this to them.

Roman love practices thus constitute a triangular system that may be compared with Claude Lévi-Strauss's famous culinary triangle.[35]

The diagram may be read in a number of ways. For example, it shows that the "cooked" kiss relates, on the one hand, to "raw virility," as a preliminary, on the other, to "rotten" passivity, with which it shares *mollitia*, a pliant, feminine sweetness. That "rotten" passivity itself has something in common with "raw" virility, namely the disgust that is linked with the lower part of the body that it involves.

Culture, Kissing, and Greek Love

In the context of this culture of kisses and breath, a few remarks on the eternal question of so-called Roman homosexuality, more recently regarded by some authors as bisexuality,[36] may perhaps be appropriate. As Paul Veyne has shown, what mattered in Rome was, to be sure, not the sex of one's partner, but rather, to borrow the terms used by Michel Foucault, one's relation to oneself in the eyes of the other, or others. However, those authors set off down a blind alley when they replace the old opposition between homosexuality and heterosexuality by another opposition that is equally inadequate historically, namely between active sexuality and passive sexuality. It is particularly inadequate in that it is founded on the affirmation (never proved) that the term *impudicitia* meant "passive homosexuality" in Rome. It is claimed that this sense of *impudicitia*, which is never made explicit by the ancients themselves, was a "euphemism."[37] But that argument does not hold water in a society in which sexual language was subject to no censorship (as a perusal of Martial and Catullus suffices to show).

It is true that free, male, Roman citizens were under an obligation to prove their priapic capacity from time to time, but that was not the basis on which they organized their sexuality. For the major question, all too often forgotten by modern historians, was that of pleasure and desire. And in Rome activity (*labor*), whether or not of a sexual nature, was never a source of pleasure either for men or for women. Sexual aggressiveness was of a symbolic rather than an erotic nature. When one man threatened another, as Catullus did, *pedicabo* 'I'll fuck you', the insult did not imply bisexuality (today, a gesture with the same meaning is frequently used between motorists). Its symbolic meaning was all the stronger in a society in which sodomization was a possible punishment for adulterers, frequently effected using a horseradish or a gray mullet.[38]

Thus, when it was simply a matter of pleasure and desire, the ancients reckoned that human beings were most inadequately served by nature. That is why, for sensualists in Rome, pleasure and amorous desire were helped along by culture, that is to say by wine, kissing, and poetry:

> Dicta, sales, lusus, sermoinis gratia, risus
> Vicunt naturae candidioris opus.
>
> Words, wit, play, sweet talk and laughter surpass the work of simple nature.[39]

All the same, in Rome as elsewhere, the pleasures of love, like other pleasures, were always slightly suspect, for they linked together and softened those who indulged in them, while at the same time being as indispensable as the delights of the table were to citizens wearied by war or politics. Certain rules were accordingly devised, to limit their corrupting effects.

The boundary that could not be crossed was not that which separated men from women, or passivity from activity. It was the line that divided society into two groups: on the one hand, men, women, and children who were free, born from free parents, anyone who was *ingenus*; on the other, all the rest, slaves and freedmen alike, without distinction of sex or age. With those in the first group, no relationship was allowed outside marriage; with those in the second group, there were no prohibitions at all.

The bodies of free men and women were sacred. Any infringement of their modesty (*stuprum*) was a crime that deprived them of their honor (*pudor*).

> Dum te abstineas nupta uidua uirgine
> iuventute ac pueris liberis ama quidlibet.
>
> Provided you respect free wives, widows, virgins, young men, and boys, love whomever you want.[40]

Conversely, slaves and freedmen could not reject the desire of a master, as the following famous formula makes clear:

> Impudicitia in ingenui crimen est, in seruo necessitas, in liberto officium.
>
> Sexual submission in the case of a free man is a crime, in the case of a slave it is one of the constraints of servitude, in the case of a freedman it is a service that he owes his former master.[41]

So dishonor was a matter not of passivity or activity in the gestures of love, but of subjection to the desire of another. It made little difference whether that submission was consented to or not: the result was the same. That is why judges were particularly severe with officers who used their authority to abuse young recruits in the solitude of the army camps.[42] But if the officer could prove that the soldier was well known to be a gigolo or that he had already lost his honor, he would be let off.

Similarly, as soon as a boy emerged from childhood, at the age of about fourteen, when he discarded the children's version of a toga, it became socially acceptable for him to indulge in every kind of sexual activity with the slaves and freedmen of the household, just as he had observed his grandfather, father, uncles, and elder brothers doing. A young Roman harbored no inhibitions with regard to either feminine or masculine bodies, or even those of children. To desire a boy or a man was neither a social failing nor a moral sin, provided, of course, he was a slave or a freedman.

We should think of Rome as a civilization in which men's desire for the masculine body was not repressed, not the object of an unspoken prohibition from childhood on, as it is in our society. A young boy would see his father maintaining long liaisons with slaves who were beautiful and gifted, whom he would free and appoint as his private secretary, his steward, or his librarian. This link, based on eroticism, which attached a freedman to his master, was one of the forms taken by the Roman *fides*, reinforced by gratitude and the law, since every freedman owed his former master loyalty. In many cases, the lover-freedman showed unswerving loyalty throughout his entire life, and the bond between the two men was never broken. Cicero's relationship with his secretary Tiro is a well-known case in point.

Furthermore, even if women were not shut away in a harem in Roman society, they were excluded from all the public and outdoor activities that essentially constituted the hub of the lives of men. The bonds of friendship that the latter formed in these public places from adolescence onward were far stronger and more durable than most of their love affairs with women, for the most part freedwomen. Plenty of political betrayals provoked emotional clashes between brothers-in-law, sons-in-law, and fathers-in-law, for a friendship would often be cemented by a matrimonial alliance, or even an exchange of wives. The story of the noble Hortensius is well known: he asked his friend Cato to lend him his wife—who would be temporarily divorced—so that he could have her bear his children, and the sons of the two friends would thus be brothers.[43]

No prohibitions impinged upon physical proximity between men among themselves. They could express their affection and tenderness with hugs and kisses and other physical contacts too, without shocking anybody. What we would call a loving relationship was so natural, so common that no blame would attach to anybody for it—unless, that is, unpleasant rumors suggested that the ultimate of infractions was taking place: namely the sexual subjugation of one or the other of the partners, for this would mean that his honor was lost.

This Roman tradition never really changed over the years, even in the period in which some scholars claim to detect the rise of exclusively conjugal love. Pliny the Younger,[44] whom they sometimes represent as a model of the new kind of husband, stirred by one of Cicero's epigrams about Tiro, on the subject of kisses (*suauia*) withheld in intimacy although promised at a banquet, wrote a few lines to his correspondent, saying that he too had encountered on the part of young freedmen similar behavior, designed to restimulate the love of their master. It may be true that during this period a man's relationship with his wife tended to replace his relationships with his friends, at least to the extent that political—and hence, public—life absorbed less of the time of the Roman nobility. But so far as their amusements with their house slaves went, nothing had changed.

If loving friendship in Rome owed nothing to Greek models, on the other hand the eroticism of the comissatio, which was one of the forms taken by leisure "in the Greek manner," had already been introduced in Rome by the end of the third century B.C., at the latest. At this date the urban aristocracy was already cultivating the refinements of the Greek banquet, claiming to be inspired by the Greek model but inventing for itself the eroticism of kissing, wine, and games, which certainly seems a Roman addition that reproduced neither the excesses of the *kōmos* nor the complex rituals of the symposion.

To be sure, this love of boys that was limited to kisses was traced back to the Plato of the *Laws*,[45] but Greek kisses were not Roman kisses. It is true that in the *Palatine Anthology* one comes across kisses that are drunk, like wine,[46] and that circulate with the wine cup. In those circumstances, the proposis retains all the erotic power of the sharing of the wine that the lips of the beloved have touched:

> If you wish to intoxicate me
> be the first to taste and pass me the cup of wine. I accept it [*dekhomai*]
> for if you have brushed it with your lips, I can no longer remain sober
> or escape the sweet cupbearer
> since the cup transmits that kiss from you to me
> and tells me of the grace [*kharin*] that it received from you.[47]

However, a Greek kiss did not involve an exchange of breaths, the intoxication from air that any liquid or contact befouls, as is shown by the following catalog of top-ranked kisses by Paul the Silent:

> Long are the kisses of Galataea, loud and soft those of Demo,
> Doris bites. Which is the most exciting?
> It is not up to the ears to pass judgment on a kiss. . . .
> I have known the sweet kisses of Demo
> And the sweet honey of his moist mouth
> So say no more.[48]

Catullus promises Lesbia and himself an eternity of kisses, eternal pleasures that are circumscribed by the ephemeral, cultural time of a Greek banquet. Here again, the Romans invented a specifically Roman way of behaving, although they called it banqueting "in the Greek manner" (*more graeco*). Greece provided them with an alibi and a reference, as it did for any wayward behavior that occurred in the context of the cultivated pleasures of the *otium*: loving Giton, loving Endymion, loving Lesbia—Roman loving in the Greek manner.

That is why most of these texts tend to represent kissing as a chiefly pederastic activity. More boys are kissed than girls. But in truth, comissatio kisses were asexual. The texts contrast two types of erotic practice—kissing and copulation—not two types of partner. Kissing authorized erotic pleasures and love talk that were otherwise forbidden and dishonoring. But these games did not lead on to pleasures of a more solid but censured kind. For the pleasures of the comissatio had nothing in common with those of the *lupanar* or the "conjugal" bed, whether or not this was shared with a concubine or even a young slave.

Under the empire, the interchange and intermingling that took place between Greek banquets and Roman banquets assumed such proportions that it may be that, through the transmission of influences from the one to the other in both directions, the Roman games played in the comissatio even came to influence the Greek *kōmos*. When, in the second century, the Greek Philostratus is asked for a definition for the *kōmos*, he says: "The *kōmos* allows a woman to act as a man and a man to wear a woman's dress yet walk like a man."[49] It will be noticed that, by the time of this definition, a *kōmos* involved both men and women and accommodated a game of role reversals in which sexual neutralization, instead of taking place within a single individual, operated through an exchange of roles in mixed company. In contrast, in love affairs that were reduced solely to kisses, each partner could assume whichever sexual role suited him, could adopt the stated "I" of his or her choice.

These sophisticated, cultivated pleasures of the urban elite may have been more widespread in the provinces of the empire than we tend to imagine. A resident of Arles, Favorinus, who lived under Hadrian and was a friend of Plutarch, wrote of the pleasure of the comissatio, in Greek: "A handsome boy is even good to taste. And what else are they doing, those whose lips touch, but 'tasting each other'? They are making contact with their souls. Ah! If the soul could only cross the barrier. . . . It seems to be knocking on the door, begging to enter."[50]

To love boys was a sign of culture, as were all the refinements of life, providing it did not involve any vulgar desire that would humiliate the boy by subjecting him to what would be no better than a sexual service, a *stuprum*. More generally, the love of free boys, young men, and matrons—that is, the married women of good Roman society, who might be no more than sixteen years old—was an eminently cultural practice that, in Rome, was developed in the world set apart in the time and space that was represented by the comissatio. This was the kind of love that was known in Rome as Greek love.

This was a world apart, but by no means marginal. It was, on the contrary, necessary for its participants to be perfectly integrated in the general social culture. Marginals were excluded from it—Trimalchio, for instance, who participated only in the *cena* and practiced consummation of a priapic nature or, to give a more historical example, the emperor Claudius. He was said to be the only one of the Julio-Claudian princes whose tastes were limited solely to women—for him, this took a positively bulimic form—and who never had any masculine love affairs.[51] The historians who record this fact do not regard it as particularly honorable. Claudius's lack of desire for boys was no doubt something to do with his strange upbringing at the hands of a barbarian groom, which turned him into an "idiot." Claudius was socially uncouth. Even though, through his own efforts, he became impressively erudite in both Greek and Latin, he was always incapable of behaving properly in public, whether in religious ceremonies or at banquets: he would stuff himself, drink, then fall asleep. Nor did Claudius have any male friends. He spent his time solely with women or freedmen and was psychologically dominated by them. Claudius was a savage, a bulimic *cena*-goer, a drunkard incapable of the finer subtleties of conviviality.

The loves of the comissatio, indissociable from wine and role playing, which demanded a coded verbal inventiveness, made it possible to explore the limits of pleasure, along with the many dangers that such experiences involved. As often happened in antiquity, a systematic deregulation of the senses—what the Romans called a dissolution of the body—coexisted with the control exercised over that dissolution by the very individual who was affected by it. At the heart of all these explorations lay play: the Roman *ludus, lusus* that made it possible to formalize everything, to escape from a judgmental world into one of pure perception, and thereby to accede to a totally uninhibited sensuality.

The Banquet Spectacle: Self-Defining Citation

In Rome one also comes across a comissatio that was of the same type as the one in which Catullus was involved but that accommodated a different poetics. The Greek symposion was at once a place of pleasure and one where each participant demonstrated how cultured he was. Rome continued that tradition but in a different fashion; for a Roman comissatio could be used to celebrate monuments of the official culture, by citing them and laying on for its participants a performance of texts preserved in writing. The comissatio was a place for commemorating a lyric that was dead, since it was written: such musical presentations of great examples of Greek lyric in no way represented a return to orality but were, on the contrary, celebrations of writing, for these lyric songs had been decontextualized, so the speech act that produced them was a delayed one.

In the second century A.D., a Roman banquet took place in a villa in the suburbs of Rome.[52] The host was a very young man, just emerging from adolescence. He was a native of the province of Asia, that is to say the Middle East, from a family which, given that he was a knight, had by then acquired nobility, and he was rich enough to own this country estate close to the town. The boy was giving a *cena*, to celebrate his birthday. He had invited his friends and also his teachers, his former professors, who had taught him grammar and rhetoric. He was a lover of the good life, a *laetae indolis*, who was naturally fond of the "musical thing," *ad rem musicam facili ingenio ac libenti*. As for that "musical thing," it meant of course not music in the modern sense, but rather a literary education. This young man had been a good student. He had been trained in mastery of the language by reading commentaries of the major texts, which he had copied out. He had accumulated a knowledge of rhetoric, history, and philosophy. He was a "museum man," rather than a "darling of the Muses."

Aulus Gellius was one of the guests, and it was he who wrote an account of the banquet. It is an account that owes much to the personality of its author. Aulus Gellius was an amateur scholar, an imperial official, and a collector of Roman antiquities, which was a very fashionable thing to be in the reigns of Hadrian and Antoninus. Like Hadrian, incidentally, he professed to prefer Cato to Cicero and Ennius to Virgil.

Let us pause for a moment to consider the significance of those preferences. They have nothing to do with the reader's personal taste. Aulus Gellius was naming the writers whom he considered to be, respectively, the most outstanding orator and the most exemplary epic poet of the Roman civilization, the Latin Demosthenes and Homer, and was thereby indicating where he himself stood in the contemporary battle between the classicists and the "antiquarians," the latter being more fashionable at that time. The effect of the choice that the age of Hadrian made in favor of archaism was to push back the moment when the Roman civilization was deemed to have reached its highest point, dating this to the time of the Punic Wars rather than ascribing it, as did the classicists, to the point at which the republic had given way to the empire, that is to say the period of Augustus.

To follow the *cena*, the meal at which all the guests ate, the young easterner, whose name we shall never know, had organized a comissatio. The servants removed the tables on which the dishes had been set and brought in the wine cups. Now was the time for wine and conversation (*poculis mox sermonibusque tempus fuit*). This comissatio was not like the one in which Catullus played his games; it had no place for the intoxication of wine, love, and song. The *sermo*, the talk that would develop, was simply conversation; its cultural status was low, and its effects would not surpass those of ordinary sociability. It was a pleasure characteristic of the meetings of old men, whose bodies were too cold and also too weak for intoxication.[53] The Greek part of this banquet was to consist solely of citations. This, to be sure, would be in the tradition of an Athenian banquet, but there were to be two essential differences. First, the banqueters would not demonstrate how cultivated they were by "singing three of Stesichorus's songs": there would be slaves to do this for them. Second, these musical citations would not be integrated into the ritual of a banquet in the course of which the singing, whatever it might be, would circulate, like the wine cup, from one mouth to another. The banqueters would certainly be expected to show how cultivated they were, but would do so simply by commenting on the songs, not by singing them. So they would be displaying their academic skills rather than their ability to take part in a ritual of conviviality. In fact, the aggressiveness of a group of Greek professors toward a professor of Latin literature was, on the contrary, to prove how very uncouth these people were and how lacking in the civilized manners befitting banqueters.

Thus, although this was a comissatio, in it the guests were treated to a spectacle, just as they had been treated to the dishes served at the *cena*. There would be no singing circulating from one guest to another. One of the guests had pressed the master of the house to let them hear his famous group of lyric singers, and it was in response to this request that the host summoned his choir of children—slaves, naturally, *pueri puellaeque*—some of whom accompanied themselves with a stringed instrument, a lyre, or played on panpipes. In all this, the rules of Roman seemliness were observed: a host had a duty never to impose on his guests anything that might resemble a sickening display of ostentatious luxury.

The children gave a recital of Greek banqueting songs, odes by Anacreon and Sappho, and elegies by more recent poets, all on erotic subjects. All these works were sung in Greek, but the music seems to have been new, as there was no flutist among the musicians, and elegies were normally sung to the accompaniment of flute music. The text adds that this *modus* 'music' was *jucundus* 'agreeable', and this epithet probably carried a precise technical meaning, as did many of the other terms, both nouns and adjectives, commonly used to describe a banquet, such as *lepidus, hilaritas,* and *benignus.*[54] *Jucundus,* derived from the root of the verb *juvare,* means "to give pleasure" and also implies consummation. A *modus jucundus* was "music designed to give pleasure to those listening to it." Cicero would have considered this only just within the bounds of morality.[55] The musical mode suited the "sweet and erotic" (*dulcia et uenusta*) nature of the songs and the graceful physiques of the singers. One song in particular was much appreciated by the assembled company, an Anacreontic ode,[56] described in the text as *uersiculis lepidissimis.* It is a striking expression, for both terms belonged to the technical vocabulary of a Roman banquet. *Lepos* meant the convivial charm that characterized the atmosphere of any successful Roman banquet, a charm created by the easy mood and the friendly good humor of all those present: the very opposite of the anxious mood brought on by cheap wine and the aggressive irritability of drunkards. As for the *uersiculi,* this term was, as we know, used to designate all the amorous poetry of banquets, but in particular the *lusus* of the drinkers. So here we are presented with a shift from the mood of the banqueters to the spectacle laid on for them, and from the Roman tradition to a Greek citation. It is a shift which, as we can see, makes it possible for the comissatio to accommodate these songs, since it is their *jucunditas* that creates the *lepos*.

But wherein lay the charm of these musical citations? Solely in the music. The delectable sweetness of Anacreon's song: "Work the silver, Hephaestus, and make me . . ." could not lie in the poem's semantic content, for it made no sense isolated from its pragmatic meaning—that is, its function in the symposion—or to be more precise, its proposis. But it is not hard to imagine that a lovely melody, the sweetness of the voices, the rhythm of the text, the graceful images that it conjured up, and the agreeable spectacle of the singers were quite enough to lull the banqueters pleasantly. However, it achieved no more than that, for this banquet without any intoxication from words was not really a festivity.

In fact, the charm of the music did not even produce in the guests the convivial good humor that might have been expected. On the contrary, the minute the recital was over, a number of Greek professors set about attacking one of their colleagues, a Spaniard who specialized in Latin letters. So the appreciation of the *lepos* and the *jucunditas* of the songs expressed by Aulus Gellius and his banqueting companions can only have been objective judgments—as it were, erudite evaluations. It did not mean that the Greek songs had truly imparted to this banquet an atmosphere of friendly gentleness and intoxicating delight, simply that they had or might have the power to do so elsewhere. Intellectually, the guests recognized the musical and poetic qualities of the songs, but without enjoying their effects. They were perfectly proper banqueting songs, composed according to the rules. It was the verdict to be expected, since these songs were ascribed to the great names of Greek lyric, Sappho, Anacreon, and one or two others. But the concert had amounted to no more than a ceremonial that confirmed the group's image of its own identity.

Through this recital of symposion odes and possibly even a few *kōmos* songs, the comissatio acquired prestigious Greek patronage. These were well-known poems recognized to be the cream of the genre, and to these intellectuals of the empire they represented the acme of the refinement of a Greek banquet, despite the fact that none of the values of such a banquet had here been respected. Reactions to the songs were not sensual and aesthetic, merely intellectual and analytical. The banqueters had not been brought together in a shared, spontaneous pleasure. Instead, they insisted on testing one another's ability to produce a good commentary on the songs and to justify the satisfaction that they claimed to have derived from them. Hence the aggression of the Greek professors, who proceeded to subject their Spanish colleague Julianus to a veritable examination. They asked him to comment on Anacreon's song and declare his opinion (*sententia*) on it, thereby demonstrating his competence when it came to Greek letters. It was not his linguistic competence, his knowledge of the Greek language that they were questioning, but his ability to appreciate poetic qualities that, according to them, were unknown in Latin letters. They were challenging his ability to recognize what he had never encountered and accusing him of lacking models. No Latin poet, they declared, had ever created in the Latin language sweet, erotic poems that could give pleasure. They denied that Rome possessed any lyric canon at all, except in the Greek language, and proceeded to enumerate all those whom they considered to be barbaric poets with no knowledge of love and melody: Catullus, Calvus, Levius, and others too, whose works have not come down to us. Thanks to this dearth of inventors of lyric songs, they claimed, Latin words had remained a succession of hoarse, harsh cries (*facundia rabida jurgiosaque*), like the barking of dogs.

The Greek professors were not denying the existence of Roman banquet poetry, but simply claiming that it was not worth memorizing and included no monuments of culture worthy of being preserved in the "Banquet Lyrics" section of the Great Universal Library.

The Spaniard, derided as a "barbarous and rustic ranter" (*clamator, barbarus, agrestis*) leapt to the defense of his paternal tongue (*lingua patria*) against these people who were condemning him for having been born in Iberian territory (*ortus terra Hispania*). Even if Spain was his mother, Latin was his father, and he defended his language "as if for his altars and his fires" (*tamquam pro aris et focis*). Julianus was rooted in his language as one is in the soil, through the fires on which sacrifices were made to the city gods and the gods of his home. In this altercation over who belonged and who did not, Julianus maintained that a civilization must be an all-encompassing whole: you could not have religion in the Latin language but love poetry in the Greek language, for the two were an integral part of one and the same thing.

But he was required to cite examples, for the love poetry about which these professors were arguing was not something being written currently. It was a matter of recognition for the existence of model texts that deserved to be remembered just as those of Anacreon and Sappho did. Ultimately, the question at stake in this argument was: had Rome created its own monuments of *otium* in the Latin language? Or did it have only Greek words to remember during its moments of erudite leisure? At this time, leisure devoted to the sophisticated pleasures of love, wine, and poetry was regarded as a criterion of civilization. On the one hand there were barbarians who, when drunk on wine, shouted, insulted one another, fought, and crawled about on all fours; on the other, there were civilized people who savored wine, music, and sweet songs of love. The Greek professors' charge against the Romans was thus that the latter had attained to this form of civilization purely thanks to contact with themselves. It was an accusation that was hard to swallow, coming as it did from men whose sole convivial pleasure appeared to be literary criticism laced with racist insults.

Julianus's response to this Greek baiting was to recall to mind airs long forgotten, Roman songs (*lusus*) from bygone days, produced by Quintus Catulus, Valerius Aeditus, and Porcius Licinius. And he sang them himself. To avoid embarrassment, he veiled his head for, as he warned, he was about to "make somewhat indelicate remarks" (*parum pudica aratione*). This suggests that the professors' banquet did not obey the same rules as a comissatio in which *lusus* were sung. As a critical spectator, you could listen to the erotic songs of Anacreon and Sappho, but you were not supposed to sing them yourself. By doing so, Julianus was assuming a role that belonged to slaves, and putting himself at the service of all his drinking companions. Pronounced outside a comissatio, the words of *lusus* would usually be found shocking. Thus, in the course of a trial in Carthage, Apuleius once found himself censured by his enemies on the score of a number of erotic poems dedicated to the son of one of his friends, which, they claimed, proved that he was nothing but a debauchee (*comissator improbus*).[57] In his own defense, Apuleius reminded them that he belonged to the tradition of Anacreon, Sappho, Aeditus, Porcius, and Catulus—the very authors invoked in Aulus Gellius's banquet—and stressed that the obscenity of his verses was far more noticeable when they were read wrongly, harshly, and in a vulgar manner (*dure et rustico*), without modulating the voice so as to render it pleasing to the listeners. Apuleius then proceeded to give a public reading (*recitatio*) in a clear and intelligible voice and a suitable tone. Even though over three centuries of history had passed since the time of the *lusus* of Catulus, his own *uersiculi* were in the perfect tradition. The verses that he recited were designed to accompany the gift of a crown of flowers to the young Critias. In exchange for the intertwined flowers and his poem, the poet asked for other intertwinings and the bouquet of Critias's mouth. And if the boy offered him a song in return, the exchange would be perfect:

> . . . redde
> proque rosis oris auia pupurei.
> Quod si animam inspires donaci,[58]
> iam carmina nostra
> cedent uicta tuo dulciloquo calamo.

> . . . for the roses, give me kisses from your dazzling mouth.
> And if you breathe your soul into the flute, our verses will
> be surpassed by the sweetness of your song.

This anecdote from Africa indicates that there were at least two possible ways of listening to loving *lusus* when these were read outside the context of a comissatio. One type of reading would convey the poetic form: this would be a *recitatio,*[59] the type used for the professors at Aulus Gellius's banquet. The other type would convey the contents: this would be a *lectio,* a reading for oneself or a murmured deciphering that conveyed the meaning of the words rather than the musicality (*numerus*) of the text, a text that, in these circumstances, would appear obscene to a listener. You could even call this a pornographic reading.[60]

Aulus Gellius does not tell us how the Greek professors reacted. That, clearly, was not what interested him: this story had simply served as a pretext for him to record in writing a number of very ancient poems, poems even more ancient than those mentioned by the Greek professors, one of which was ascribed to the great general Lutatius Catulus (consul in 102 B.C., and the conqueror of the Cimbri at Vercellae). By introducing them into the encyclopedia that he was preparing for his son, Aulus Gellius hoped to raise them to the status of canonical models. That is why, instead of bothering with the opinion of the Greeks, he himself proceeded to provide a critical commentary on the three cited poems, declaring that they certainly possessed all the necessary refined and sophisticated qualities: they were "neat," "terse," "polished," "graceful," and full of seduction and love.

Learning of this quarrel between professors, modern readers of Aulus Gellius may find it surprising that Julianus did not riposte to the sneers of his attackers by citing the works of the author whom we, today, consider to be the greatest writer of Roman banquet poetry, namely Horace. The Greek professors had barely committed themselves to a grudging recognition that the poetry of Catullus and his friend Calvo may have possessed just a few good points. But, of course, this account by Aulus Gellius was an invention, the purpose of which was to secure for the monumental value of the ancient Roman poets he was citing as much recognition as was granted to the great Greek writers of lyric. He was writing as an admirer of the more ancient writers and was seeking to dethrone the classics. That is why he committed these poems to *writing*, copying them out for his son, in the compendium of knowledge that he dedicated to him. Reading Aulus Gellius many centuries later, we find ourselves presented with an episode in the invention of Roman literature.

Eventually, those ancient eroticopoetic games of Catulus and his friends, lifted out of the intoxicated atmosphere of a comissatio, decontextualized and reduced by writing to the status of statements, were to acquire a double destiny, depending on the type of reading to which they were submitted: professors would appreciate them for their form, lewd readers for the erotic excitement engendered by their content. But whether the reading of these *lusus* was distinguished by shameful bodies or an absence of bodies, it would lack the pleasures that had accompanied their initial, appropriate speech act. To cite them was to deprive them of all efficacy, and hence of all meaning. Nevertheless, once set up as models, they continued to have a role to play in that they served as references for the erotic games of sophisticated Romans, as we have seen in the case of Apuleius. In this manner they again became a part of life. If citation was one of the pleasures of the comissatio, it was a pleasure of self-identification: the banqueters celebrated their Greco-Roman culture by citing not only the gestures but also the words of the Greek symposion.

Eventually, we can see a ternary structure emerging, corresponding to three types of speech acts for *lusus*, one immediately relevant, the other two out of step with them. Within a comissatio, the *lusus* were an integral part of an eroticism that was a compound of kissing and the slight intoxication provoked by breath and wine: they were part and parcel of the social ritual. But once deprived of their speech-act context, they entered upon a twofold destiny as statements first decontextualized, then recontextualized elsewhere: either they became objects for formal study that were transcribed in books, in which case they could be classed as nourishment—albeit intellectual nourishment, for sure—to be chewed over by scholars in encyclopedic banquets; or, alternatively, reduced to their erotic content, they became material for pornographic readings whose only effect was to excite Priapus. More generally, we can now see that no poetic reading at all was practiced in Rome—that is, reading that simultaneously took account of both content and style. A fortiori, nor did there exist any type of reading that made the style play upon the content, as happens today in a literary reading in which the reader produces new meaning from the text, refusing to be limited to discovering the sense placed there by its author. Finally, with a *lectio,* or pure deciphering, it was not possible to appreciate the form of a text. That kind of appreciation required an oralization, either a musical citation as described in Aulus Gellius, or a public declamation or *recitatio.*[61] On the other hand, a *lectio,* a muttered deciphering, did suffice for the reader to become aware of the written message, which in these circumstances was reduced to a *sermo.*

Erudite Banquets and the Books That Provided the Nourishment

In Aulus Gellius's banquet, philological abrasiveness was tempered by the pleasure provided by the songs. But there were other, more austere banquets, in which the comissatio, with all its pleasures, was forgotten once and for all. Roman culture had its own way of commemorating not only the young Plato of kisses, but also the Plato of the symposion, who confined the living words of his master Socrates within lifeless signs. This dialogue, which was to serve as the reference for what literary history usually calls the "banquet" genre, is a philosophical version of the aristocratic Athenian symposion. In this banquet, the conversation of cultivated men is the only amusement that the drinkers allow themselves.[62] Having made that decision, they also agree to dismiss the flute player and not to become intoxicated with Dionysus. Those present are feeling the after-effects of the excesses of a banquet held on the previous day, when they had celebrated Agathon's victory in a drama contest, so they decide to drink "inoffensively," without risking intoxication.

So the model of the philosophic banquet is a banquet without Dionysus in which there is to be talk *about* love but not a word or, a fortiori, a song of love.[63] It introduces the idea of an association between drinking without drunkenness and the pleasures of conversation, which we shall come across again in the practice of storytelling.[64] In the philosophical banquet both the words and the drink are purely human, so they deconstruct the religious ritual of the symposion, reducing it to a social ritual. Instead of "making love" together, the drinkers just talk about it. It is not hard to see how this intellectual deviation from the symposion came about: Socratic philosophy, in the vanguard of the struggle against democracy, chimed with the aristocratic resistance organized by the Athenian symposion. However, philosophical speech excluded Dionysiac speech, even if it did circulate on the model of wine; and the final eruption of a *kōmos* of drunken revelers puts a stop to the philosophical talk of this banquet and, at the same time, brings Plato's transcript of it to an end.

Much could be said about this banquet without intoxication whose host has the face of the Satyr Marsyas or some Silenus, yet in which wine is resisted.[65] Marsyas was a flute player and Socrates, in the manner of a female banquet flute player, "possesses" the other participants, but only metaphorically, through his "music," that is to say his philosophical discourse, which, however, is simply "spoken," without musical accompaniment. In a way, Socrates takes the place of Dionysus as the sovereign of the symposion. The philosophical conversation is delightful (*kharis*), for the one proferring it as for those receiving it.[66] It resembles an exchange of gifts, and as it circulates among the men present, its charm is solely that of conversation—that is, it stems solely from its content. That is why these Socratic words do not need the physical presence of the master: "reported" by someone else, even by someone inept, they still retain all their power to intoxicate any and everyone.[67] The definition of reading itself is just such an affirmation of the all-powerful nature of a statement separated from its father, and it implies absolute confidence in the realism of words.

Socrates' philosophy circulated in Athens like waves of rumor. Glaucon asked Apollodorus for an account of this banquet held in Agathon's home, having already heard somewhat uncomplimentary talk of it from Phoenix, the son of Philip. Apollodorus had not himself been present, but Aristodemus had told him of it and he had asked Socrates to confirm the story. Apollodorus's account whiles away the time of their walk from Phalerus to Athens. Plato halted the waves of rumor by committing to writing this, the most reliable version of the famous symposion, thereby arresting the rumor and, at the same time, turning his book into a monument to it. The way in which he effaces from the text all the different strata of information—that is to say, the fact that Plato had heard the story from Apollodorus who himself had been told it by Aristodemus—confirms his confidence in the realism of written words, capable of representing things perfectly and freed from the subjectivity of the narrator.

It was thus Plato who made known these banquets of learning, imaginary spaces of a cold culture preserved in books that were later reproduced in Rome. A banquet became a place and opportunity for erudite discourse, subsequently committed to writing. A philosophic banquet thus constituted a kind of fictitious speech act.

Some banquets were veritable scholarly congresses to which each man brought along his basketful of knowledge to share with his fellows around the table. The acknowledged model for the banquets, in which Greek or Latin was spoken, was the Roman *cena*, a *cena* at which one could be nourished at once physically and intellectually. The metaphor was quite commonly used in Rome.[68] These banquets of knowledge became encyclopedias and served as fictitious speech acts for a whole series of ancient compilations such as Macrobius's *Saturnalia* and Athenaeus's *The Learned Banquet*. There were a great many of these banquet books, most of which have disappeared, such as Maecenas's *Symposion*, in which this friend of Augustus's brought together Horace, Virgil, and Messala.

Macrobius dedicated his book to his son, hoping to provide him with nourishment for the rest of his life when he presented him with this perpetual store cupboard of fictitious friends gathered in a kind of banquet planned to last for the whole duration of the Saturnalia. His idea was to produce a synthesis of all that he had read in the course of his life, so that his son would not need to read it[69] and so would be able to extend his father's knowledge by adding his own to it. It was a Roman father's duty to provide nourishment for his children, and Macrobius was extending this obligation to the field of education.

Plutarch drew a contrast between these learned banquets—*deipna* in Greek, *cena* in Latin—and the banquet, or symposion of Plato.[70] In his view, Plato and Xenophon, instead of writing down what had been said at Callias's or Agathon's table, which was after all only "philosophical banter," would have done better to preserve in writing "the food, the cooked dishes, and the tidbits" that had cost so much effort and money. Plutarch does, in general, tend to set more store by anything nourishing, be it food or scholarly discourse, at the expense of whatever brings no nourishment with it, such as wine and chatter. It is the same very Roman distinction as that drawn between the substantial and the lightweight.

Athenaeus's *Deipnosophists* suits Plutarch's project perfectly. The very title sets the scholars (*sophistai*) in their places at a *cena*—in Greek *deipnon*—and the preface introduces the banquet as follows:

> The subject is a banquet given by a wealthy Roman named Larensis, who has summoned as guests the men of his time most learned in their several branches of knowledge. Not one of their excellent sayings has Athenaeus failed to mention. For he has contrived to bring into his book an account of fishes, their uses and names with derivations; also vegetables of all sorts and animals of every description; historians, poets, philosophers, musical instruments, innumerable kinds of jests; . . . drinking cups in all their variety. . . . In short, the plan of the discourse reflects the rich bounty of a feast [*deipnon*], and the arrangement of the book the courses of the dinner. Such is the delightful "feast of words" [*logo deipnon*] [of] Athenaeus.[71]

It was no longer simply a matter of accommodating citations with which it was possible to identify. Now the banquet, thanks to its many participants, could forge ahead with the frantic business, begun by the Alexandrians, of first collecting all the knowledge possible (it being taken for granted that this must necessarily be written down), next putting together a preselected compendium of knowledge, for not everything was worth preserving, and finally summarizing and condensing it all.

The author of an encyclopedia would cook the foods that he had collected from all over the place, so as to turn them into tasty semipredigested nourishment. The preface of Macrobius's *Saturnalia* makes that point explicitly. The metaphors mount up: first the book is a store cupboard that will supply the young man with all the intellectual nourishment he needs. Then the father explains that he has gathered pollen like a bee in order to make a uniquely flavored honey from the nectar of a hundred flowers. The rewriting is first like the leaven that makes pastry rise; then it is compared to the kind of cooking that makes it possible to assimilate all foodstuffs. The aim of the book is to replace all others: "If you need an account of a historical fact, generally unknown and hidden amid the mass of books, or a word, or an action worth remembering, it will be easy for you to find them in this book and to extract them from it." For, of course, these encyclopedias are bursting with tables of contents and indexes so that, as their authors naively say, it will not be necessary to read everything. The Romans did not like reading purely for the sake of reading.

One famous example of this frenzy for purely nourishing reading is provided by Pliny the Elder, whose feverish activity of a bulimic reader is described by his nephew Pliny the Younger.[72] All his leisure time, that is to say every moment not devoted to public affairs, he spends reading, then rewriting more concisely. He has books read aloud to him by a slave and either takes notes or dictates them. After his bath, while being massaged, while being conveyed somewhere in his litter, during his meals, and even during his sunbathing, he never stops. The result of all this: the thirty-seven books of his *Natural History* that have come down to us and sixty-five books that have been lost, devoted to subjects as diverse as grammar and hurling a javelin when on horseback—not an easy feat without stirrups, but the author had, after all, been a cavalry officer in Germany. For the Romans, all this belonged to the category of letters (*letterae*), but we ourselves would hardly call it literature.

Books were present in Rome, even played an important role there, but it was not to provide pleasure from words. Reading for oneself was a nourishment that had to do with the body. It was not wine. The intoxication of words could only be experienced in orality and—what is more—only in a relationship with the body of another, with his breath and the fragrance of his breathing. Reading erotic poetry on one's own could only create a pornographic excitement; it was the kind of reading of the contents in which Cicero refused to indulge on the grounds that it had a softening and putrefying effect. The metaphors used to illustrate these two kinds of reading associated them with the belly, likened them to the two kinds of nourishment with which the Romans were familiar, the kind that was actually nourishing and the kind that delighted the "gullet."

Trimalchio and Mythology

In Trimalchio's banquet the participants are simply bellies; no room is made at the end of the party for a comissatio without food. This banquet is a *cena* in which erudition rubs shoulders with priapic excitement, but Eros and love are totally absent.[73] During the meal, actors dressed as warriors from the *Iliad* come in and recite the Homeric epic, in the Greek language, in dialogue form. Nobody understands this archaic language at all, and Trimalchio, as a good student, follows it using a Latin translation that he reads out in a singsong voice.[74] In itself, that is not particularly ridiculous: the master of the house is keen to show that this old Greek culture presides over his banquet and gives it a certain prestige, an intellectual dignity not conferred by the Roman *cena* on its own. Having decided to introduce a citation spectacle, he does so with the greatest solemnity and, by following the acted story (*fabulam*) on a libretto, he hopes to avoid the criticism of not understanding the first thing about it, the kind of criticism that the Greeks heaped on Julianus. However, any perception of form is beyond Trimalchio.

In introducing players of Homer in the course of the *cena*, when the guests are busy eating, he has mixed up musical culture and culinary delights, a comissatio and a *cena*. He is, anyway, quite incapable of suspending the consumption of food for a while, to make room for a comissatio, for the *cena Trimalchionis* is a Major Blowout. Possibly to make the presence of the declaiming warriors more enjoyable, Trimalchio makes use of Ajax in a pantomime in which the hero uses a sword to cut up a boiled calf with a helmet stuck on its head, pretending to be frenziedly massacring the poor beast. This feat requires incredible virtuosity, and it is known that the Romans were experts when it came to classy carving. So the guests are open-mouthed with admiration when Ajax passes them their slices of veal on the tip of his sword.

Trimalchio's second mistake stems from the fact that he can neither remember nor follow the slightest mythological story. His way of summarizing the story acted out before him by the players of Homer, which he is supposed to be reading out from his book, is hilarious: "Now Homer is telling how the Trojans and the Parentines made war. He, naturally, was the victor and his daughter, Iphigenia, he gave her to Achilles. That is why Ajax is so angry." Each time Trimalchio tangles with mythology, the same narrative debacle ensues. A fine vase of his is painted with a scene that, according to him, represents "Niobe imprisoned by Daedalus inside the Trojan Horse"; on one of his cups Cassandra is to be seen, "killing her children."[75] Trimalchio suffers from a paralysis of "literary" memory because in Rome an ability to cite from the Greeks was the mark of an educated man, that is to say a man who was free and born of a free father and who had received a liberal education. Clearly, citing Greek or Latin poetry was a way of affirming one's cultural and social identity. Liberty, the *libertas* of a genuine Roman citizen, free and born from a free father, was demonstrated by his "liberal" education.

Petronius also tells us of another Roman, Calivinius Sabinus,[76] a contemporary of Trimalchio's and a multimillionaire. He too came from servile origins and suffered from the same selective amnesia as Trimalchio. He muddled up Achilles and Odysseus and could never remember the name of Agamemnon, despite claiming to have assiduously courted their company at school. He would pay fantastic prices for slaves more gifted than himself, or rather who did not have to prove that they had received a liberal education—which, of course, they had not, any more than their master—but were able simply to recite poetry in a mechanical fashion. Each of these slaves had his own speciality: one knew Homer by heart, another Hesiod; and Calivinius Sabinus had distributed Greek lyric poetry between the nine others. At meal times they would crouch at the foot of their master's bed and prompt him with the requisite citation at the right moment.

In Trimalchio's banquet, as in the one described by Aulus Gellius, two kinds of speech coexisted, citation and conversation (*sermo*). Culturally, both were manifestly inferior. Conversation was only to acquire a certain efficacy when freedmen took to telling stories,[77] but in itself conversation was anyway a weak kind of speech, and as for citation, well, we have already seen to what depths it could sink: freedmen could acquire knowledge and their libraries could be full of books (Trimalchio possessed three), but their knowledge was limited to the contents of those books. They could not accede to a mastery of language or to an aesthetic appreciation of it, as these citation celebrations show.

All Banquets . . .

At the heart of hot culture in both Greece and Rome lay the intoxication of singing, wine, dancing, and kissing. But we are separated from all that by so many years and so many kinds of distance that we can do little more than guess at those ancient forms of intoxication, most of which no doubt escape us.

It is in Rome, rather than Greece, that I shall try to anchor the idea of a hot culture, for in Latin that "heat" expressed the gratuitous surplus of vitality that fired all those taking part in a festivity. In those moments their lives were as distant from death as they could ever be. They were intensely conscious of whatever was most human about them, whatever distinguished them from animals and brought them closer to the gods. Roman wine, the blood of the earth, the liquor of life, the drink of eternity, concentrated within it the same dry heat as that of vital breath, which ignited in a kiss. A body in love was more alive, because it burned more fiercely, and its vital breath (*anima*) became violently active and animated. The fire of love was a divine fire in that it partook of immortality, but an immortality experienced only for a fleeting moment. The whole art of kissing lay in prolonging that moment for as long as possible. Clearly, intoxication could arouse a human being's most purely human—or divine, it comes to the same—dimension, without automatically involving an explicit religious ritual in the form of a prayer or an invocation. Ancient polytheism in any event set the gods at the heart of every human activity. However, that presence of the gods could take different forms. Although intoxication was a ritual of possession in Greece, in Rome it was not—hence the interest in comparing two types of ancient intoxication, the Greek and the Roman, the former dependent upon a religious ritual, the latter not.

A culture of intoxication, constructed through ritual, whether or not religious, is always shared, extreme, perilous, and confined to the event. Hot culture cannot produce monuments since, by definition, a monument serves to commemorate something that is over—that is, an absence. It is on the side of whatever is fixed, frozen, dead; it belongs to cold culture. Hot culture can only be lived in the fever and fervor of the present moment. It is inevitably limited in time, since the intensity that it demands and the energy that it burns up would consume its participants to the point of death, were it to be overprolonged.

Whether it involves a minority group or an entire community, it brings with it an experience of otherness, such as sexual indifferentiation. In consequence, hot culture cannot create normative models of humanity for the civilization in which it is practiced, nor can it produce transgressive models. For the experiences of intoxication take place elsewhere. They do not belong to the everyday world: in his intoxication, a drinker does things he would not do in the everyday world. Normality is thus circumscribed from within by people who belong to it but who probe its limits at the risk of swinging outside it.

Because hot culture concentrates intense moments of collective life, wherever the group sets a high value on those moments, representing them as one of the highest manifestations of humanity, the acme of the refinement of which the society is capable, a hot culture tends to be treated as that society's distinctive emblem in its relations with the world outside it. Take gypsy flamenco, for example, or the Ionian banquet lyric. It is at that point that a self-identificatory tendency creeps in. Threatened with genocide or perhaps simply required to define themselves in terms of common norms, those of panhellenic Greece in the past, or of Western culture today, the Ionians defined themselves by the banquet lyric, the Gypsies define themselves by flamenco. As they do so, both groups systematically turn their art into a model, fix it, theorize about it—in short, objectivize it and make it normative. Above all, when presented to the gaze or ears of others, that art turns into a spectacle; it is uprooted, wrested from its real speech act, its sole raison d'être. The Gypsies give concerts, the painted dreams of the Aborigines are collected together in exhibitions, the Ionians sang at the festivals of Olympia and Delphi. Eventually, flamenco is recorded on compact disks and Ionian lyric became a subsection of the lyric genre, on the classified shelves of some library.

But once a self-identificatory culture, that is to say a culture by which certain people identify themselves, is reduced to commemorating its past, it is on the way to becoming a distinguished kind of boredom. A cold culture is not costly and is furthermore easy to integrate into an economy of accumulation. Hot culture, on the other hand, is costly in terms of expended energy, wasted time, and declining productivity. Living culture is ruinous, calls for a frugal day-to-day budget to allow for special uncontrolled spending sprees, such as the Roman games. Hot culture is a fire that is all-consuming.

We have traced the development of what we have called a self-identificatory trend in both Greece and Rome, involving the invention of mythical poets and the fixing of emblematic poems. Then, moving on from festivals to books, we have sketched in the last stage, in which texts, now written down and memorized word for word, begin to circulate like fetishes, to be commemorated in cold ceremonies such as recitation contests or recitals for erudite banquets, or fed as a daily diet to children in schools.

In this behavior of civilizations posturing before eternity, it is not hard to detect what much later would become the cult of "great literature." The fetishes of the French, collected into a pantheon of literary histories, are Molière, Corneille, Racine, Voltaire, Montesquieu, Rousseau, Vigny, Lamartine, Chateaubriand, Stendhal, Balzac, Zola, Baudelaire, Verlaine, Rimbaud. Other choices are, of course, possible, always selected according to ideological criteria. It is amusing for us today to remember how there was a time when the left and the right each laid claim to its own heroes of literature. Left-wing France identified with Rabelais, Molière, Rousseau, George Sand, Hugo, and Zola; right-wing France claimed affinities with

Corneille, Bossuet, Chateaubriand, Vigny, and Claudel. They were at daggers drawn over whether Balzac and Racine were progressive or reactionary. Recently, literature has been aligned with human rights, with Condorcet and Julien Benda on one side, and Tocqueville on the other.

However, transition from a hot culture to a cold one through the celebration of fixed texts or through their digestion, depending on whether it was a matter of content or of form, does not necessarily bring about the birth of literature as an institution. Roman readers either concentrated on admiring style or else absorbed the knowledge contained in written works, leaving no room for an interpretative reading or an aesthetic and polysemic hermeneutics such as we use today, which is what makes something that is written down function as a text.

When the culture with which a civilization identifies is socially predominant, hot culture does not necessarily disappear but it does become marginalized, diversify, and sink into the obscurity of traditional microsocieties.[78] Seen from outside, that hot culture now no longer produces anything but vulgar, abnormal, and dangerous forms of festivity: "Nothing good ever comes from it," "It's a whole lot of superstition." The hot culture of the "have-nots" is an enigma to the "haves," who despise or fear it. However, this marginal hot culture cannot take the place of the kind of hot culture that an entire society may bring into being in great, consensual festive events. We have already glimpsed this in connection with Plato's *Symposion*, in a situation in which the culture was to turn away from Dionysiac intoxication, which was then replaced by an (unfortunately metaphorical) philosophical intoxication; and it is a development that will become more manifest in our study of the ancient story, which will, in turn, lead on to the idea of cultural entropy.

III

THE STORY CULTURE: BOOKS THAT WERE NOT FOR READING

In my quest for the hot cultures of antiquity, my point of departure was the Homeric banquet and the song of the bard. After proceeding by way of the Greek symposion, followed by the Roman comissatio, I now find myself back where I started, ready to set out again along a new path, one that leads to the popular story. In the Homeric *dais*, mythical speech and the speech of stories were combined in two narrative forms, the song of the bard and the traveler's tale, both of which opened windows onto the world of banquets and kings, in which each was defined in relation to the other.

In the *Odyssey*, to hear a traveler tell his tale was one of the pleasures, alongside the song of the bard, that was offered to those who were sharing the same food, whether as kings or as servants, although it was a pleasure that was culturally inferior since it possessed none of the charm, the *kharis*, of the Muses: a story was not sung. In the swineherd's hut, Eumaeus and Odysseus, disguised as a beggar, feast meagerly as they tell each other their extraordinary life stories. This is the same kind of pleasure as that which we come across much later, at the time of the Roman Empire, in the form of the story, which may likewise be recounted at banquets but may also be told in other circumstances. Such stories are a considerably later phenomenon, for the most ancient of the documents that we possess date from the first century, although stories, in themselves, must have existed much earlier. However that may be, storytelling, in the form in which we thus come upon it, belonged to a time when the consensual culture had split apart, and an official elitist, self-referential, and unified culture had been put together by collecting monuments to canonical works and then transmitting them through the teaching of rhetors. But in its margins it left room for a popular culture to develop, shifting and shadowy and based on the weaker forms of speech.

The official Roman culture had nothing but scorn for these storytellers and the noun used to designate them, *circulatores*, was an insult that intellectuals enjoyed bandying about together.[1] The word evokes not only the groups of loiterers that would form in the streets around all illusionist artistes, jugglers, fakirs, imitaters, charlatans, and tellers of untrue stories, but also the wandering lives of these peddlers of stories, people with neither hearth nor home, who eked out a meager living telling boring tales whose only charm was the whiff that they brought of the elsewhere out of which they had materialized and into which they would subsequently, soon disappear.[2] The denigratory overtones attached to their name also resulted from the fact that these *circulatores* demanded payment, so their stories fell into the category of merchandise, and cheap merchandise at that: "Have your copper ready and hear a first-rate story."[3]

Alongside the exquisite refinements of wine and kisses, cultivated by the Greek and Roman aristocracies, refinements that were certainly sociologically of a minority nature but were socially prestigious and constituted the dominant model, here is evidence of another culture, also of a minority nature but less resplendent, a culture that has to be tracked down along caravan routes and among working women. Yet even if, as we shall see, a story lacks what lies at the heart of a hot culture, namely physical pleasures, intoxication, and musical delight—hence, its humility—it was without doubt the only genre that prolonged the line of epic orality: these stories are all linked together, never closed off in a text; they weave around the world endless garlands of words that unite the storytellers with their public, within a common culture. Under the Roman Empire, stories were certainly a living culture.

The Saying of the Bard and What He Said

However, before going off to listen to a story, we must first return to the Homeric banquet, to renew contact with speech designed for communication in which what is said is not totally abolished by the saying of it, in other words the pragmatic meaning does not altogether cover the semantic meaning. When we left the *dais* for the symposion and the Roman comissatio, in a sense we entered a world of meaninglessness. The intoxicated words addressed to Cleobulus and Calvus eluded the narrative mode: it was a matter of singing or of speaking with nothing to say. Between the subject of the speech and his addressee, the only thing that counted was the saying of it, not what was said, for the information that passed from the one to the other amounted to nothing at all.

In the case of the Homeric bard, that was not so. The bard, like the drinker at the symposion, sang at a banquet, inspired by a deity. But that was certainly all the two had in common. In the first place, the bard was not a guest at the banquet, but a professional. His musical ability was a gift to the guests from the master of the house, on top of the generous portions of wine, cooked meats, and bread. The bard's speech did not make the banquet work religiously, even if it did make it work socially, whereas the drinker's song, for its part, certainly was one of the mechanisms that made the symposion work. Furthermore, the bard's speech was distributed equally to every guest, in the same way as the portions of meat, cut up and offered by the master of the house: it too was a gift of hospitality. It did not circulate, was not passed from one guest to another, like the wine cup in the symposion. Nor was the bard possessed by the wine; instead the voice of the Muse penetrated him directly, with no drug mediating, thanks to the music that he played. The Homeric bard was a professional initiated into the art of the cithara. His song put him in contact with the mother of the Muses who, as her name indicated, was the mistress of divine memory, the one who knew "the past, the present, and the future," as the now famous formula puts it.[4]

Finally, the Homeric bard did not sing with nothing to say. Through his exploration of myth, he revealed to his listeners the hidden connections within the culture that they shared.[5] His way of divulging these truths was to tell improbable stories that the entire audience agreed to recognize as such. Although his speaking of the mythical truth was wiped out when the speech act came to an end, what he had said, the fiction that he had recounted, which was so to speak the syntax of mythical speech, remained in his listeners' memories: what the bard had said, which survived beyond its context, was, in other words, a story that operated as a structure.

The Cyclops, Odysseus, and the Satyrs

Thus, the meeting between Odysseus and Polyphemus, the Cyclops, who wanted to devour him raw, along with his companions, and Odysseus's cunning ruses to escape formed a narrative schema that was, as we know, put to a number of mythical uses in Greece. The two best-known versions are book 9 of the *Odyssey* and Euripides' satyr play, the *Cyclops*. In both, the Cyclops is a cannibalistic monster who is alien to the human race because he is nothing but a shepherd who drinks milk, eats cheese, and lives alone; since he does not till the earth or sacrifice to the gods, he eats no cooked meat. The cultural field explored in the two cases is close enough, since it concerns the hospitality organized when a banquet takes place, along with the reverse of this, the cannibalism of the Cyclops who, instead of inviting travelers to feast with him, eats them instead.[6] Only the reference for conviviality differs in the two versions of the story.

In the *Odyssey*, the banquet that constitutes the reference is the Homeric *dais*. In the *Cyclops*, it is the Dionysiac symposion. Without going into a long comparison between the two myths, it is worth noting that, although in both myths Polyphemus is a victim of drunkenness, in the *Odyssey* his mistake is to have drunk pure wine; in Euripides' tragedy it is different: the wine that he drinks is properly mixed with water and drawn from a krater, but he drinks it alone, without the company of the other Cyclopes and surrounded by the Satyrs whom he has taken prisoner. One of the myths reveals the necessary correlation between watered wine and hospitality, while the other shows the equally necessary link between hospitality and sociability when drinking.

In Homer, Odysseus's divine protectress is Athena; in Euripides, his protector is Dionysus. In the one case, the pure, Poseidonian violence of the monster is opposed by the cunning, or *métis*, over which Athena presides and which is superdeveloped in Odysseus; in the other, the violence of Polyphemus is overcome by the spells of Dionysus-wine. In Euripides, Odysseus is saved with and by the Satyrs who, for their part, are capable of withstanding drunkenness indefinitely. The hero brings the wine from the outside world, and the Satyrs set up the deceptive symposion that intoxicates Polyphemus, by drinking to excess with him without succumbing to the huge quantities of the wine that they knock back unscathed yet that totally overcome the Cyclops.[7]

The structure of space in the two myths is also different: in Homer, the world of men and the world of Nowhere, in which Odysseus—No One—is traveling, are strictly separate and, apart from the hero, nobody has ever been to the latter or will ever go there. Odysseus meets nobody from the world of mortals, nor is there the slightest sign that any mortal has ever set foot there. In Euripides, the Satyrs, companions of Dionysus, make the same journey as Odysseus. They set out in search of the god, who has been carried off by Etruscan pirates, but are shipwrecked on the reefs of Polyphemus's island. The Satyrs who, not being human, are inedible, are there reduced to slavery by the Cyclopes, but soon, thanks to Odysseus's arrival, they are set free and are able to return to the world of light where mortal men worship the Immortals and where they meet up with Dionysus again. Although this is a god who customarily frequents wild places such as the mountains or the seashores, he never ventures beyond these into the world of the Cyclopes. However, it is because of his affinities with the furthest reaches of the world that his drinking companions and fellow wanderers, the Satyrs, are accidentally marooned on Polyphemus's island, from which they eventually manage to return. They do so aboard Odysseus's ship and had landed on Polyphemus's island in the first place only as a result of an error of navigation, just as Odysseus only reached it as a result of being blown there in the course of a series of storms. The king of Ithaca and the Satyrs have been tossed about by the same fictional sea squalls. The Satyrs thus appear as mediators between here and Nowhere, just as does the hero of the bard's song. Perhaps this was a way of making the point that, in the theater, Dionysism could produce mythical fiction, for a Satyr provided an exaggerated and inaccessible image of a symposion drinker and *kōmos* dancer. Perhaps it was also a way of showing how, in Athens, theater, established as part of the trappings of Dionysus, was also an heir to Homeric myth.

Myth and Representation

The bard's performance of myth, like the song of the symposion drinker, stemmed from a culture that expressed itself in terms of otherness. It excluded all forms of representation through resemblance. It used "the other" as its mirror. Epic did not show Greek civilization as it was. What was real to the listeners was always twisted and distorted so as to construct the fiction. The Greeks' own self-referential culture—meat that was cooked, studded armchairs, ships with oarsmen, girls doing the washing—although certainly present was dislocated by situations that were not humanly possible. Even Odysseus's palace in Ithaca, which seems so realistic, was an improbable house, for its master was neither living nor dead. An absence of over ten years was one of those situations that were humanly, culturally impossible, the kind that epic was always constructing: a fiction. Furthermore, ten years was not a precise number of years, but a way of indicating an infinite space of time, an excessive period of time, a duration that could no longer be controlled by expectation. In the real world, Odysseus's wife would have remarried, or else his estate would certainly have been ruined by all the festivity that the suitors had a right to insist upon. Alternatively, with Telemachus killed and his possessions dispersed, she would have returned to her father. The effects of Odysseus's absence were irreparable for hardly was he home than he had to leave again. The destruction caused by his return, when he wanted to reclaim his wife and his house, was too great and the island community rejected him.

The performance of the myth explored a civilization that was an accepted fact and did not need to be either described or represented, for it could be defined quite simply in the following terms: "The Greek civilization is wherever epic is sung." The identity of the Greeks had no need of affirmation, for it was consubstantial with their existence. They were not men painted in Greek colors, a particular species of the human race. Rather, they were indissociably both men and Greeks.[8] That is why those many, shifting, mythical performances of the bards, split into a thousand idiosyncratic versions, incompatible with any form of political union, were crushed by the city culture and panhellenism, and became fixed in a self-referential mythology.

Only at that point, when myths were fixed in a mythology and had lost their exploratory function, did they come to be used as representations and reduced to stories. Once their pragmatic meaning was lost, all that remained was fiction. Meanwhile, as this fiction continued to be fabricated, to create impossible situations, these mythological stories came to take the form of extravagant, immoral lies. Only allegory, hermeneutics, or some other kind of semiological reading could render them tolerable. Let us at this point abandon mythical fiction, which no longer had any pragmatic meaning, and return to the banquet, from which we can set off once again, following in the tracks of ancient travelers. This trail will lead us to discover among the travelers of the Roman Empire a kind of speech that, having become autonomous and in the absence of exploratory myths, turned into stories: both Greek and Roman stories, since the period in which they emerged was the period when the whole Mediterranean was united under Rome and was resolutely bicultural.

FIVE

The Golden Ass Stories

Walking with One's Ears

In a Homeric banquet, the host would offer good food and a bard, as part of his hospitality; and a stranger would produce his name and his story. It was an exchange of gifts that amounted to mutual recognition. The host proved that he was civilized by showing that he sacrificed and listened to the Muse's songs, common to all civilized men; the stranger indicated that he too belonged to the society of men: his own name situated him in a lineage and the name of his city attached him to a land. He thereby created a geographical distance that he then proceeded to fill in with his stories. With its travelers' tales and the songs of its bard, the Homeric banquet opened itself up to the whole world by means of the combination of its exploration of mankind and its exploration of fiction.

Because Odysseus is a hero like no other and because Odysseus is at the same time No One, when he tells of his travels to the land of Nowhere at the Phaeacians' banquet, those two explorations merge, since the voice that his listeners, the Phaeacians, hear is the voice of Odysseus, which the bard produces from his own speech. The epic song gives the heroic traveler the same ability to explore as it gives the inspired singer.

Because any traveler, heroic or not, was an explorer, whether he stayed in the human world or left it, as Odysseus did, in a banquet of hospitality he brought as his gift the story of his adventures. That held not only for the Homeric poems but for the whole of Greek and Roman antiquity. A stranger from elsewhere told of his own country; a traveler returning home told of lands elsewhere.[1] Why travel if not, among other things, to tell stories about faraway lands to people who would never visit them?

Tell stories about them, not describe them, because those lands could only be revealed through the extraordinary adventures that the traveler had himself lived through there. Elsewhere was necessarily different and strange, otherwise it would not have been elsewhere, would still have been here. In a world in which geographical space was seldom represented by maps, and even then only in a very schematic fashion,[2] people could only construct imaginary representations of that space if they heard stories about it, for it could neither be measured nor drawn. Distance was calculated according to the degree of strangeness of the people encountered. To go elsewhere was to come face to face with varying degrees of otherness, to meet blue men, witches, ghosts, and vampires gorging on blood. The further you went the more the chances of returning diminished. The farthest reaches of the world were still those from which no one returned, as in Homer. It was not necessarily a matter of being devoured by cannibals. If the path was too long, the years that elapsed would cost a man his personality: his town and his wife would forget him, and when at last he did return, white-haired and gaunt, no one would recognize him. Socially, he would be dead, like science-fiction characters who spend light years exploring the galaxy and return to planet Earth to find that men of their own age are their great-great-grandchildren, piously tending the tomb of the long-gone cosmonaut, a hero of the conquest of space.

There was no way of distinguishing travelers' tales from fantastical stories. A marveling explorer resembled nothing so much as a clever inventor of fables. Pythias of Marseilles, known as Pythias the Liar, had sailed away to the distant North, too far for anyone to believe the tales he told upon his return: for instance, he said he had seen the seawater change into a "marine lung." After Euhemerus (330–240 B.C.), the traveler's tale turned into a medium for philosophical discourse. Today, people speak of Euhemerus's "novel": Euhemerus recounted that, during a journey to the Red Sea, he had copied a sacred inscription on the imaginary island of Panchaie, far out beyond Happy Arabia. This declared that all the gods of Greece had been mortal kings and queens, deified by men after their deaths. So, Euhemerus claimed, the stories about them in mythology were really simply human adventures.

Euhemerus's allegorical use of the voyage of exploration shows that what was expected of travelers' tales was an account of an experience of the unknown. A traveler's audience "traveled with its ears."[3] It did not need to go far afield; it was pointless to run risks in barbarian countries in order to see incredible things. In Greece itself, ancient Thessaly was a land of witches. If you went there, you never returned—unless, that is, you were one of those people of high rank who scoffed at anything the least different from their own habitual, narrow horizon. If you were one of those, you would encounter vampires and ghouls without even noticing them. And then you would return home having seen nothing and declaring to anyone willing to listen that "those women who attract the moon and change into owls are nothing but nonsense."[4] To travel, you needed to know how to use your ears as well as your feet.

Ears were a most excellent vehicle, for the best way for a traveler to walk was telling stories or listening to them. We should imagine these people plodding along on foot beside the donkey carrying their luggage. Within the Roman Empire, roads, though dusty, were more or less well maintained and you could usually travel in peace.[5] There were certainly a few brigands holed up in the mountains or lying low in the forests, just as there were a few pirates at sea, but rumors greatly exaggerated the dangers. So the various stages of the journey would seem endless, particularly as the ancients showed scant appreciation of picturesque landscapes. They knew nothing of the Rousseauesque pleasures of meditation surrounded by nature and daydreams, savored by the solitary walker. For the Greeks and the Romans never talked to themselves, or to God, which really comes to the same thing. They were far too civilized for that. For them, the worst thing of all was to travel without a companion, with only a slave for company, a man who, by definition, had nothing more interesting to tell you than a horse. The more bored they were, the more tiring the journey felt. Other travelers, chanced upon round a bend in the road or in some empty landscape, were a positive blessing.[6]

What can those two men over there in the distance be doing, spotted by a man on his own, trudging along by his horse? One is telling a story about what happened to him in Thessaly, the land of witches. The other is refusing to believe him and laughing stupidly: "Stop your absurd tales!

What a bunch of lies!" But Lucius, the solitary traveler, draws closer. He is a man who knows how to travel and is prepared to believe anything, for although he is traveling to Thessaly on business, that is just a pretext: what Lucius really wants is to learn about witchcraft, and besides, as he says, "The charming delight of some story [*fabularum lepida incuntidas*] will smooth out the ruggedness of the hill we are climbing." He makes his request in a friendly way. In exchange for a story, Lucius promises to offer the storyteller the pleasure of a dinner in an inn, that evening. The pleasures of a story are a fair exchange for those of a meal, since both help to restore the weary traveler.

Aristomenes, the storyteller, recounts his adventure, which incorporates an account of the adventures of another traveler, his friend Socrates. Both are appalling and extraordinary stories that completely changed the lives of their protagonists. Aristomenes, for his part, has never returned home. Originally, he was a native of Aegina, a cheese and honey merchant. But afterward he settled in Aetolia, where he remarried. Predictably, the story comes to an end just as the journey does. The skeptic is still grumbling; nevertheless, he has listened to the story from beginning to end. Lucius is delighted; listening to Aristomenes' tales, he has forgotten the tedium and fatigue (*labor et taedium*) of the long steep path. He has traveled with his ears (*me . . . meis auribus pervecto*). The pleasures of a story are like the pleasures of good wine and good food; they make you forget your everyday worries, creating a protected space within which men are relaxed and good-humored. But the story of a man on the road, a traveler on foot, is better than intoxication as it does not affect the entire body. The legs go on walking while the walker forgets about them. That is probably why stories are not sung: the storyteller might lose his breath. A story is told quite simply, following the rhythm of a conversation, *sermo*; no oratorical histrionics are required. However, a story does need to make up for its lack of musical charm by being particularly interesting. The worth of a story is measured by the distance that it helps you to cover effortlessly. So long as the storyteller makes the other travelers forget their weariness, so long as they are not conscious of their aching muscles and their bleeding feet, the story is a good one.

And if the road is too long, the storyteller fits a second story into the first, as Aristomenes does, inserting into his own story the tale of his friend Socrates. In this way, the suspense never fails. All of which goes to show that the pleasure in a good story depends on the narrative strategy. To capture the listener's attention, you have to embark on a whole sequence of events: his attention will be yours until it is completed, but then it will flag.

Whoever has heard a story will himself retell it, if he thought it was a good one that helped him on his way. The story will thus pass from one caravan to another, spun out, inserted into another or shortened, depending on the length of the road. A story is not a fixed text. Each time it is told it is the same yet different, constantly recomposed. It may alight in a banquet, in which the storyteller may possibly tell it as if it is his own, in a bid to get his listeners to suspend their disbelief in the extraordinary adventures that he is recounting. Like the song of a bard, a story is a telling, which is why it cannot be immortalized as what has been told. The only difference is that a story may be told in many different speech-act contexts. But that does not turn the story into a text, or decontextualized speech, as is proved by its "disbelievers," whose very existence shows that a story is a social institution. All the same, the contexts in which it is told do vary and its pragmatic meaning is less arresting than that of a song.

The Sociability of Stories: Watery Speech

All Greek and Latin "novels," which are really collections of intermeshed stories, introduce other incorporated stories into the course of the principal account, which is itself a story. The effect of this is to create an addressee listening to the story, a character whom French "narratologists" sometimes call *le narrataire* ("narratee").[7]

The setting in which a story is told is often a banquet. At the request of the host, the storyteller, like Odysseus among the Phaeacians, recounts the strangest episodes in his life: "Dear guest, why do you not tell us your story? It seems to me to contain adventures that are not without interest, and such accounts make an excellent accompaniment to wine."[8] The fact that a story is a convivial gift likens it to the song of a bard, and the role of the storyteller likens him to a singer in a symposion. Like the bard, he tells a story, does not speak with nothing to say; like a symposion song, storytelling circulates from one guest to another, each with a story to tell. But what a story fundamentally lacks is the intoxication of wine and music, and that lack sets it apart from both the singing of the bard and the song of the symposion, and finds expression in the kind of beverage with which storytelling is often associated. While bardic singing is characterized by a sharing of meat and the symposion song by the wine cup that circulates, storytelling, for its part, is often associated with water:

> Nausicles took hold of a cup of pure water and passed it to Calasiris, saying "My dear Calasiris, I offer you these chaste Nymphs, just as you prefer them, unaccompanied by Dionysus and truly still with all their purity. If, in return, you served us the words we wish to hear, you would be treating us to the most delicious of drinks. The tale of your travels would, were you willing, be the sweetest of pleasures to accompany the banquet."[9]

Here, the story is like the pure water that is added to wine, to temper drunkenness, just as the name of the beloved is added to a song, except that singing fans the fires of wine and love. Here, the information given is cold, it circulates with the "chaste Nymphs," the water that is mixed with wine in the drinking cups. And the god of stories is, as might be expected, the god of travels and of speech that circulates, namely Hermes.[10] Cnemon, another guest at this same banquet, addresses Nausicles, the master of the house, who has organized the party after a sacrifice to Hermes, as follows:

> It seems to me that you are well versed in religion, you who install Hermes alongside Dionysus and arrange for the nectar of words to flow at the same time as the wine. I have admired the sumptuous nature of your sacrifice, but it would be impossible to celebrate Hermes better than by getting each guest to contribute to the general joy with what the god prefers, by which I mean talk.

The pleasures of storytelling at a banquet are essentially astonishment and commiseration for whoever tells of his misfortunes. This pity (*sympatheia*) involves an affective identification with the storyteller: "Sorrow softens the soul . . . and this changes commiseration into friendship."[11] The fact that those present at the banquet all exchange stories of the same kind makes it all the easier to identify with what is recounted.

Identification and a softening of the soul: these two effects of storytelling rightfully belong to the world of the *cena* and Roman conviviality in general. It is this relaxation of the body and the soul that produces the good-humored benevolence and the atmosphere of *benignitas* in which the *cena* is bathed, thanks also to the warmth of the bath that has preceded it, the sweetness of the soft foodstuffs, the reclining positions assumed by the guests, and the wine diluted with water. The listeners' identification with the storyteller is a kind of recognition: the similarity of sentiments draws those experiencing them closer together, suggesting that they share the same social origin. Polycharmes, in chains, working as a slave, and on the point of being crucified, is immediately saved and given his freedom by his master Mithridates, when the latter hears his story. They both love Callirhoe; so Mithridates forthwith invites him to his table.

One does not share one's life story with just anyone. Even if the person to whom one tells it is not already a friend or a relative, he is nevertheless marked in some way that distinguishes him and shows that he belongs to the world of stories:

> "And what have you suffered, my good friend? For I can see from your face that you are not far from being a devotee of the god Love." "You have stirred up a whole swarm of stories," he replied, "but what has happened to me has the air of just a tale." "Then hesitate no longer, my excellent friend," I answered. "In the name of Zeus and Love itself, do me the pleasure of recounting it, even if it does resemble a fable."

Although tales are often linked with banquets, they convey the idea of sociability even when told outside the context of a *cena*. For, unlike Catullus's games and the song for Cleobulus, the speech-act context of a story is not physical intoxication. A story is like the water that slakes a traveler's thirst as well as like that which weakens the banquet wine. When two storytellers meet far from anywhere, by exchanging their stories they create a new bond that, in some cases, proves strong enough to turn them into companions in new adventures.

A Tale as an Alternative to Dionysiac Intoxication

However, the fact that a tale can be told in all sorts of places and can be extended to include what is virtually conversation—or communication—as is suggested by the term used to designate it, *sermo*, also contributes to its cultural inferiority. It is only accommodated in a banquet because it amuses those present. It does not enchant them, for it possesses neither the beguiling power of *lusus* nor the intoxicating grace of Dionysiac songs. By dint of astonishing his audience, a storyteller certainly captures its attention, but does not intoxicate it physically: he only aims for the partial pleasures of the mind. That is how it is that travelers can tell and listen to stories as they walk along and women can tell one another stories while they spin and weave. Social tasks need not be interrupted for a story, nor does the body need to be totally relaxed. A story leaves both the teller and the listener in their ordinary, everyday context. It is modeled on the speech of ordinary social communication and, in this respect, constitutes an extension of the speech of a Homeric guest who volunteers his own name and that of his place of origin. A story as such has a legitimate place in a hospitable banquet, but does not in itself suffice to turn it into a festivity.

In Ovid's *Metamorphoses,* to work and tell stories or to be festive and sing is the alternative that divides the women of Thebes.[12] What happens is that Dionysus, as so often, performs a miracle to impose his cult among the people of Thebes. Most of the women there are only too happy to celebrate the cult of the god. They abandon their woolwork for a while, leave their homes and, clad in animal skins, crowned with wreaths of ivy and with their hair flowing loose, become intoxicated by dancing and singing of the exploits and power of Dionysus. But a few, the daughters of Minyas, refuse to leave their daily tasks and enter the time of festivity. They remain at home, spinning and weaving with their servants. And, immersed in their labors, without ever breaking off the movements necessary for spinning and weaving, each in turn tells a story.[13] This, they say, is how they try "to lighten their task, linking together story after story" (*Utile opus manuum uario sermone leuemus*), for the time seems long to them, just as it does to travelers on dusty roads that seem to go on forever (*quod tempora longa uideri non sinat*). The interwoven stories continue until the task is completed, just as we have seen them coincide with the duration of a journey. Speech passes from one to another in the circle of working women. It is artless speech (*sermo*), a murmur that slips from lips to ear and that makes no use of the body, speech without *actio,* without dramatic impact, in which neither the voice nor the gestures of the body are projected expressively.

Ovid draws an opposition between this sensible, everyday speech and the songs of the Bacchae who fill the air with their voices lifted in praise of the god. The Bacchae form what the ancients called a chorus, an organized group singing and dancing in honor of a deity. They praise Dionysus, listing his names, then sing a hymn that recounts his exploits and grows naturally out of the naming that constitutes the kernel of their praise. To proclaim the power of Semele's son, the Theban women celebrate the miracles of Dionysus, the death of Pentheus, and the mutilation of Lycurgus. Their entire bodies are mobilized by the music of the singing and the accompanying instruments, music that is their offering to the god and that both possesses them and, at the same time, establishes a ritual space. Their singing tells stories that everyone knows—Ovid contents himself with a few brief allusions—but its charm lies elsewhere, for the aesthetic pleasure of such festivity stems from the music and the dancing, not from the astonishment produced by a story.

In contrast, the hallmarks of a story are the novelty and the marveling produced by the unknown; these are, in fact, its only merits: *et factum mirabile ceperat auris*. For the daughters of Minyas, the best story is the one least known (*non vulgaris fabula*), so the second storyteller chooses a new tale rather than that of the all too familiar loves (*amores vulgatos*) of Daphnis, wishing to captivate her audience with the delights of a story as yet unknown (*dulcique animos . . . nouitate tenebo*).[14]

However, the charms of astonishment do not possess the seductive power of music. Because a story is a completely human form of speech, coldly human and untouched by any divine grace, it can easily provoke incredulity. The stories that abound in the most marvels and that are on that account the most captivating are also the ones most likely to be suspected of being untrue.[15] The audience made up of the daughters of Minyas divides into those who believe and those who do not, just as did Apuleius's travelers as they listened to Aristomenes' tales.

The story of the overzealous Theban spinners has an unhappy ending. Dionysus is so irritated by them that he turns them into bats.[16] The light, shrill cry of these creatures that only live indoors will resemble the charmless murmur of their storytelling voices, but is furthermore inarticulate and therefore stripped of the power to tell a story, which was its only asset.

The daughters of Minyas tell each other stories of the miracles of the other gods, then in their turn become a miracle of Dionysus. But the Bacchae too sing of the god performing miracles. The point here is that the nature of stories depends not on the narratives into which they are woven but on the context of the speech act through which the storyteller practices his or her skill and the effects of its reception. The body is sadly lacking in storytelling, despite its orality. A story does not make a festivity—hence, its low-grade status, its cultural mediocrity. It has nothing to offer Dionysus. Instead of raising man to the level of the gods, it confines him to the ordinary, unrisky humanity of a drinker of water. When stories reproduce narratives that belong to the world of epic myths, it is fair to speak of a phenomenon of cultural entropy since, in a way, a degradation of energy is involved in the transition between the one kind of speech act to the other, in the switch from the intoxication of singing that mobilizes the entire person to chatter that passes from lip to ear, leaving the hands and feet free to be otherwise engaged.

This cultural entropy that characterizes stories as opposed to inspired song and speech of a spectacular nature accounts for the way that storytellers recycle dead myths preserved by mythology or even by comedies or mimes. Thus, in *The Golden Ass*, Lucius-the-ass hears the story of Phaedra told in a manner that reduces it to the dimensions of a petty incident in some provincial town.[17] The narrator does explicitly point out that the story comes from the tragedy: "From now on, dear reader, understand that it is a tragedy, not just a story, that you are reading and that, discarding the lowly slipper, we are being elevated to the lofty buskin."[18] Even so, the narrator exaggerates the horror: through a terrible coincidence, the son of the stepmother who is so much in love drinks a poison that the pseudo-Phaedra intended for the pseudo-Hippolytus. He dies from it and his mother accuses her stepson of the crime. The indignant populace is on the point of stoning the supposed culprit to death, but is foiled when he is granted a trial, in which he is condemned to death on the basis of false testimony, when . . . surprise, surprise, the truth is suddenly revealed in court thanks to an old man who turns out to be the doctor who sold the poison and who now reveals that, instead of a real poison, it was just a powerful sleeping draft. They hurry to the cemetery, exhume the child, who wakes up and falls into his father's embrace. The story does not say what happened to the stepmother.

The mythical fiction of the tragedy, reduced to an informative tale, undergoes the same cultural degradation as in Aristotle's *Poetics*: in both cases speech becomes a mere vehicle of representation. But there is one difference: in Apuleius, the story is presented as a manipulation of the story of Phaedra and thus offers the reader-storyteller a model of transformation, thereby reinjecting into the story potentialities for oral recomposition that are altogether absent from Aristotle's theory.

A Tale as an Alternative to Eroticism

Yet a tale does bring forgetfulness. The suspense created by the narrative utterly monopolizes the listener's attention. And that suspense is enjoyable enough to dispel his own worries. In *The Golden Ass*, a very beautiful, very noble, and very affecting girl is carried off by robbers on the day when she was to have been married to the most handsome and most noble young man in the city.[19] Kept prisoner as a hostage by the band of robbers, she shrieks, weeps, and laments incessantly. Even when she falls asleep she is engulfed by dreadful nightmares. The old woman appointed to watch over her decides to try to keep her mind off her misfortunes by telling her agreeable old wives' tales (*lepidus narrationibus anilibusque fabulis*),[20] and embarks on the interminable but famous tale of Love and Psyche. However, the oblivion that the story brings is not the oblivion of intoxication but is, in a sense, a substitute for sleep; it is water that slakes a thirst.

Like the old retainer of Apuleius's robbers, many storytellers are strategists of oblivion. The storyteller of *A Thousand and One Nights* must be the most famous of them all. Scheherazade will serve to provide us with a long-distance perspective and also to amaze us, albeit rather differently from these Latin tales recounted by a Greek-speaking ass.

Ever since Antoine Galland produced his translation in the early eighteenth century, everyone in France has been familiar with the story of Scheherazade, who tells her husband, the sultan, stories every night, in order to cheat death.[21] The sultan Shahriar, disappointed by the infidelity of women in general and his own wife in particular, has decided to marry a new bride each day and then to kill her in the morning, after a single wedding night. So Scheherazade, unable to win her husband's love by the usual means, for no woman can now do that, instead uses storytelling to attach him to her.

In the nuptial bed, Scheherazade's stories take the place of the eroticism to which the sultan is insensible. Love, for Shahriar, has been reduced to impersonal sexual consummation. It makes no difference who his partner is. The same is true of all those who surround him. When their husbands are absent, women are unfaithful simply because they are temporarily condemned to abstinence. Love has become anonymous, quantitative. Any woman is as good as any other. In Greek terms, these people know nothing of Aphrodite—nothing of the desire that is addressed to another because he is he or she is she. They know nothing of the shared dialogue of desire that allows a man and a woman to become a social couple through marriage and friendship.

What eroticism cannot bring about, a broken-off story can. It can bind Shahriar to Scheherazade in expectation of the night that is to follow. For, although all women can procure him the same sexual satisfaction, only

Scheherazade can tell him what happens next in the story that began one hour before dawn the previous night. The thousand nights that follow constitute a single story into which dozens of other tales are incorporated, thereby endlessly deferring the denouement. This goes on until the day comes when Shahriar forgives women and pardons Scheherazade, having realized that he will forever be captivated by her stories.

Here, the culture of storytelling takes the place of a culture of love and intoxication that bound lovers together. Why does the young and beautiful Scheherazade, the daughter of the vizir, voluntarily take this risk? She is not ambitious, nor is she in love with the sultan. But she does love order and social peace. "What I intend to do," she says, "is put a stop to this barbarity that the Sultan is inflicting upon the families in this town. I wish to dispel so many mothers' justified fear of losing their daughters in such a tragic way."[22] At the rate of 365 a year, the nubile female population is in danger of extermination. The sultan is a tyrant, a pestilence that threatens his town with sterility and death. Storytelling can put an end to the sultan's murderous madness.

In Apuleius's novel, storytelling is similarly a substitute for love, for the hero, at the beginning of his adventures, is forced to choose between eroticism and stories. Lucius faces the same choice as Scheherazade. By deciding to enter the extraordinary world of magic, he is led to abandon the world of love in favor of the world of stories. For he changes his body for a different one and, having undergone metamorphosis into an ass, moves from the position of a lover to that of a storyteller. Present, though invisible in his ass's skin, Lucius becomes a story thief—for who would expect an ass to enjoy the pleasures of a story?—and also a thief of human delights. First though, he is faced with a choice between two women, a witch and his mistress. The witch is Pamphile, the wife of Milo, his host at Hypata, and the mistress is Photis, a young servant of Milo's, with whom Lucius has shared moments of intense eroticism.

But Lucius can think of nothing but the witch, and his mistress comes to act as his intermediary. Lucius manages to persuade Photis of the lovely locks to forgo their amorous play for one night and help him to spy on the witchcraft of her employer, Pamphile. Having seen the latter change herself into a bird, Lucius begs Photis to steal the magic ointment that Pamphile used. Photis steals the wrong pot of ointment and Lucius, instead of changing into a bird, finds himself with the body of an ass.

Here, he was certainly safe from love. For to the ancients an ass was the ugliest of creatures, with its long ears and its thick, furry pelt.

> My body hair was thickening into bristles and my soft skin hardening into hide. At the ends of my palms my fingers were losing their number, all being compressed together into single hoofs, and from the end of my spine came forth a great tail. My face was immense now, mouth spread, nostrils gaping, lips sagging. My ears too grew immoderately long and bristly. I saw no consolation in my metamorphosis except for the fact that, although I could not now embrace Photis, my generative organ was growing.[23]

An ass, a beast of Priapus,[24] the god who combines ugliness with sexual bestiality, was the antithesis of a bird, the tender companion of young women and an innocent partner in their kisses. Debarred from love and rejected by his mother Aphrodite as by all those, both men and women, whom he longs to court, Priapus is a loquacious god because words are all that are left to him. Similarly Lucius, once reduced to an ass, is separated from Photis but becomes a storytelling beast. It comes as no surprise to learn that his way of coping with the situation is to munch roses, the flowers of Aphrodite.

The degradation of Lucius, who passes from eroticism to storytelling, resembles the degradation involved in moving from the intoxication of song to the kind of oblivion procured by extraordinary tales: what is at work is the same cultural entropy that we have detected to be the source of the cultural inferiority of stories. However, humility does not, in itself, suffice to define the position of stories in ancient culture. Another thing that needs to be said is that all a story can do is create oblivion by producing astonishment and that those who decide to "believe" stories count solely upon that oblivion and are content with fiction because of the pleasure that it gives them. But is it true that stories, for the most part derived from mythical fiction, really do retain only their fictitious mold, and none of the potentiality for mythical exploration? Or does the fiction of stories also, potentially, if in a different fashion, possess exploratory effects?

Lucius and Odysseus

Where do the travels of Lucius in his ass's skin lead him? Can they be compared with the travels of Odysseus? In other words, is the space through which Lucius travels an elsewhere to which no man, No One can accede?

First though, what exactly has he become by smearing himself with the wrong ointment? The metamorphosis of Lucius is not the same as those of which we read in Greek mythology. For although his body changes, he retains his human intelligence, his *sensus humanus* and his *mens.*[25] He perceives his surroundings as a man, remains capable of opinions and plans, and is still endowed with a memory. In other words, Lucius, although he cannot speak, is capable of being the subject of a statement. He is a potential narrator who lacks nothing but speech. He is still the subject telling a story.

In contrast, mythological metamorphosis strips whoever undergoes it of all human perception.[26] If a hero loses his body, it is really because he has already lost the soul and heart of a human being. Hecuba, too violently wounded by grief for her children, who one after the other have died, and for her husband and her city, wails endlessly amid the ruins of Troy. Plunged into an everlasting grief that has already excluded her from humanity, truly "maddened by grief," Hecuba, her mouth distorted by her shrieks of despair, has already become a bitch, even before she assumes the form of one. And once she has undergone metamorphosis, she loses her identity, ceases to be Hecuba and is lost, anonymously, amid the race of dogs. Her human intelligence is extinguished in the same way as Lycaon's when he becomes a wolf and the Heliads' when they turn into poplar trees. Metaphorical metamorphosis brings a story to an end, curtails the narrative by wresting its hero out of human temporality. Young Syrinx, pursued by Pan, when on the point of being caught and raped, changes into a forest of reeds. When the wind blows through them, scattered snatches of sound can be heard: the dispersed voice of Syrinx. The god cuts a few reeds and fashions them into the pipes of Pan, so as to gather those dispersed sounds together. When he plays his flute he reconstitutes the girl's voice; and this flute, the heroine's final metamorphosis, is known by the generic name syrinx.[27]

Lucius, in contrast, is simply a man concealed inside an ass's skin. Even his appetites remain human; he prefers raw barley cakes to his manger and beautiful women to female asses. As a dumb and invisible servant, he is an ideal witness of human societies. When he recovers his face and his voice, he remembers all this and tells of it. As both a domesticated animal and a tireless traveler, he makes his way through Greece, passing from one master to another.

This Lucius-ass is like the seafarer-Odysseus, an impossible man who travels where no mortal can venture. The travels of Odysseus take him beyond the world. Lucius, for his part, remains in the world but accedes to an ultimate understanding that is normally inaccessible. Odysseus is a superman, with superhuman *mētis*, cunning intelligence; Lucius is subhuman, a beast just as an ass is, but the exploratory fiction is the same. The stories of Lucius are those of Odysseus among the Phaeacians. But they are told by an anti-Odysseus who, instead of acquiring the *mētis* of the bird of Athena, through his metamorphosis possesses the stupidity of Priapus's ass. We should not forget that he would have been changed into an owl had Photis not stolen the wrong jar of ointment.

Stories of Robbers

The robbers' cave where Lucius is brought the first time he is kidnapped is every bit as dangerous for a man as the cave of the Cyclopes.[28] To be sure, the robbers are men whereas the Cyclopes are the monster-sons of Poseidon. But neither the robbers nor the Cyclopes intend to allow any man who ventures among them to depart with his life. The Cyclopes eat their visitors raw; the robbers kill them to prevent them revealing the secret of their hideout. The result is the same: men will never learn what happens in robbers' caves unless some fictitious hero comes to spy upon them.

The thieves' den is far removed from all civilization. It is a cavern hollowed out from "a terrible mountain, in the depths of a dark forest." The surrounding area contains not a single human dwelling. Bushes conceal the entrance. This is a place that exists only for those who tell of it. Lucius-the-narrator ends his description as follows: "You can take my word for it [*dixeris*] that here was the atrium of a band of robbers [*latronum atria*]." The expression shatters any illusion of realism. Just as the Cyclopes exist solely for and through Odysseus in the *Odyssey,* and have no reality except that of epic fiction, the robbers' cave exists solely for and through Lucius-the-ass. The cavern where he arrives is exactly as anyone would imagine a robbers' dwelling to be. The expression *dixeris,* literally "you would have said," although certainly a current way of expressing the impersonal "one would have said," is one of many used that presuppose the presence of an addressee and make an appeal to him. Has he properly recognized a robbers' cave from the ass's description, not as such caves are seen to be, since nobody can ever find them, but as they are always imagined? Lucius, for his part, who—inevitably—had never seen one, was in no doubt about it. The narrative is founded on the effects of recognition based on not experience but the logic of a culture: a robbers' cave could not be otherwise.

Here then, in this rocky crevice, is where the robbers rest and recover and it is here that they hold their banquets. The Cyclopes, for their part, never hold banquets and the fact that they do not is not the least of their defects, since it is what makes them cannabilistic vegetarians. They know nothing of sacrifice, hospitality, and the singing of bards. The robbers, however, are still men. Cruel and barbaric they may be, but they are not such savages as not to hold banquets. Whatever can a robbers' banquet be like? This is where Lucius-the-ass is indispensable, for he is the only one who can tell us.

The ass with an exploratory gaze recounts what he has seen. These robbers, although rather rough with the old woman who keeps house for them, seem to behave as civilized people when it comes to banqueting. Weary after the day's labors, they strip, sweat by the fire, bathe in hot water, rub themselves down, and anoint themselves with perfumed oil. Then they come to table, reclining on beds (*accumbunt*). Like Homeric kings, they eat bread accompanied by meat stew washed down with wine. Yet it is clear from the disorder that reigns that the banquet is a robbers' feast. The food is piled up on the tables, and they all fall on it at once, not sharing it out and passing it round. Then comes the time for the comissatio. Just like civilized men, the robbers play (*ludunt*), sing (*cantilant*), and joke (*iocant*). Yet the disorder and confusion that reign ruin the harmony and conviviality normally created by the songs and wordplay. The wordplay is lost in the din (*clamore*), the music is drowned by their shouts and the clatter of tableware (*strepitu*), and the jokes turn into insults (*conuiciis*).[29] The feasting robbers are not comrades in arms but a horde of looters.

Their banquet is also graced by stories. But these stories are not told in order to give pleasure to one another or as a gift for some passing guest. The robbers are no more hospitable than the Cyclopes and their banquet is not an occasion for the sharing of pleasures. As the watching ass sharply remarks, they are like the centaurs at the famous banquet of the Lapiths at which the centaurs, monsters that were half man, half horse, invited to the wedding of Pirithoos, the king of the Lapiths, got drunk and tried to carry off the young bride, at which point the nuptial banquet turned into a free-for-all. The robbers, who had split into two separate bands on separate expeditions, having reassembled around the table, set about challenging one another, each group boasting of having accomplished the greatest exploits and attempting to outdo the other in its tales of brigandage. In this company of Mars's devotees, every subject is eventually reduced to warfare.

One after another, three stories are told, each an account of a heroic death. Three robber chiefs were killed by their enemies and theirs were fine deaths since they demonstrated their courage and their loyalty to their comrades.[30] The sociability that signally fails them amid pleasure and conviviality appears in its highest form amid the solidarity of armed men. The three warrior-chiefs in question, Lamachus, Alcimus, and Thrasyleon, with their terribly epic-sounding names, appear to have stepped straight out of the *Iliad* or the *Seven against Thebes.*

The story of Lamachus is particularly striking. His band of robbers had gone to rob the safe of an extremely miserly and unpleasant banker and Lamachus was delegated to gain undetected access to the house. He crept up to the door and slipped his hand into the large keyhole so as to remove the bolt that barred the door. Chryserus, the wily banker, who had heard him approaching, was on the watch, crouching the other side of the door. As soon as Lamachus's hand emerged through the keyhole, he nailed it to the door and hastened to arouse his neighbors. Lamachus was trapped. To escape from the inhabitants, his companions, with his agreement, lopped off his arm at the elbow and dragged him away, leaving the arm behind and mopping up the streaming blood so as not to leave a trail. The wounded man slowed them down and their pursuers were about to catch up with them. At this point Lamachus, expressing himself in magnanimous terms, begged them to finish him off:

> Our hero of lofty spirit and preeminent valor plaintively exhorted us with many an appeal and many a prayer. "By Mars's right hand," he pleaded, "and by the loyalty of your oath, free a good fellow soldier from torture and capture alike. Why should a brave robber outlive that hand of his which alone can steal and murder? Happy is the man who can choose to die by a comrade's hand!"[31]

Despite his pleas, which were those of a model Roman soldier, his companions refused to kill him. The god Mars, not generally known as a protector of thieves, was then invoked, for the rhetoric was that of military courage, as it was for the appeal to the oath that bound Roman legionaries to their general: "When he had failed to persuade any of us to slay the willing victim, he drew his sword with his remaining hand, kissed it again and again and drove it with a mighty stroke through the middle of his chest." He died like Cato of Utica, untouched by pain or fear and identifying himself with the right arm he had lost, the arm that had wielded his sword.

There is, however, an obvious crack in this facade of sublime nobility: the sacrificed arm is the arm of a looter and murderer and Lamachus's exemplary death is the death of a bank robber, just as that of Alcimus, which is equally painful, was to be the death of a robber of old ladies. These robbers thus remain ambiguous. Although civilized in the acts of war, in peace they remain savages. And instead of waging war outward, against enemies, their strikes are directed inward, against their fellow citizens, and where they should be at war they feel quite at home. Their only god is Mars.

The manner in which they are honored in death by their companions conveys the full extent of this ambiguity. Here is the account of Lamachus's entombment. "We then paid homage to the strength of our stouthearted general, carefully wrapped what was left of his body in a linen cloth, and committed it to the concealment of the sea. Now lies our Lamachus with an entire element for his grave."

Following a fine death, a glorious hero is normally provided with a tomb (*monumentum*), which reminds passersby of his illustrious deeds. No such tomb can be erected for Lamachus, for his glorious deeds are also criminal acts that would earn him from passersby nothing but execration and the destruction of his monument. His corpse would be mutilated and thrown to the wild beasts. The very best his companions can do is bury him anonymously. So rather than give him an obscure tomb of that kind, they decide to commit him to the sea, the wild space that is their own, as is the solitude in which they live. They provide the same tomb for Alcimus, who fell on the same day.

Lacking any human monument, the three dead leaders are commemorated by the stories told by their companions, but told in places as inhuman as the sea, their last resting place. There can be no fame unless it is socialized, and theirs would have been lost forever had not Lucius-the-ass witnessed the banquet from the back of the cave. The fame of these ruffians is thus contradictory by nature, neutralizing the alternative between blame and praise.

The stories restore order among the banqueters because they turn them into warriors celebrating the memory of their leaders who have fallen in battle. It is on that account that this is the only moment when their words and their actions are in harmony: "That was the end of his story. The robbers poured a libation of unmixed wine from golden cups to the memory of their deceased comrades-in-arms, sang some hymns to flatter the god Mars, and then went to sleep for a while."

In the last analysis, what do these robbers' stories relate? At the beginning of this chapter the question posed was: does the story undertake an exploration of the same kind as a mythical exploration? Is the fiction that it creates put to serve anything but itself? Or is the story simply a device to produce amazement? The answer is that these robbers' tales do explore an imaginary society and do thereby, to some extent, show how such "internal Cyclopes" function. Apuleius's robbers are culturally impossible beings, living in a wild space, with no techniques for life apart from warfare, no economy—not even of a pastoral nature. In order to live in any but a bestial fashion, they have to pillage civilization. They have no proper home, no wives, no hearth. They constitute a band of young men who know nothing of culture except what immediately concerns their own age group: warfare and banqueting. They have just one woman among them, who is indispensable for the preparation of their banquets. Their only way of relating to civilization is through violent robbery. This enables them to gain access to all the things men need to live: bread, wine, clothing, pots and pans, tableware, and good food; it also makes it possible for them to develop the warrior virtues of courage, obedience, and solidarity. However, living as they do, far from the towns and the humanized countryside, what they lack is the peaceful complement to war, namely socialized fame. So they wage a "private war," an "economic war" that respects none of the values of civic society. In a way they bear a certain resemblance to the society of wolves as imagined by the ancients, who attributed to those wild predators a soldierly discipline that involved sharing out the booty fairly once the pack's hunt was over.[32]

In a banquet, these men are incapable of playing games or singing. Such pleasures are inaccessible to them, as is the pleasure of sharing out meat and wine. Where Mars reigns as sole master, Dionysus, Eros, and the Muses are absent: the robbers never get beyond warfare, the values of which exclude those of the other three graceful deities. The feast in the cave would be nothing but an orgy of savages were it not for the storytelling that restores calm and an ability to communicate among the banqueters. Once again we find that, as has been glimpsed earlier, storytelling can coexist with all kinds of occupations that rule out singing. Here, it finds a place in a space devoted to warfare, just as it does in spaces devoted to traveling or working with wool.

This is a clear indication of the marginality of the position held by storytelling as compared with other linguistic forms of the banquet culture. Storytelling made an appearance where epic could not and was substituted for the latter, as a second-best. To succeed, the social ritual represented by the banquet, whether Greek or Roman, required participants who were altogether cultivated and civilized. In fact, it was the banquet that provided effective confirmation that its participants belonged to the social elite, whether they happened to be Homeric heroes, Athenian aristocrats, urban Romans, or young knights of the Roman Empire. In one way or another, the banquet's success was achieved in and through poetic singing. Because the robbers were marginalized by civilization, they were incapable of celebrating a banquet correctly, so their feasts in the cave could only be a fiction. For the right granted to the storyteller, by virtue of the contract that bound him to those who "believed" him, gave him the power to, among other things, pretend that improbable things did in fact exist and, in particular, to describe the unfolding of a social ritual whose very context should have blown its components apart.[33] To put that another way, the robbers' banquet is a feast of centaurs that should have disintegrated into violence but that, thanks to the narrator and the stories told during it, runs its full course.

The cultural logic revealed by this fiction shows that stories belonged to a lower strand of banquet culture that could perhaps be termed its subculture. The fact that storytelling secured a place and a way to function in this banquet of robbers testifies to its hidden relations with barbarian society. Stories, like warrior values, had, in theory at least, no need of the city in order to flourish. These stories that come from the margins of the world also belong to the margins of culture. And, of course, those margins of culture can only be conveyed through fiction. That is why the story resurfaces in another impossible banquet in another imaginary society: the banquet of the emancipated slaves gathered in Trimalchio's home, another place where it was possible for a deficient culture to flourish.[34]

Stories of Emancipated Slaves

Like the robbers' cave, Trimalchio's house is a fiction, a place too strange to be believable, with its door that only opens to let you in, like the gates of the Underworld, and its mosaic dog that barks. In Trimalchio's house, likewise, the banquet offers neither the delights of love nor those of music, quite apart from the fact that it is impossible to organize proper cultural "spectacles" there. We have seen how the freedmen are unable to cope with the Greek poetry that provides Roman *otium* with a self-referential element.[35] As slaves, they could act as auxiliaries in the pleasures of their masters; but even so, once freed, they never learn to master them. However, even if they are incapable of correctly summarizing an episode from the Trojan War, when it comes to stories they are in their element. At Trimalchio's insistence, one freedman, Nicerus, tells a story about a werewolf: "Do please, to make me happy, tell us [again] of your adventure."[36] Nicerus is a frequent visitor to Trimalchio's house and is always expected to tell the extraordinary story of what happened to him. A story is always worth retelling: "Well, it shall be pure fun then, though I'm afraid your clever friends will laugh at me. Still, let them. I will tell my story." He thus agrees to proceed, albeit not without qualms, for the *scolastici* who are present, Encolpius, Ascyltos, Giton, and Agamemnon, all either students or professors, might indeed laugh at his story and jeer at him, just as Aristomenes' traveling companion in Thessaly refused to believe him. Unlike mythological narratives, stories were not part of the official culture. They possessed neither the prestige of epic nor the sweetness of music. Stories were simply fictitious tales, which was why respectable people, the cultivated elite, scoffed at them. Nevertheless, stories brought gaiety to banquets. "Let unalloyed good humour prevail!" (*Itaque hilaria mera sint*), says Nicerus. Good humor (*hilaritas*) made for the atmosphere that normally reigned at banquets, a cheerful, relaxed goodwill that was the primary condition for a successful *cena*. Stories clearly contributed to this, demonstrating that they definitely were part of the culture of the *cena*.

Nicerus's story is a dark tale about a werewolf. The narrator was traveling by night to join his mistress, an adorable girl who answered to the sweet name of Melissa. He had asked a soldier, a huge giant of a man, to keep him company. As they were passing through a cemetery, the soldier changed into a wolf. Nicerus arrived at his mistress's house more dead than alive. There, he was told that a wolf had broken into the stable, where it had savaged all the sheep before running off. However, one of the house slaves had managed to wound it in the neck with the thrust of a spear. On returning home, he found the soldier lying in bed with a bleeding neck, which a doctor was bandaging; and he realized that this big fellow was a werewolf.

The listeners are speechless with astonishment, even though most of them have heard the story before. Trimalchio himself has come out in goose pimples over it (*mihi pili inhorruerunt*). He proceeds to cap it by recounting another adventure of the same type, an even more gruesome tale, that had happened to him. One story always does tend to elicit another, with a second storyteller hastening to support the first, proving with his own story that such things really can happen. For stories, strength lies in numbers. The more people tell them, the stronger they become. The more there are, the more they are believed. Stories are a social affair.

Trimalchio's story is about the Stryges. A child had just died when those present heard the shrieking of the Stryges, the deities who suck out the intestines of babies.[37] A giant of a man with a courageous heart drew his sword and threw himself in pursuit of the Stryges, managing to run one through in the courtyard. It could be heard howling in agony. Everyone returned to the bedroom: the child had been reduced to a dummy stuffed with straw. As for the brave giant, he turned blue and died shortly after without regaining his color.

Nobody scoffs at Trimalchio's story. All present, freedmen and academics alike, believe it, kiss the table for luck and offer up a prayer to the goddesses of the Night.

On the one hand a story about the fine death of a robber, on the other a couple of incredible old wives' tales: in both cases, the stories produce a consensus among all those at table and bring them together, thereby creating sociability where, without them, it would not have seemed possible.

Mysteries of the Empire: Stories and Mythical Exploration

For the ancients, stories were a feature of the lower reaches of society, or were told in the context of strenuous effort or daily tasks. The reason for this was that the culture of stories was deficient, since it was not a culture that involved the entire body. It lacked the intoxication and pleasure of music and love, the more civilized kind of sociability, the rituality that admitted one to a more refined culture. On that very account, the culture of storytelling found an imaginary place on the margins of a settled, civilized way of life. The stories told by travelers on the road were also told by freed slaves and robbers and tipsy old women trying to console young girls—and by one particular ass. A story could be retold endlessly with equal pleasure for both listener and narrator; and wherever it was repeated, the narrator would pretend either that it had happened to himself or that he had heard it in person from the lips of its hero himself. Although no stronger than water or the speech of ordinary communication, a story was a fiction that explored the culture in which it was told, and the means that it employed to do so were analogous to those of mythical exploration.

Apuleius's *Golden Ass* could well have been entitled "The Mysteries of Greece." Lucius-the-ass never sets foot (or hoof) outside Greece, but the Greece that he discovers is a strange and impossible world. As the robbers wrangle over which one of them is the most heroic, the ass hears of greedy, cunning, cruel bankers, bloodthirsty old women, and touching young newlyweds who are the victims of abominable treachery. All the love stories in *The Golden Ass* have sad endings. To be sure, the dead emerge from their tombs to denounce the criminals, but by then it is too late; all the victims can do is take their revenge on the traitors, piling horror upon horror. Ghosts, apparitions, prophetic dreams, sadism, and pornography are the stuff of these stories that deal in all that is excessive or contradictory. Just imagine: to punish the beautiful, touching bride whom they have taken hostage, those magnanimous robbers plan to sew her alive into the ass's skin, after killing and disemboweling it, and then leave her out in the sun with her head sticking out of the carcass! She is to die slowly, ravaged by vermin, weakened by hunger and thirst, amid an appalling stench; and when scavenging birds set about devouring the carcass, they will tear her own entrails to pieces.[38] But the robbers do not hold a monopoly over sadism. A woman, following a series of complex intrigues, murders her husband's sister, believing her to be his mistress, by sticking a burning brand up between her legs, then poisons her husband and her daughter. Eventually she is denounced by the wife of the doctor who sold her the poison, whom she has refused to pay. The governor sentences her to be thrown to the wild beasts and organizes a whole spectacle around this death, the opening sequence of which is to consist of the violation of the prisoner by Lucius-the-ass.

People who tell each other stories are bound by a pact constituted by their belief in the stories. To believe or not to believe the stories is an act of social and cultural faith. Anyone who believes the stories becomes a link in the chain of those who tell them and who listen to them, those who "travel with their ears." In default of belonging to the elite and possessing other, stronger cultural links, those who specialize in stories in this way create for themselves a sociability of a minimal kind. This is the source of the story's power and truth. But the pleasure derived from stories can also be dangerous, as the example of Lucius shows: as a result of listening to so many tales of witchcraft, he tried to enter the land of witches himself and in his turn became both the subject of an adventure and also its direct storyteller. Storyland is a bourn from which no traveler returns. To be sure, the traveler will reintegrate into the world of ordinary men in order to tell them his story, but he will no longer be the same, his identity will have changed. Apuleius's storytellers are travelers who are lost, when—that is—they do not succumb to their adventures immediately after recounting them to some other traveler. In many cases, as in that of Telyphron who, at every banquet given by the noble and wealthy Byrrhenus, tells the story of his life, the storyteller bears on his body marks that testify to the veracity of his tale: his eaten-away nose and absent ears prove that he has indeed been the victim of witches. His hostess treats him as a machine for recounting his mutilations.

To justify attributing an exploratory function to stories, it is not enough to show that they are fictions. It is also necessary for each story to constitute one in an open-ended series of performances. Exploratory fiction and textuality are not compatible. A story only functions within a context of creative orality. When storytellers reuse fictions borrowed from the epic or the tragic tradition and given a fixed form by the mythographers, they literally recycle them, by relaunching them into a circuit of permanent recomposition. Reduced to the state of *something said* by being formally memorized, they come back to life when they become a *saying*. Yet this saying, or telling of a story, is culturally weaker than a mythical song or even a tragedy. Cultural entropy has taken its toll.

It would therefore be quite mistaken to assess these stories that are so improbable despite their authors situating them in Greece, Italy, or some other civilized region of the Roman Empire against the yardstick of French (or English) novels of the eighteenth or nineteenth century. They are subjected to no ideology of representation and do not stem from either social realism or philosophical utopianism. They are the product of an exploration of cultural—not social—margins, in the same way that other narratives explore geographical frontiers. In both cases the exploration of those borderlands is carried out purely by means of fiction and serves to mark out the boundaries of the world. The fragments of humanity of which these narratives tell are always imaginary and are constructed by dint of perverting reality, by scaling it either up or down and thereby creating a fiction that diverges from the norm. What makes it rather confusing for us is the fact that these margins of civilization are explored not through fictions from the outside, as in Odysseus's travels, but from the inside: the imaginary microsocieties created by the stories and in which stories are also told are composed of robbers or emancipated slaves—social groups that really do exist but that, in these stories, are defined by a culture that is deficient, too deficient to be believable. They are fantastical representations of the majority culture. It is as though that majority culture was unable to speak of those who constituted its cultural margins, except through fiction.

To say that the story belonged to popular culture is to situate it culturally, not socially. It was not simply a form through which the lower strata of the population—freedmen, wet nurses, traders, and shepherds—expressed themselves, while the elite expressed itself in rhetoric or poetry. Everybody listened to stories, the nobility included, everybody told them and everybody concurred in regarding them as a form that constituted a subculture, like the soaps of television or the penny dreadfuls purchased by sailors in the port of Toulon. The banquet of the robbers and the banquet of the freedmen were a mythical way of conveying the moral and aesthetic deficiency of stories and the vulgarity of the pleasures that they provided.

This cultural inferiority of the story, which rendered it equivalent to the water served in a banquet, may explain how it was that it came to be used to compose what are known as "Greek novels," books consisting of a collection of stories destined for we know not whom. It should be noted in passing, however, that the transition from story to novel implied yet a further cultural degradation, since the novel forfeited the last link with orality. A written story provided a zero degree of poetic pleasure. It was no more than "a good read," transparent to the words that recounted it, like an opera libretto or tape-recorded chatter.

SIX

Writing Sandwiched between Two Voices

OF COURSE, THE GREEK and Latin stories that we read today had to be written down at some point for them to finish up in our hands in the form of paperbacks or scholarly tomes. The very number of papyri that have been discovered proves that numerous copies were made of them. What did the people who bought all those books do with them? Let us beware of speaking too hastily of "popular literature" or even of "the invention of the novel."[1] Papyri were costly and under the Roman Empire books, though no longer luxury articles,[2] were still expensive and cannot conceivably have been widely distributed. Above all, however, as in the case of an archaeological object, we need to reconstruct how they were used in the ancient world. The discovery of a Roman book, which we of the twentieth century, assimilating it to a modern genre, classify as a "novel," does not necessarily mean that the contemporaries of that text used it in the same way as we do; in other words, it does not necessarily mean that it had a public of readers to whom it was intended to be addressed.

With regard to *The Golden Ass*, then, the question that is posed is the following: how were stories turned into books in Rome? Amid what kind of writing and reading were these books classified? And after what ups and downs? For stories were at home in orality as fishes are in water. Voices gave them life and breath and enabled them to multiply. The speech that carried them along dispersed them in a thousand bursts of sound, from banquet to caravan and from merchant to wet nurse. How did they come to die and be frozen in writing? After all, thanks to the scorn that respectable people poured on them, they were well protected from the machinations of self-referential culture. The collection of stories of which *The Golden Ass* is composed was not a cultural monument, for sure. A story's life could only continue in an open-ended chain of performances, and its exploratory function, which linked it with epic, implied perpetual *recomposition* and *shifts*,[3] which ruled out any fixing and pinning down of model statements.

Books as Machines for the Telling of Tales

The preface to *The Golden Ass* provides one, if not *the* solution to the puzzle. It states that this book of stories is not made up of tales first recounted and later fixed in writing. Apuleius's first pages are quite clear on this point: he presents the book as a text constructed by writing, which can only become a reality thanks to its reader. He dispels any illusion of a narrative recorded in writing and presented just as it was recorded. This preface offers the reader a book from which a hundred stories may be drawn, a machine designed to enable him to tell stories.[4] It is a complex preface, in which three successive "I"s in turn speak.

I, the Book, Am Beginning

At ego tibi: the first three words of *The Golden Ass* seem to constitute the opening words of a hero-narrator about to tell his story: *At ego* 'as for me', and who is speaking to an interlocutor to whom his narrative is addressed. The language of this kind of situation in which communication takes place is known in Latin as *sermo*; and the fourth word in the text is indeed *sermone*. This term, for which "conversation" is too narrow a translation, is, as has been mentioned, the word used in Latin to designate a story. It reminds us that what we have here is neither a song (*canticum*), nor an act of oration (*oratio*), nor a verbal game (*lusus, uersiculi*), but speech for communicating.[5] The word *sermo* denotes speech with no stylistic polish, no "writing," and therefore not speech intended for a large number of listeners, a public. A *sermo* presupposes a very limited speech-act context, man-to-man speech, which cannot be extended to more than a few listeners. It is suitable for banquet conversation or for a philosophical dialogue, but has not the strength to carry further afield. The assumption is that it establishes communication between people who know each other well, belong to the same social circle and already enjoy some special kind of relationship, such as *amicitia*. *Sermo* is only effective if a measure of complicity exists between those talking together, and this is even more essential in the case of a written *sermo*. That is quite clear in, for example, a letter-writing relationship, which can only be established between private persons within the framework of a preexisting and socially defined personal relationship such as *amicitia*, without which letter writing is impossible.[6]

Ego . . . *tibi*: two anonymous persons. The anonymity presupposes a speech-act situation that is implicit in the statement. Who do this *ego* and this *tibi* latch onto? If *tibi* is the reader, the one who is deciphering the letters on the papyrus, as the text declares in the following line—for the modality of the speech act implied by this preface is, without doubt, a reading—who is *ego* (1), the first "I" in the text?

Ego . . . *tibi*: in Rome, the speech-act situation of a letter was defined as mimed dialogue, or what we have earlier termed epistolarity. Is that the model in operation here? If so, *ego* would be the person writing, *tibi* the person to whom the written message is addressed. But in this case, the anonymity of the two actors involved in communication is abnormal, for every letter presupposed that they be named in the opening formula that was used in letter writing (*adscriptio*). This book would thus be a letter from nobody to anybody. A fiction. So the type of reading proposed here could not possibly be epistolary. Besides, the material used, papyrus, and above all the tense, which is the future, are both incompatible with the practice of letter writing. A letter would be written on tablets of wood coated with wax, and the tense used would be the imperfect. For the time of reference for Roman epistolarity was that of the reading of the letter, not the writing of it, which implies that, for the Romans, a letter was not recorded orality but rather an act of writing designed to produce a speech act. It was not a matter of an original oral speech act subsequently trapped in writing, to be reconstituted through a reading. Although the reading enabled the absent person, the subject of the statement, to speak, the writing, for its part, was not a means of addressing the absent person for whom it was intended. There was no such thing as a written epistolary statement; there were only epistolary statements that were read. Epistolary writing was not autonomous; it was simply a preliminary to a reading-speech act. Finally, generally speaking every epistolary statement, once read, was destined to disappear: it was a link in a chain of dialogue that was covered over by the reply that followed it. That is why it was inscribed on wax, then wiped out with a sweep of the thumb. Egyptian papyrus, on the other hand, was the material for written texts intended to be preserved.

Ego speaks in the future tense: "I shall weave together garlands of tales for you" (*ego tibi . . . uarias fabulas conseram*). This future tense could indicate that the voice aroused by the reading is that of the writer, for by addressing the reader at the moment when he picks up the scroll of papyrus, the preface sets the act of reading the stories in *The Golden Ass* in the future. This would make the present the time of the writing of the book, which is destined to come to be in the future if a reader will at that point lend it life. However, this *ego*, who is also present at the moment of the reading, cannot be the writer since he, by definition, is absent from the book. The *ego* must therefore be the book itself, which is here promising the reader to present him with a series of interlinked stories. This is what is conveyed by the image of the intertwined garland: there will be no break between one story and the next. The one will not come to an end until the next has already begun. The system adopted is that used in *The Thousand and One Nights*. And the setting for the text, the adventures of Lucius transformed into an ass, is a device to gather all the tales into one single story, which serves as a guiding thread, albeit admittedly a somewhat loose one.

To his first promise, *ego* tacks on two, if not three others:

> auresque tuas beniuolas lepido susurro permulceam modo si papyrum Aegyptiam argutia Nilotici calami inscripam non spreueris inspicere.
>
> I will caress your ears into approval with a pretty whisper, if only you will not begrudge looking at an Egyptian papyrus inscribed with the sharpness of a reed from the Nile.

The pleasure of stories has to be conveyed through the ears, so the reader must read aloud, even if it is only to himself. Furthermore, his ears must be "sympathetic," he must behave like Lucius, believe in the stories, not be skeptical or scornful, but accept the story culture. Finally, the reader must be willing to read, to put himself at the service of the letters inscribed on the papyrus. In antiquity, reading a text by someone else was by no means a neutral act, for it meant lending him your voice and subjecting yourself to his writing. Jesper Svenbro has shown that in Greece this kind of reading was sometimes even perceived on the model of pederastic submission,[7] and there are signs of the same being true of Rome, as is suggested by the following Latin inscription: "I, who am reading, am buggered" (*ego qui lego pedicor*).[8] However, an Egyptian papyrus, which was a costly and fragile material, and the quality of the writing were of a kind to attract a reader and encourage him to read, if only for the pleasure it afforded his eyes.

The book thus promises something that does not yet exist but will come about through the reading, if only the reader is prepared to take the trouble and place himself at the service of the writing: namely a delightful murmur (*lepido susurro*). The verb *sussurare* suggests not only a whispering, muted speech, but at the same time the act of passing on the stories. The oralization of the papyrus, forecast but not yet realized, indicates that so far the reader has only had a chance to run his eyes over the text; next, he must produce this murmur, which is another way of reading to oneself.[9] By reading in this way, he will reproduce the sonorous model of storytellers and will thus give the potential stories of the papyrus the reality that comes with a speech act. *Lepido* 'delightful, soothing' reproduces the *lepos* of a Roman banquet, which created a friendly goodwill that brought the participants together in a conviviality that fell short of intoxication, the conviviality that seems to have constituted the minimal culture of the Roman *cena*. The reader will be his own storyteller as he oralizes the book, and also the addressee for whom the story is intended, as he listens to the murmur he himself is producing. The act of reading thus consists of making the manuscript work as a machine designed to produce stories, provided it is plugged into the speaker's apparatus for producing sound through the use of his eyes. To read *The Golden Ass*, you had to be neither deaf, blind, nor dumb.

The delight promised by the book is thus the delight in the stories that a murmured reading of them will produce, the stories that the reader will be telling himself, stories about changing forms and fortunes: "figuras fortunasque hominum in alias imagines conuersas et in se rursum mutuo nexu refectas." Such shifts of bodies and fortunes are a characteristic feature of the imaginary travels of the heroes of stories. And the pleasure that the reader will derive from these stories, *ut mireris* 'to make you marvel', is the pleasure that is expected by all listeners to stories, Trimalchio's guests[10] just as much as Lucius himself in the course of his travels: it is the pleasure of surprise.

So here is a first speech-act situation: it involves a book and a reader who must oralize the book for himself, the reader whom the book addresses in its preface. It is a situation that is quite similar to that of a reader of funerary inscriptions.[11] Jesper Svenbro has produced a striking description of this very special kind of speech act in which the stone itself speaks to the passerby in the first person, whenever a passerby stops to read the inscription:

> What is written is present, the writer is absent. . . . Just as he foresees his own absence, the writer foresees the presence of his writing before the reader. . . . He counts on the reader and the reading aloud that the reader will accomplish. . . . The reading aloud is a part of the text, an integral part of it. . . . For on its own this writing is voiceless. It is silent; it keeps quiet. . . . The most it can do is *provoke* a reading, prompt its own rendering in sound, get the reader's voice going. . . . At the moment of reading, the reading voice does not belong to the reader, even though he is the one using his vocal apparatus to ensure that the reading takes place. . . . His voice becomes the voice of the written text. So the "I" that denoted the funerary monument does not have to be changed to "it" at the moment of reading, for while he is reading, the reader is not speaking . . . as the subject of the statement. He has lent his voice . . .

Clearly then, when the words of Lucius, the narrator-hero of *The Golden Ass* and the subject making the statement, are oralized through a reading, the reader identifies himself through his voice with that narrator-hero: he becomes the storyteller.

A public inscription on the plinth of a statue hails the passerby, as a possible reader: "You, whoever reads me" (*Tu quicumque leges*). The situation is the same as that of *The Golden Ass* addressing the reader, with the same intriguing implication of a future tense and the same anonymity. In return for agreeing to make the effort to read the inscription, the traveler might be promised all sorts of benefits, happiness, success, health, and wealth. The book, for its part, promises only what it has to offer, namely stories.

Some inscriptions ask whoever stops to read aloud a particular part of what is written, even if reading it to himself, in other words reading it in a whisper. The particular words that the reader of the epitaph is required to oralize are, essentially, the name of the dead person and a few prayers "for the earth to lie lightly on him or her." Unlike in Greece, in Rome the reading of epitaphs was not a declaration to all and sundry, speech loud and clear that brought fame (*kleos*). Instead, the reader, talking to himself, added to the murmur of rumor (*fama*). We detect a qualitative difference between the sound of Greek fame and that of Roman renown, a difference that can perhaps be explained by the absence of heroic songs in Rome. Greek fame was sung and was proclaimed by poetic and rhetorical inscriptions or odes by Pindar or Simonides or, in Athens, by funeral orations. Roman renown was something that passed from mouth to mouth, through rumor and murmured gossip, and this explains the fact that, along with funerary inscriptions, it came to serve as a symbolic model for the diffusion of stories.

The Third Man

This epigraphic model helps us to understand the way in which the text continues. Hardly has the book declared "I am beginning" (*exordior*) than a question is asked, in the direct mode: "who is this?" (*quis ille?*). The question comes from the reader, and is addressed to the book, even if it is the book itself that has just prompted him to ask it. This is a type of dialogue also to be found in funerary inscriptions.[12] *Ille*, in Latin, is the demonstrative form of the third person singular, the equivalent of the Greek *ekeinos*, and it designates the third party in this situation of communication between "I" and "you." On funerary inscriptions, where "I" is the inscription and "you" the passerby, "he" is whoever commissioned the monument—that is, the writer, the one who dictated the text to the stonemason.

A modern reader would, in the case of a book, be inclined to assimilate this third person to the author, in this instance Apuleius. It is a temptation to which at least one editor of *The Golden Ass* has succumbed, coolly translating this as "Who am I?" Another, equally imperceptive, produced "a few words on the author."[13] But, in reality, this third man who is taken to be the writer has nothing to do with Apuleius. His name is to remain unknown, but his history and origins make him the Greek double and negative of the Roman Apuleius. So far as we can tell, Apuleius was born in Africa—that is, in the province of Africa—in about A.D. 125, in Madaurus, now Algeria, then a prosperous Roman colony. This Latin-speaking Berber came from a rich and noble family. He went to study Latin rhetoric in Carthage, then the capital of Africa. He then proceeded first to Athens, to learn Greek and study philosophy, next to Rome, after which he returned to Africa. But never mind. The third man (*ego* 2) has Greek as his maternal tongue and in his childhood learned the pure Attic language. He then went off to Rome to continue his studies and learn "the language of the Forum," Latin. He is presented as the writer of what is written because he is the Greek translator of this book written in Latin.

What is the truth about this *ego* (2)? To judge from a careful perusal of what is claimed to be his biography, he is a pure fiction: "Attic Hymettos and Ephyrean Isthmos and Spartan Taenaros, fruitful lands preserved forever in even more fruitful books, form my ancient stock."

Everything about this statement is peculiar. No Greek was ever a native of three cities (these three, designated figuratively, being Athens, Corinth, and Sparta): one city was all that was needed and was quite enough to make one a citizen. Descended on the paternal side from a particular lineage, he could not possibly be from all over the place without being from nowhere at all. Moreover, all the three cities to which he claims to belong are defined by a single characteristic modeled on a traditional descriptive format, but instead of being "rich in harvests" or "rich in mares," they are said to be "rich in books." So this translator is not the citizen of a particular city, but the son of a tongue rather than a land, a man from nowhere whose homeland is constituted by libraries. This writer is a fiction of the writing, a Greek book concealed inside a Latin one.

It is writing that has endowed him with speech, for it is he who, using "I," answers the reader's question. Such a shift is not unprecedented in epitaphs where the person dedicating the epitaph produces speech from the inscription.[14] In this case, however, you can tell that the writer has no social reality, he is simply the process of translation and writing. He is a part of the statement, the part that will provide the text with its Latin sonority, for it is he who will be present at the moment of the oral speech act, the reading. It is as if every reading summoned up a Greek text translated into Latin; as if the papyrus needed to be oralized not only to exist, as any inscription did, but also so that the translation could become a reality. The third man is the mute intermediary between a Greek voice and a Latin one: "This very changing of language [*uocis*] corresponds to the type of writing [*stilo*] we have undertaken, which is like the skill of a rider jumping from one horse to another."

The expression *stilus,* which designates the physical effort of writing, places on the same level the translation from Greek to Latin and the rendering from composition to inscription. The book, a speech-producing machine, is not a recording of already oralized Latin stories, but a translation machine. The imaginary writer has moved from an oral Greek speech act, the story, to a written Latin statement, the book, which is designed to produce an oral Latin speech act, the story. To put that another way, there is as much or as little difference between the Greek story and the Latin story as there is between the written statement and its oral speech act. It is all a matter of sonority.

The first "I" was the inscription book; the second "I" is the transcription book, which is why the fictitious writer expresses himself in the past tense as well as in the future, when the translation excuses itself in advance and in the present tense for the Latin mistakes that it may make in the course of the reading: "I beg your pardon if, as a raw speaker of this foreign language of the Forum, I commit [future tense] any blunders." The future tense draws this "I" once and for all away from the fiction of a writer. It certainly designates an element present in the reading, namely the translation. And the "we" that is used connects the two aspects of the text, the book of Greek stories and the Latin text. The same "we" recurs at the end of the paragraph:

> Fabulam Graecinam incipimus. Lector intende: laetaberis.
>
> We are about to begin a Greekish story. Pay attention, reader, and you will find delight.

This "we," which combines the "I" of the book and the "I" of the Latin language repeats *in duo* the *exordior* 'I am beginning' that concluded the first paragraph. Perhaps the reader could also be associated with these. It all depends on how *Lector, intende* is understood; the verb *intende,* which means "pay attention" can also be interpreted as "read carefully" or as "listen carefully." The verb *laetaberis,* which means "you will be rewarded for your efforts" or "you will not be disappointed in your expectations," can also be interpreted in two ways—in fact, three ways, since the reader, according to the program that the book has indicated for him, is both the storyteller and the person for whom the story is told. He will be satisfied as a listener if he has read the story well to himself, that is if he has correctly deciphered the written text.

If one tries to, it is quite possible to believe that *incipimus* 'we are beginning', concerns all three—or even four—of the speech-act actors: the Greek book, the Latin translation, and the storyteller-listener. But it should be noted that this whole bunch of *egos* remains anonymous and that, although this preface certainly does function on the epigraphic model, the latter is here diverted from its commemorative function: what this book is about to perpetuate is certainly not the fame of one man, the author.[15]

I, Lucius, Once upon a Time

The third "I," *ego* (3), is that of the storyteller hero, the "I" of the statement who will tell the story of Lucius from beginning to end. He starts off without introducing himself, as if he was already there, in flesh and blood, with friends at a banquet or walking along a road. He is a man whom they can all see, whom they all know, and whose story some of them have heard before. This "I" will still be there at the end, but by then he will have greatly changed. For the reader will eventually discover that Lucius's story is that of the conversion of one of the great priests of the cult of Isis and Osiris in Rome.

This storyteller-hero is thus introduced by a fictitious speech act that reproduces the speech-act position that the storyteller can be seen to occupy through *The Golden Ass*. It is a fictitious speech act, which is presented as such through the device of the three "I"s of the preface. Without a fictitious speech act, without a machine for translating and for producing Latin sounds, how could one possibly hear a Greek storyteller telling his story "in the language of the Forum," as Apuleius puts it?

A Book for a Single Reading and a Single Reader

But why such a long digression? Apuleius was a Roman who spoke Latin, and his hero, Lucius, the priest of Isis in Rome, earns his living as a lawyer, which proves that he too speaks perfect Latin. So why or for whom is the translator there? Why the book, and for whom? For it certainly could not take the place of a storyteller. There were so many storytellers in the square of an evening, so many travelers to invite to one's table. What was the good of a story without the conviviality that it created? Whatever pleasure could there be in telling a story to oneself in this way? It was not something that was done in a banquet, where you shared everything with your neighbors, nor as you trudged along the road (it would hardly have been convenient to unroll a *uolumen* as you followed your ass or even when perched astride it) or while engaged in spinning or weaving wool. In antiquity it was not the custom to take a book along as a traveling companion. What would be the point? Where was the dust-covered storyteller, leading his weary horse by its bridle? Where was the adventurer maimed by vampires who, at the end of the story, would uncover his face, revealing its ravaged nose and the absence of its ears? A story could not be told just anywhere or to just anyone. Its extraordinary veracity would not ring true except in particular places and at particular times.[16] Where was the boulder-strewn, windswept desert, the bivouac in the depths of an Anatolian forest that would make it possible to listen to a tale about the heroic deaths of brigands, bank robbers with an appalling kind of courage and immersed in hatred and despair? Solitary reading was always disappointing because it meant an absence of the body of someone else, an absence of that person's voice and breath, an absence of the body that made the story believable, that was marked by the scars explained in the story, or of the body that had changed its identity and that had a gaze that was from elsewhere. Solitary reading was in touch with neither heaven and earth, nor with day and night.

So how could *The Golden Ass* have been read and reread just for the pleasure of reading? The reader must have had another purpose. A book suffered from a double disadvantage in that it either mobilized the body too much or too little: too much in that it hampered the gestures of whoever was reading, whose head and arms were engaged in perusing and holding the book (besides which it would appear that the reader needed to be seated);[17] and too little in that it left the listener's body vacant, untouched by the pleasures of music. The fact is that even if Romans seeking from books the knowledge that they lacked were willing to submit themselves to the austere discipline of reading, they would do so without pleasure; and it is hard, anyway, to see what reading stories could teach them, except the stories themselves. Any interaction between storyteller and listener presupposed a situation in which speech circulated in a social manner and the body was otherwise occupied. A book object had no place in such a situation; clearly the storyteller would not be reading for others.

But one last possibility remains: an autonomous reader reading Apuleius's stories to himself and deriving pleasure from the narration of the extraordinary tales he was murmuring to himself. The hypothesis is not ruled out, even though it may well be thought that at this point cultural entropy would reach its maximum level since the effect of the sociability of the story would have disappeared totally, with the solitary reader closed in on himself like some monad. Even if the reader addressed by the preface did derive a certain pleasure from being his own storyteller, that pleasure, which stemmed from amazement, solely from amazement, could only be produced once. Are we to believe that so precious a manuscript was designed to be read but once? For a fixed story could never possess the life of an oralized story, recounted over and over again, but each time differently.

I am more inclined to think that that first reading was just the starting point for a new kind of orality and that Apuleius's book was a kind of *compendium* that provided storytellers with material that they could then reuse. This would be how it worked: the first reader of *The Golden Ass*, who read it in a murmur for the very first time, would be the first Latin storyteller of the tales recounted by Lucius. He did not read the book purely for the sake of reading it or just for the pleasure of hearing himself tell a story. He read it in order to recount stories himself, in his turn, launching onto the waves of rumor a new generation of stories from elsewhere. He read the stories of *The Golden Ass* in the same way as all the Romans who "fed on" books, in quest of material for their own words.[18] The book represented a "cellar," a "store cupboard," a "granary": the storyteller could take what he wanted from it and proceed to recount whichever episode he had chosen, just as nowadays publishers lift "The Travels of Sinbad" out of *The Thousand and One Nights*, or some other story in isolation, such as "Aladdin and the Magic Lamp," so that parents can read them or tell them to their children. To tell stories in a different way—adapt them to a particular audience and endlessly recompose them—is to create orality out of writing. That is certainly the promise made to the reader in the preface of *The Golden Ass*. But at the same time it is true that the reader's murmured reading to himself is already the murmur of an oralized story and that the reader, by lending his voice to Lucius, receives from the book, as he would receive from a storyteller, stories that he will subsequently recompose for himself. This is made possible by the particular nature of a *sermo*, by the cultural humility of the story, speech with virtually no sonorous substance, which has no need to be "acted out," and also by the practice of storytelling, which, on the model of travelers' tales, confuses the narrator with the hero so that each storyteller is supposed to be telling either his own story or else a story told him by the person to whom it happened.

In the last analysis, one single reader and one single reading would suffice for this precious and fragile papyrus, the very material of which ruled out frequent or careless handling—one single reader whose effort to decipher the text would be rewarded by the pleasure that he would derive from becoming a storyteller in his turn. The fiction of a narrative told by a certain Lucius would make it possible for him to tell the story in the first person. And he would certainly tell it, not read it. It is true that some philologists have suggested that what are nowadays known as "Greek and Roman novels" may have been read by groups gathered together to while away the long evening hours.[19] Their hypothesis is based on a confusion between what one of them eruditely calls intradiegetic narratees and extradiegetic narratees, in other words the people listening to the stories in the narrative and the reader of the book. For those scholars, Lucius trudging behind his mount or at the banquet given by Byrrhenus reflects an image of a reader of *The Golden Ass*. But to believe that hypothesis is to forget about speech-act situations and to confuse stories that are told and stories that are read, reading for oneself (*lectio*) and live speech. It is impossible to imagine these stories being read publicly, given a *recitatio*, for such a reading had its own rules and its own speech-act conditions, and only particular kinds of texts would be used.[20] The speech of ordinary communication, *sermo*, had no place there. Finally and perhaps most importantly, it is hard to see why, if that kind of collective reading did occur, the book itself did not envisage the possibility. For the book suggests only two models: a solitary reader and a listener to a storyteller well placed to tell the story, either a solitary listener or one in a group of others.

If my own hypothesis is correct, Apuleius's book was thus a staging post in between two kinds of orality. It was not a *monumentum*, a cultural masterpiece intended to immortalize its author, since there is no author, given that not one of the three "I"s of the preface refers to Apuleius of Madaurus. No doubt Apuleius was not in so great a hurry to die as to erect his own tomb while still alive. His book was not dedicated to his own personal fame but simply served to reinject into popular rumor a new generation of stories, by creating a first time, but without that first time being stamped with the mark of a particular inventor. Only writing was capable of producing a narrative without a real subject, in which the "I"s that do the recounting all fit into one another, the central one being the "I" of an ass, which itself reminds the reader that this is a fiction created by the story: "So ran the story told to the captive girl by that crazy, drunken old woman. I was standing not far off and, by Hercules, I was upset not to have tablets and stilus to write down such a pretty tale."[21]

To remember the story of Cupid and Psyche, Lucius the ass would have needed to write it down—a hypothesis doubly unrealizable: first, no writing materials were available and, second, even had they been, they would have been no use to him, for how could he have written using his ass's hooves? So it is not him telling this story from memory; it is purely a creation of the text, as is the robbers' cave.[22] The ass *is* the writing.

Apuleius's book should therefore lead us somewhat to modify our traditional view of the possible relations between writing and orality, for we tend to imagine a purely one-way process in which stories, initially transmitted by the oral tradition, are subsequently, one day, fixed in writing. Here, manifestly, that is not what happened. The book was used not to fix or arrest an earlier orality but to seize hold of the latter, transform it through writing and translation, and then to relaunch the new stories into the circuit of orality.

Pornographic Reading

We know of another Lucius, from the same story of a man transformed into an ass, attributed this time to a Syrian, Lucian of Samosata (or rather the Pseudo-Lucian),[23] and also of yet a third *Lucius-ass*—the text of which, however, is lost—by a certain Lucius of Patras. Are these earlier or later than *The Golden Ass?* It does not really matter which; in the present work we are, after all, concerned not with imitation or rewriting, but with oral recomposition: each new story wipes out all the rest the moment it is told; it is not trapped in a web of intertextuality.

A comparison of the account by the Pseudo-Lucian and that by Apuleius shows that the difference between them is that the one is simple, the other multiple. In sum, the story is the same but the tale written in Greek stands on its own, without incorporating other intertwined stories and with no preface and no final episode telling of the hero's conversion to the Isiac religion: Lucius simply "returns home, safe and sound." There is no intertwining of stories and no writing presented as such. The account starts with the words "I, Lucius" and is simply a transcription of a fictitious speech act. This Lucius too is curious about witchcraft; on the other hand, he is not avid for stories. Inside his ass's skin, he pays no attention to the stories of men. This, for example, is how he sums up the robbers' banquet: "They were served an abundant repast and the conversation of those robbers went on interminably."

Instead of being bathed in the mystic atmosphere created by the two Egyptian gods, first Isis, then Osiris, appearing to the ass, the ending of the story is an obscene farce. Lucius, who in his form as an ass had provided one lady full satisfaction as a lover, looks forward to continuing his relations with her, now that he is once again a handsome young man. However, upon seeing him naked, the lady has her slaves throw him out:

> "By Jupiter," said she, "it was with the ass that I was in love, not with you; it was with him, not you, that I went to bed. I thought you would have retained the large, splendid specimen that distinguished my ass. But I can see full well that instead of being that charming and useful animal, now, after your metamorphosis, you have become a mere monkey. . . ." At break of day, without having had a chance to recover my clothes, I ran to the ship and, laughing, told my brother of my misfortunes.

The lady, devoted solely to Priapus, regarded love as nothing but bestial copulation; she was blind to the beauty of the human body (Priapus was the ugliest of gods) and had eyes only for his sexual organ. To her, Lucius, once reduced to the proportions of an anthropoid, was a monkey.

The Lucius of the Pseudo-Lucian belongs to the genre of Milesian stories of which there are other Roman examples in the *Satyricon*, such as "The Matron of Ephesus" and "The Ephebe of Pergamum."[24] The stories invariably revolve around erotic adventures in which women or young boys reverse the expected modes of behavior by manifesting extremely healthy sexual appetites. They are told in unusual situations: Eumolpus, for instance, tells the story of the matron of Ephesus in the course of a banquet on a ship belonging to Lichas. The participants, who had been quarreling among themselves only moments earlier and have only just been reconciled, remain silent and the atmosphere lacks convivial warmth. The old poet, for once abandoning the idea of declaiming anything that would put everyone in an even worse temper, captures the whole assembly's attention by promising them a story about a woman of light morals. Having undertaken to spare them "tragedies from the olden days and heroines known to us for centuries," he announces that he will tell them of "an adventure that happened in my own times." The effect of the story is remarkable: the sailors greet the ending with laughter and the banquet guests, for their part, are infected by the atmosphere of the Milesian tale.

As a result of gaps in the manuscript, the precise context in which Eumolpus recounts the other Milesian tale in the *Satyricon*, about the ephebe of Pergamum, remains unclear. In any event, its effect upon Encolpius is equally gratifying: the young man who, before it, had been overcome by the infidelity of his lover Giton, perks up enormously on listening to this lewd story: "erectus his sermonibus. . . ." The Latin expression is no doubt a euphemism.[25]

In all likelihood then, different types of stories corresponded to different speech-act situations, Milesian tales being reserved for banquets in which what the participants expected from the *sermones* passing from bed to bed was erotic stimulation. From this point of view, Lucian's *Ass* is a narrative that is all of a piece: in English it would be classed as "erotic fiction." For it is devoted solely to the erotic adventures of first the young man, then the ass that he becomes, some of which are spiced with sadomasochistic touches. The fiction is limited to the domain of Priapus in which the emblematic animal is the ass. Was this story transcribed for a particular reason? Unfortunately even the ardor of the Greek Hellenistic archivists throws no light upon the matter.

A Handbook for the Use of Storytellers

In any event, Milesian tales had no need of an introduction to the Latin scene at the time of Apuleius. As the work of Petronius shows, the genre was already current in Latin in Nero's period.[26] *The Golden Ass* certainly comprises a number of Milesian tales in which wives trick their husbands, tales that could very well be entitled "The Baker's Wife," "The Day Laborer's Wife," "The Decurion's Wife," and so on, but it also includes plenty of stories in other styles, in particular melodramatic accounts in which innocent victims and deplorable traitors all come to a bad end. This very diversity supports my thesis: in *The Golden Ass,* the story of Lucius is not a single tale, but a compendium into which the process of writing has introduced different types of stories, all destined to be multiplied many times over, thanks to the many storytellers who will recount them, suiting each type to the particular speech-act situation that fits it best. It is a kind of encyclopedia of stories, setting out models for the making of stories, models based on examples grouped into different series, from which it is possible to work out the rules of their composition. The book itself shows how the stories collected together in the episode of the robbers can be used. The young man betrothed to the charming girl taken hostage and imprisoned in the cave manages to pass himself off as a robber by the name of Haemas of Thrace, by dint of inventing a story about robbers in which he is represented as the hero, a story modeled precisely on the stories told in the course of the banquet. There are only two means of gaining access to the robbers' cave: either as an ass or as a storyteller, which in the last analysis boils down to the same thing.

So, even if the reader of *The Golden Ass* did perhaps enjoy discovering new stories by deciphering Apuleius's manuscript for the first time, that pleasure of his was not the goal of his reading and would assuredly not accompany any rereading. What he was really after was fresh knowledge for a storyteller, and it was that quest that made the effort worthwhile: *intende . . . laetaberis.*

Translation Reading as a Means of Transition between Two Oralities

Much could be said about the figure of Lucius who, inside his ass's skin, is an ideal cultural intermediary or exploring interpreter for the mysteries of Greece: this narrator-hero, who himself moves geographically and linguistically from Greece to Rome and religiously from Eros to Isis by way of Priapus, is also a man who, after three separate initiations, eventually becomes the priest of an Egyptian cult and thereupon leaves the oral, risqué Milesian tale behind him, to devote himself instead to sacred writing set down on papyrus.

The unusual character of this narrator-figure and the puzzle posed by the preface do, however, fit in with one particular Roman representation of translation and, more generally, with what Romans had to say about the transfer of Greek culture into Roman culture.[27] They spoke of translation using metaphors of scriptural weaving. For example, when Catullus wrote his long work *The Marriage of Thetis and Peleus,* the poem changed into a fabric. "It is as if Catullus was using a Greek warp—the traditional material of his poem—and introducing into it his own Latin woof; as if the best kind of text was a compound of a Greek warp and a Latin woof."

Another form of translation was likewise represented in Rome using an image of weaving of this type: the translation that made it possible to interpret the *Sibylline Books.* These books were a collection of Greek texts in verse attributed to a Sibyl. They were consulted upon the appearance of omens that Rome needed to expiate in order to restore concord with the gods. The oracles were interpreted in the following fashion. The priests responsible, the decemvirs, selected a line from the book at random. Next, the letters that composed the line were set out in a vertical column, constituting the first letters in the lines of a Latin poem that the priests thereupon composed, a poem prescribing what expiatory Roman rituals were to be performed. This vertical column of letters taken from the Greek text formed the edging, *praetextum*, of the textile constituted by the Latin poem. The text, as the word itself indicates, thus resulted from a weaving that "signified the union between the selected hexameter, fixed and unalterable, and the sequence of lines that were to be produced in view of the crisis situation that obtained. It signified the intertwining of the 'hard,' traditional statement and its exegesis, which was pliant and took account of the present,"[28] or—as I myself should put it—of the speech-act conditions.

This reading of the *Sibylline Books*, the *interpretatio* produced by the decemvirs, was at once a translation from Greek to Latin and an oralization of a written text, but as well as that it constituted the transfer of a statement linked with the Greek culture into a statement inserted into the Roman culture: a reading of this type made it possible to step back from the original statement and reformulate it to suit the new circumstances. What we have here is a technique of oral recomposition applied to a text—whose reader is not the writer's slave, not subjected to his words—a technique that (if you follow me) could well have been that used by the reader-storyteller of *The Golden Ass*. The writing does not serve to fix an oral performance in order to preserve the statement that it makes; instead, it is used to recompose a new oral performance on the basis of that statement, which in effect implies the creation of a new statement, never before oralized.

What we have here is the use of a combination of writing and oral composition, which creates a particular kind of memorization that includes both a written memory and an oral memory. A creation of monuments is certainly involved, for texts are preserved and turned into archives that will be used for reference, but at the same time all this results in an ongoing evolution of texts that truly are pronounced orally.

The cultural model for this very particular use of writing is to be found at the very heart of Roman culture, in religion and its rituals. I refer to what E. Valette-Cagnac calls "a double speech act,"[29] which would take place when ritual formulae were read out, at the same time and together, by both a priest—often a pontiff—and a magistrate. The formula (*carmen*) was first pronounced by a priest, who either read it out from the tablets that made up an old book, a *uolumen*, or else recited it by heart; and it was then repeated aloud by the magistrate. The priest thus acted as a "prompter" (*praeit*) to the magistrate and as an auxiliary to the collective memory. The magistrate had the political authority that gave the pronouncement its performative power. But legally neither one of them could proceed without the other.

The explanation for this manner of proceeding was certainly the very Roman need for formal precision. The formulae had to be pronounced without hesitation, without stumbling, without confusion, word for word (*uerbatim*). But it should also be noted that between the first reading and its reproduction there was room to slip in changes that were necessary so as to make the formula suit the present circumstances. Scipio Aemilianus,[30] for example, was obliged, as censor, to preside over the completion of a *lustrum*, the five-year period during which censors carried out a census of the population. On this occasion he was required to say prayers following the traditional formulae that were prompted to him by a scribe reading from tablets. In the past, the censor had always prayed that the empire should continue to expand and to prosper. But the conqueror of Carthage, worried by the rate of Roman expansion eastward, altered the formula and prayed only that the gods should preserve its existing boundaries. The alteration was recorded and the formula for which the subsequent censor was prompted was that which Scipio had had registered in the minutes of the ceremony.

This constitutes a very particular example of the way in which writing and orality could be combined to produce a flexible, public memory. The scenario itself was a fiction. Scipio pronounced his formula of words just as if it was the one prompted by the scribe, and the scribe proceeded to write down Scipio's formula as if it was the only one that had ever existed. Similarly, in the oral tradition, the newest formula is always the most ancient, for tradition is constantly being brought up to date even though there is assumed to be never any history, never any evolution, only a contextual renegotiation. However, instead of this being the prerogative of priests of Memory such as the Homeric bards, whose authority was subject to no political control, in Rome that negotiation was organized by the political authorities, checked by the priests, and confirmed by a written memorial.

Ancient Roman religion thus provided the model for a two-voiced reading that left a space free in between the deciphering of a text and its oral reintroduction into social life. It is within that space that I would situate the reactivation of Apuleius's stories by reader-storytellers, the recomposition and translation of Greek erotic poetry recycled in the *lusus* of the comissatio, and the transfer of Greek theater to the stages of Rome. The fixed text was no more than a moment of memory petrified in between two kinds of living speech. It was reanimated just once and thereupon replaced by its successor, which would encounter the same fate. At best it would fetch up in the archives or in a library, smothered in dust. It is the kind of memorial for which the only technique of preservation in writing took the form of the writing of minutes.

Reading for More Than One Person: The *Recitatio*

In contrast to this writing–reading–oral recomposition upon which the culture of stories was based, there also existed another sequence that likewise associated writing, reading, and orality, but in which it was oral reading that effected a transition between two kinds of writing preserved in books. It was on this sequence that the official culture was based. I refer to a practice well known under the empire, the *recitatio* or public reading.

At the end of the republic, a passion for fine writing seized Romans of high rank.

> Mutauit mentem populus leuis et calet uno scribendi studio . . . scribimus indocti doctique poemata passim
>
> The fickle public has changed its taste and is fired throughout with a scribbling craze . . . skilled or unskilled, we scribble poetry, all alike.[31]

They devoted all their leisure moments to turning out, sometimes in record time, tragedies, scholarly poems, philosophical or rhetorical treatises, and historical accounts. These writings brought some of them new fame, possibly ensuring that their names would be attached to some monument book for having introduced a new form into Latin culture or else for having contributed to the literary prestige of Rome in the Alexandrian spirit, by imitating some predecessor. With the advent of the empire this passion became a frenzy. But writing was no longer enough. Now these writings had to enter the public domain in order to spread the fame of the author. This became the function of the *recitatio*.

To read one's work aloud to one's friends was now the ambition of every author, for a book would not be published until it had passed the test that the Romans called a *recitatio*.[32] In Rome, a civilization of books, archives, and writings,[33] only oral speech was prestigious, only oral speech could prove a man's ability to control language. Even when the text in question was intended to be "literature," when the work created was a written one and was destined eventually to become a book, it did not exist, nor did its author, until such time as it had been read aloud publicly before a select audience of friends, who were themselves likewise potential authors and would be accompanied by their own clients. Furthermore, the *recitatio* was not simply a preamble, allowing the book to be presented to a handful of people before being read by a wider public. Those two readings constituted different types of speech act, for the first was part of the system of gift giving and gift receiving (*officia*) that constituted the very fabric of aristocratic Roman friendship.

A Self-Defining Ritual of the Roman Nobility

The recitation stemmed from a social ritual that had become rapidly established as early as Augustus's reign and that made it a self-defining practice of the Roman aristocracy, to a certain extent (but only a certain extent) replacing the more ancient *oratio* or public speech.[34]

Under the republic public speech was, for a politician (i.e., the ideal citizen), a way of behavior that affirmed his identity in the sociopolitical hierarchy of the *populus* (i.e., his rank). The practice of the *oratio* thus situated it in an oral culture, since the reflexive effect of the *oratio* upon the *orator*—that is, its social efficacy from the point of view of the subject—was only realized when the speech act took place. The orator needed the forum or the *curia* and the presence of other citizens listening to him. To exist as an orator, he needed the event constituted by the delivery of a speech and he also needed the unique and fleeting relationship that this created between him and his audience. A written or even a read speech, one that was not an "action" but was reduced to a text, would have ruled out any "event." The subject of a statement could never be substituted for the subject of a speech act, nor could a *lector* play the role of an orator. So an *oratio* was always an improvisation. To prepare a speech was not to compose it in advance but to train oneself for its performance. Reduced to the statement that it made, an *oratio*, recorded in writing, was speech that was socially dead and that lacked any oratorical efficacy. That was necessarily the case, as was socially and culturally obvious, for had it not been so any Roman without breeding or honor but who was a good actor and capable of reading out a speech written according to the rules would have been able to usurp the social prestige or *dignitas* that attached to the figure of an orator.

The *recitatio* thus came to produce the same social effects as the erstwhile *oratio* although, as a speech act, it lost its political effects. With a *recitatio*, it was no longer a matter of winning people over but simply of demonstrating that one was capable of creating speech that was persuasive. The *recitator* would be judged not on a real performance but on a fictitious one in which he would manifest his skill. He made use of a combination of writing and orality that conferred on his written and read text the qualities of fictitious oral speech. The text had to be written since there was now nowhere that the kind of speech mastered by an orator could be created on the spot. Any prestigious words that were now mastered were confined within monumental writing, the kind that produced the self-reflexive monuments of Roman culture by rewriting earlier works and thereby becoming part of a long chain of imitations based on the canonical texts of the library of Alexander. A text was a statement fashioned out of a fictitious speech act. What a *recitator* did was give these future mummies a few short moments of life.

Thus a writer—or, strictly speaking, a *scriptor*, that is to say a man who had composed a text committed to writing, whether or not he himself actually wrote the letters—would read that text aloud in the presence of a circle of friends. The text might be a lyric or epic poem, a play for the theater (a dramatic poem), a historical narrative, or even a legal speech or a ceremonial piece.[35] It is important to note that these public readings excluded any works that made use of *sermo*, such as philosophical dialogues and stories, since in the eyes of Romans *sermo* was the "zero degree" of writing. It presupposed a purely communicative use of language at the very lowest level and implied an ideal of transparency, which ruled out the kind of reception that concentrated on style (*verba*) rather than subject matter (*res*), as was the case, as we shall see, in a *recitatio*.[36]

A singular feature of the *recitatio* was that it constituted a speech-act situation without a specific statement. The statements made were always produced by fictitious speech acts. Tragedy was written as though it was to be acted, lyric poems as though they were to be sung; as statements in a *recitatio*, they were accordingly bound to seem incomplete. Moreover, most of these fictitious speech acts—lyrical poetry, for example, and epic—did not even belong to the Roman tradition. So they were not only fictitious but also Greek. For written texts such as these, the only speech act possible in Rome was therefore a delayed, out-of-step speech act such as the *recitatio*. The interplay between a fictitious speech act and a delayed one was underpinned by the phonetic ideology of writing that turned writing into the transcription of oral speech, producing the illusion of a recording. Such an ideology was clearly connected with the alphabetic nature of Roman and Greek written texts, which, according to the ancients, used letters to "represent" sounds.[37]

The discordancy between the speech act implied by the genre of the statement—tragedy, lyric, legal speech—and the nature of the speech act peculiar to a *recitatio* removed any pragmatic meaning from the text, in short prevented it from creating any effect. In consequence, the listeners could not pass any direct judgment on the effects of the text as a speech act, but could only imagine them on the basis of the statement, through an appreciation of its style, *compositio*. The kind of reception elicited by a text in a *recitatio* puts one somewhat in mind of that elicited from the public in the poetry festivals of classical Greece, except that in the case of the *recitatio* the suspense engendered by the competition would be lacking. The listeners were in the position of professors, that is to say critics, in relation to what was in effect a stylistic exercise on which they would pass a purely technical judgment. They were in the same position as the professors invited to the banquet described by Aulus Gellius.[38] Speech in a *recitatio* was listened to with all attention focused on its purely formal aspect; the truth (*res*) of what was said was not relevant. Pliny the Younger thus recounts how he attended the first *recitatio* of a very young man from the excellent Calpurnia family, who read out a poem to do with astronomy.[39] The members of his audience were enchanted, not by the boy's scientific knowledge in itself, for they themselves no doubt knew very little about the subject, but by the excellence of the verse and the varied beauty of the style. The stars were no more than a pretext for a literary exercise. Thanks to what was essentially simply a school exercise, the young man proved that he possessed a perfect mastery of language, in other words all the technical abilities of an orator. He made no attempt at all to convince them of the truth of what he said, but simply demonstrated his rhetorical virtuosity, which at one time would have been enough to herald a fine career in the Forum.

An Indispensable Reciprocity

A *recitator* depended absolutely upon the presence of listeners who took an active part in the lecture. It was they who asked him to begin—which he only did at the request of his public—and who then spurred him on with their applause and, finally, voiced their criticisms. A *recitatio* was such an important element in the life of a Roman noble that, for any client of his, it was a moral and social duty to attend.[40] And it was a matter of not simply listening passively to the reading but also expressing an opinion on the merit of the text.[41] The event put the participants' qualities of friendship to the test: the intellectual rigor, honesty, and openness of each one would be assessed by the other listeners, as would the lucidity and modesty of the *recitator* as he accepted criticism and altered his text accordingly. A whole code of ethics attached to the *recitatio*: a gentleman would never refuse to listen to a friend giving one, not even if this duty ate inconveniently into his time, just as he would never refuse to help him in his lawsuits and other public affairs. Indeed, he was expected to press him into giving such *recitationes*, overcoming his modesty and reproaching him for his lack of ambition (which would, naturally, be more or less feigned).[42] Similarly, along with the rest of the audience, he would encourage him throughout the reading, insisting that he kept on right to the end, even if this took several more days. Finally, when he himself had written a work that deserved a hearing, he would not ask his friends to come and listen to it, as if they owed this to him, but would wait for them to force him, with pressing insistence, into a *recitatio* of his own.

Reciprocally, a reader would repeatedly proclaim his indebtedness to his friends, declaring that the text that would eventually be published would be a collective creation, rather than his own personal work.[43] He would insist that he could have achieved nothing alone and that one genius on its own was always inferior to a gathering of average talents. All this was a far cry from the romantic vision of the solitary creator.

A text read out in a *recitatio* was invariably as yet unpublished and that reading was never repeated. This conferred upon a *recitatio* the status of an event, even if the text later turned into a monument. It was an event that had to take place in town: a man would do his writing in the country, during his *otium*, and it was there too that he would read the great writers of the past, drawing nourishment from them (for this would be a purely utilitarian type of reading); but to read out his work, he would return to Rome.[44]

For a *recitatio*, the physical presence of the author of the text was essential, for he was defined not as the subject of a statement but definitely as the subject of a speech act. Even if he did not himself read out his work, he had to be present. Pliny, who was a poor reader of verse, entrusted the reading to one of his freedmen, who took his place at the *recitatio*,[45] but he was bothered about what he should do during the reading. Where should he sit? How should he behave?

> Ipse nescio quid illo legente interim faciam: sedeam defixus et mutus et similis otioso? an ut quidamquae pronuntiabit murmure, oculis, manu, prosequar? Sed puto me non minus saltare quam legere.
>
> I don't know what I am to do with myself while he is reading, whether I am to sit still and silent like a mere spectator, or do as some people and accompany his words with low voice, eye and gesture. But I don't believe I am any better at mime than at reading aloud.

One imagines the author miming his text as if to a playback, or sitting alongside the reader with an apparently distrait air. This comical passage proves that the *recitator* truly was first and foremost a physical presence, a living body. It was fitting that he should live through the agony of this social trial in person, himself confronting the verdicts of his peers, accepting their views and advice and making the requisite corrections. Only if he did so could he garner the fruits of his labor and acquire the social prestige that accompanied the exercise of public speaking. And only then would his circle of friends grow, attracting other writers-*recitatores*.[46]

Recitationes thus constituted a practice in which the values of the old republican nobility truly were revived, creating a sociability that was based on giving and countergiving and therefore implied a reciprocity. Every listener was a potential reader, and vice versa. The practice of writing followed by a public reading was a way of preserving the unity of the Roman political class, essentially the senatorial class, as a group of peers who offered one another mutual recognition on the occasion of each *recitatio* through the celebration of common values, first and foremost a rhetorical mastery of language.

Literary relations consequently reproduced the framework of clientship. The fact that here the clientele was called a literary circle should not mislead us: to applaud a patron's stylistic exercises and present one's own works in his presence was certainly a means of social promotion. It was in this fashion that Suetonius advanced his career and eventually became one of the most important officials in Hadrian's palace. As a modest knight, he became a protégé of Pliny the Younger, who got him excused from military service, interceded for him with the emperor Trajan, and at the same time encouraged him to write.[47] Suetonius was one of his *recitatio* colleagues, albeit clearly in the position of a debtor.[48] When Pliny died, the future historian was bequeathed as a client to an eminent member of his former literary circle, Caius Septicius Clarus. It was he who, as prefect of Hadrian's praetorium, made Suetonius the palace secretary-general. *The Lives of the Twelve Caesars* was probably composed within the framework of this clientship, with Suetonius offering his writings and Septicius offering his attention, in the company of all their friends who belonged to the same circle.

The satirists poured plenty of mockery on the dependent position of the wretched *scriptor* who by himself, with neither money nor social relations, would be unable to organize a *recitatio*.[49] His patron might lend him some scruffy premises, provide him with a public made up partly of freedmen, to make up the numbers, and of clients who were used to shouting or applauding at the right moments. The poet would be required to pay out of his own pocket for the hire of chairs and a stage and also for the musicians who would help to make the reading a pleasant occasion. The very same men described so gravely and respectfully in Pliny's letters are elsewhere represented as a mob of writers on every subject under the sun, always short of cash and respectability and striving to pull themselves, through their works, up to the level of the elites. Juvenal, being more or less one of them himself, puts in a plea for these wretches who in the long run would become disenchanted with being always relegated to the ranks of the listeners. He begins one of his satires as follows:

> Semper ego auditor tantum? Numquamne reponam
> uexatus totiens rauci Theseide Cordi
> Impune ergo mihi recitauerit ille togatas hic elegos? . . .
> Nota magis nulli domus est sua quam mihi lucus
> Martis et Aeoliis uicinum rupibus antrum
> Vulcani . . .
> Expectes eadem a summo minimoque poeta.

> What? Am I to be a listener only all my days? Am I never to get my word in—I that have been so often bored by the *Theseid* of the ranting Cordus? Shall this one have spouted to me his comedies and that one his love ditties, and I be unavenged? . . . No one knows his own house so well as I know the groves of Mars and the cave of Vulcan near the cliffs of Aeolus. . . . Such is the kind of stuff you may look for from every poet, greatest or least.[50]

Prevented from giving their own *recitatio*, plenty of Romans would force their works on anyone available. Horace who, for his part, was well content with a public of handpicked friends and manifested the same aristocratic scorn as his own patron, Maecenas, describes authors declaiming their works in the Forum, or even in the public baths, where their voices would resound with a powerful echo.[51] Many a host was guilty of inflicting readings of his works upon his guests. They constituted insipid and indigestible fare. So generally recognized was this that the best dinner invitation was considered to be the one that promised the guest that he would not be subjected to a reading of his host's verse.[52]

In Rome, everyone wanted to write but no one wanted to listen to the works of others; the position of a *scriptor* was socially gratifying but that of an *auditor* was humiliating. That is why, in a *recitatio*, the two positions were indissociable. Ideally, there were no *auditores* who were not also *recitatores*.

A Rite of Passage

Under the empire, a *recitatio* was so much part of the identity of the nobility that the first public reading of the young scion of a great aristocratic family served as a rite of passage to mark his accession to the adult class. Under the republic, the same purpose had been served by a young noble's first lawsuit, in which he would attack his family's traditional enemy.[53] As we have seen, Pliny tells of how he attended a public reading given by the young Piso.[54] His account lacks neither bite nor social significance. We follow first the anxiety of the family, then its relief once it sees from the reactions of the public that their latest fledgling will emerge with flying colors and so will follow in the glorious footsteps of his ancestors. Pliny, present in the audience, embraced the *recitator* with emotion after the performance. He was delighted to see the future of a great family assured and its continued nobility guaranteed, just as, on other occasions, he declared his satisfaction at having witnessed the flowering of other *recitatores*.[55] Literary writing served solely as a necessary stage in the transmission of rhetorical techniques that could only be demonstrated in oral performances.

In order to achieve such a result, a young Roman received a special education, described at length by Quintilian in his *Institutio Oratoria*. The training was essentially based on reading and writing, seen as preparatory exercises for eloquence, which, ideally, remained an ability to improvise.[56] The orator is compared with an athlete who will have to confront competitors and tricky situations. First he needs to be "nourished," just as athletes are "fed up," by reading widely so as to accumulate a store of words and facts (*copia uerborum et rerum*). Next, his education involves three exercises: first, the writing of imaginary general speeches; second, the improvisation of imaginary legal speeches—both of which exercises were often based on a study of causes pleaded by great orators of the past such as Cicero and Demosthenes. The boy would be presented with models that he was expected to imitate or, if possible, surpass. It was a process of what the Romans called *aemulatio*. The third exercise consisted in the improvisation of real speeches.

The knowledge that a boy accumulated through reading was of two kinds. On the one hand, he had to extend his vocabulary, and not simply by learning lists of synonyms, as some did, for he needed to memorize them in context. On the other, he had to acquire as much information as possible in every domain, in order to enrich his speeches. He had to read "what was useful":

> Knowledge increases day by day, and yet how many books is it absolutely necessary to read in our search for its attainment, for examples of facts from the historians or of eloquence from the orators or, again, for the opinions of the philosophers and the lawyers, that is to say, if we are content to read merely what is useful, without attempting the impossible task of reading everything?[57]

Quintilian thus developed the very Roman idea of a store of collectible knowledge. Earlier generations had made discoveries that their descendants inherited.[58] Plato, Aristotle, and all the other ancients had put together knowledge (*scientia*) that the moderns could simply learn. They did not need to criticize or sift through what the great men of the past had bequeathed them. All of it could be used, provided it was used knowledgeably. Detectable in this attitude is what might be termed an ideology of jurisprudence, of a knowledge that was entirely pragmatic, in total contrast to mythical exploration.

Desperately Seeking a Reader

The *recitatio* was not only a self-referential, identity-confirming practice of the Roman nobility. For others, it was a necessary preliminary to the publication of a book from which they hoped to derive fame. The invention of prestigious public speech, unconnected with politics, thus gave rise to the creation and recognition of *litterae*, monuments of the Roman culture.

Studious Books

All this "literary" activity of adolescents, which the Romans called *studia*, continued into adulthood for some, those who prided themselves on their literary culture, such as Cicero in his day and Pliny under the empire. Most were men for whom letters were a means of social promotion, who published their exercises in order to turn them into canonical works, as did the intellectuals under the protection of the Ptolemies, in Alexandria. Let us call their works "studious books," since they were a pure product of such studies and were intended to enter the pedagogical circuit, once their monumental nature had been recognized.

These people too were reading in order to write. They included Virgil and Stacius; and Horace was behaving no differently when he read the *Iliad* in search of "what was bad, what was good, what was useful, and what was not" (*quid turpe, quid pulchrum, quid utile, quid non*).[59] His reason for reading and rereading the *Iliad* was to find examples and illustrations of the vices and virtues of his own contemporaries. As a writer, Horace needed not only paper and peace and quiet, but also his box of books: "calamum et chartas et scrinia posco."[60] When he went off to his country retreat he piled a whole library into his carriage.

From some books these studious authors sought subject matter, from others they borrowed style. To be more precise, what they were seeking were the traces of a stated speech act, in order to imitate a fictitious speech act. Thus Pliny, in one of his famous letters to Tacitus, declared that a written speech (the word he used was *oratio*) was the archetype or paradigm of an oral speech (here the word used was *actio*): "Est enim oratio actionis exemplar et quasi αρχέτυπον."[61] So it is that, sometimes, in speeches that were never actually delivered, only published (Pliny cites the later *Verrines*), one comes across expressions that are typical of an improvised speech (*figuras extemporales*).

The reader thus seems, once again, to have been living in a total fiction: even if he really was the sole intended reader of the book and what was written in it, the speeches themselves bore the traces of a fictitious speech act whose intended addressees were supposed to judge its merits. The reader could therefore not appreciate the effects of the book directly, but had to work them out in his imagination. Wherein lay the interest of such books? In the fact that they provided model legal speeches, like those composed in schools, whose imaginary efficacy owed nothing to chance or the ineptitude of an opponent—legal speeches written according to the rules.

We have seen first the reader wiped out, next the author monumentalized, now the text petrified. A book, in Rome, was definitely not an instrument of social communication. Wherein lay the advantage in reading such legal speeches? They taught the reader how to write others, which in their turn would likewise be petrified, and thereby ensured the survival of a type of speech that was politically dead but lived on in the social practice of the *recitatio*. So the sole use of reading was that it made it possible to write imaginary legal speeches and then read them aloud. A studious book was certainly an instrument of memory, but only of dead memory. Thanks to the repetitive process of writing–reading–writing, techniques for producing oratorical statements were preserved even in the absence of any appropriate speech act.

The Book-as-a-Tomb and the Elusive Reader

Meanwhile, a *recitatio* generally led to publication, and the studious book that came to be published thus diffused the speech of the *recitator* who, through it, became an author and the owner of that speech.[62] However, the expansion of the author's public, which might have been expected at last to bring him the kind of fame that had been enjoyed by the republican orators who addressed a real *populus*, in fact led to a further depreciation of the speech act. The *recitatio* had, of course, deprived the author's statements of an appropriate speech-act context, but on the other hand it had reestablished a real speech-act subject, the *recitator*, and real addressees, his public—still referred to as *populus*—and had thus created a form of social communication between the two. What the book would subsequently ruin was that communication between the reader (who was the author) and the listener, since the two would become confused, and the author, absent at the time of this speech act, would become nothing but a name on an object, a book.

Publication led to the disappearance of the subject of the speech act, the *recitator*, who was also the *scriptor* and whose place was now taken by a new subject of the speech act, the *lector*. All that a book did was commemorate the event constituted by the *recitatio*, an event never to be repeated. The book was a *monumentum* to that event, set up to preserve the fame of the *recitator*. In all likelihood, the astronomical poem written by young Piso was published in a limited edition of copies that were then distributed to his relatives and friends, who hastened not to read it, but to express their gratitude and admiration most effusively.

The Latin word *monumentum* is a loaded term that frequently designated a funerary monument; and a book published after a *recitatio* had definite affinities with a tomb. To persuade one of his friends to publish his works, Pliny used the following commonplace argument: we are all mortal and only fame, that is to say human memories, can save us from that dire condition, memories that are kept alive by a *monumentum*:

> Habe ante oculos mortalitatem a qua deserere te hoc monimento potes
>
> Bear in mind that you are bound by man's mortality, but that this one memorial of yourself can set you free.[63]

And that *monumentum* was, of course, a published book. "I have finished a monument more lasting than bronze" (*Exegi monumentum aere perennius*), wrote Horace, at the end of the book that he decided to make of his odes.[64] The fame that a book brought extended throughout the empire, since a book was available to all those who knew Latin. So long as Rome and its culture survived, knowing Latin was thus a sufficient condition for becoming a book's addressee.

> Non omnis moriar multaque pars mei
> Vitabit Libitinam usque ego postera
> Crescam laude recens dum Capitolium
> Scandet cum tacita uirgine pontifex.
>
> I shall not altogether die, but a mighty part of me shall escape the death goddess. On and on I shall grow, ever fresh with the glory of after time. So long as the Pontiff climbs the Capitol with the silent Vestal.[65]

Pliny made the same point as follows:

> Sine per ora hominum ferantur isdemque quibus lingua romana spatiis peruagentur.
>
> They [your books] should be on all our lips, to travel as widely as the speech of Rome.

But who was the *ego* commemorated by a book, if not the subject of the statement that the poem constituted or the name inscribed on the book's cover? The writer-poet thus took the place of a dead man. For he would be forever absent and the book would speak in his name, just like a funerary inscription.[66] In fact, this eternal absentee, the author of the book, only existed through his absence and was thus condemned to be mute. He had turned himself to stone by becoming a speaking statue. And this was indeed how authors were perceived by their readers. If a handful of intellectuals from the furthest reaches of the empire arrived in Rome to visit an author, they looked at him as though he were a statue:

> Si quis requirit ut semel uidit, transit et contentus est ut si picturam aliquam uel statuam uidisset.
>
> If anyone does happen to ask for him, when once he has clapped eyes on the poet, he passes on his way, quite satisfied—just as if it had been a picture or a statue that he had seen.[67]

An author did not communicate with his contemporaries, for he was already dead; or else he had had to resume his life as a citizen.

A studious book could thus not establish any relationship between a living author and a public (*populus*) of readers. In Rome, only three cultural pigeonholes existed for such a book: the *recitatio*, but in that case it was reduced to a single oral performance; the *monumentum*, but in that case the author was assimilated to the dead; or finally, the *epistula*, in which case, the book would be sent to a correspondent in exchange for another book, thereby establishing a symmetrical dialogue between two writers-readers.

A famous example is provided by the letters that Pliny wrote to Tacitus on the subject of the latter's works, assuming the position of not a reader but a corrector, that is to say a listener at a *recitatio*.[68]

> Librum tuum legi et quam diligentissime potui adnotavi quae commutanda, quae eximenda arbitrarer
>
> I have read your book, and marked as carefully as I could the passages which I think should be altered or removed.

And he hoped that Tacitus, to whom he had sent his own book, would render him the same service:

> Nunc a te librum meum cum adnotationibus tuis exspecto.
>
> Now I am awaiting the return of my book from you, with your comments.

This exchange established an exceptional bond, realized through reciprocity and the practice of the traditional values of aristocratic friendship:

> O iucundus, o pulchras uices! quam me delectat quod si qua posteris cura nostri usquequaque narrabitur qua concordia, simplicitate, fide uixerimus!
>
> . . . a fair exchange which we both enjoy. I am delighted to think that if posterity takes any interest in us the tale will everywhere be told of the harmony, frankness, and loyalty of our lifelong relationship.

Two writers, in their lifetimes, thus did manage to overcome the constraints of books, thanks to their letter writing, which enabled them to reestablish a dialogue, albeit at a distance, and consequently also a symmetry between reader and writer.

In the last analysis, the trouble with reading books—and the aspect that invalidated it as an honorable practice—was that it did not allow for the reciprocity of exchange that was the basis of a relationship between peers and that *was* effected in a *recitatio*. For what mattered above all was the reversible social relationship between its author-reader and its listener, which was precisely the aristocratic type of relationship that such an occasion created.

The Three Panegyrics to Trajan

The story of the *Panegyric to Trajan* published by Pliny provides a striking illustration of the strange situation of the studious book in Rome. Pliny composed three panegyrics, two of which he delivered orally. The third he published. Only the first was real. The other two, one of which is the one that has come down to us, were false.[69]

This is what happened. As was customary, it fell to Pliny, who was consul in the year 100, to declaim before the whole Senate the panegyric in praise of the emperor on the occasion of the latter's assuming office. He accordingly made this official speech, paying due attention to the speech-act situation, as he himself explains: "taking account of the place and the circumstances, in conformity with the tradition" (*ad rationem et loci et temporis ex more*). The ceremony in the Senate appears to have been a trying one for everyone involved. According to Pliny, this was always the case with panegyrics, because of the speech-act constraints on such occasions. He then wrote another panegyric, intended for a *recitatio*. This one was not affected by the constraints of the official ceremony. It took three days to read it (although that does not mean three *whole* days). All the same, Pliny's friends seemed pleased with it and he was himself very satisfied with this false panegyric, which, he claimed, was the only real one since he had been able to express himself freely. Then, following this reading and "in the presence of just a few," he corrected his text, as any good recitator would. Then he published it. At this point, Pliny's addressee changed. Up until then the addressee, real in the Senate, then fictitious in the *recitatio*, had been Emperor Trajan. The addressees of the book, however, were future emperors to whom Pliny wished to offer instruction by setting the example of Trajan before them.[70] What is interesting about this change is that it took into account both the funerary nature of books—when dead, Pliny would become the teacher of Trajan's successors—and also the fiction of an oral transcription. It thus changed from being a studious book to being a book that served as a store of information for pedagogical ends. Yet was not this too, in truth, a fiction, for if Pliny's book was intended for the education of future princes, why did he offer it to the people of the empire? Besides, the listeners at the *recitatio* had appreciated only the style of the panegyric, as was normal since that was what was intended in the case of studious writing.[71] Nor was anything different expected of future readers. The third panegyric thus comprised two fictions, one contained within the other: the fiction of a panegyric and the fiction of a political handbook for the use of princes.

What this false panegyric really served to commemorate was simply the two faces of the fame of citizen Pliny, the ceremony in the Senate that had set the seal on his political career crowned by his appointment as consul, and the public reading that had set the seal on his competence as a political orator.

But Who on Earth Read the *Satyricon*?

In the last analysis, the only books that presented themselves as such and were solely intended for the reading of a *lector*, without passing through a fictitious speech act that emptied them of their pragmatic meaning, were those that fitted into a system for storing knowledge, with no stylistic effects. The type of writing in these was that used for commercial records or the archives of storekeepers or priests. It belonged not to the ideology of alphabet, according to which writing served simply to register an oral performance—the text did not claim to transcribe an oral event—but rather to an ideology of transparent signs, either oral or written. These books did not connive with public orality, for their function was not to celebrate the poetic or rhetorical mastery of their authors. They employed only the language of ordinary communication (*sermo*).

This ideology of transparency—the signifier = the signified, the word = the thing—related the writing more closely to a series of pictograms.[72] Quite often, abbreviations, not to mention coded notations, such as numbers, the titles of magistrates, the names of coins, and sometimes layouts of lists, made it impossible for a simply alphabetical reading to latch on to any intelligible phrase. Oral discourse needed to recreate itself on the basis of whatever information was supplied. An extreme form of this phenomenon was the Roman funerary inscription: one could only decipher it after having been initiated into the peculiarities of epigraphy. Without such an initiation, the Roman tombs remained dumb. Writing used to store knowledge is often associated with an oral creativity. Discourse produced from this type of writing was not simply an oralization of what was written.

As we have seen, *The Golden Ass* proves that point. But there is one specimen of Roman writing that still poses a problem, the *Satyricon*. Petronius's "novel"—to make do with this word that had no equivalent and no reality in antiquity—or rather the bits and pieces of it that have come down to us pose an insoluble problem for the archaeologist of words: what kind of addressee can we reconstruct? Most commentators have been distracted by the question of the author (Who was this Petronius? Was he really one of Nero's courtiers, known as an arbiter of elegance, whom the emperor forced to commit suicide?) and by the preponderance of male love affairs in the narrative. But those are not the greatest puzzles. From where we stand, in the twentieth century, it is hard to see who could have been the addressees of this messy hodgepodge, this *satura*, a potpourri of neoclassical poems, erotic and fantastical stories, and conventional declamations.

To be sure, the construction of the narrative is certainly "Odyssean" and the travels of Encolpius, like those of Apuleius's ass, are those of the hero of the story, an impossible person since he is a man with no family, home, patron, or slave, a free man yet one without citizenship, a Roman whose Greek name turns him into a fictional character. The only social link that he recognizes is the "fraternal" pact that binds him to Giton and Ascyltos. The three call themselves brothers and their fraternity implies a solidarity between them and potential amorous relations. However, the only function of that link is a narrative one; it suggests no form of sociability known to exist under the early empire. Meanwhile the text withholds from us what might have provided the key to the book: a preface or a beginning, for the opening of the book is lost and the narrative starts right in the middle of a diatribe against the new rhetoric and new painting, put in the mouth of the story's narrator and hero, Encolpius, who is attacking the corrupting influences of eastern and Egyptian art.

Today's reader's only option is to scrutinize the Latin text in the hope of finding, as in *The Golden Ass,* the model of some addressee, even a fictitious one, in order to reconstruct the fictitious speech act that presided over the composition of the statement. The *Satyricon* does in fact suggest several addressees, all incompatible with one another, but it does not introduce any model of a reader who might be the addressee of the real speech act.

In this book, nobody ever reads a book to himself, with of course the exception of Trimalchio, who uncomprehendingly mumbles his way through a translation of Homer during the spectacle put on by the Homerists, and the only two public readings mentioned are two incongruous *recitationes* of epic poems written by the poet Eumolpus. He is a ragged vagabond, crazy about versification and always on the lookout for listeners. In a picture gallery where he has just met the hero Encolpius, he inflicts upon the latter sixty-five lines on the capture of Troy, on the pretext of commenting on a picture of the same subject.[73] The other visitors to the museum, who are much annoyed by this *recitatio,* eject him, with a volley of stones to send him on his way. Encolpius, who is forced to flee with Eumolpus but is not at all keen on his poetic production, promises to invite him to dinner in exchange for his silence.[74] This is a flagrant paradox, if one thinks of the meeting between Lucius and Aristomenes, in which the hero promises his companion a meal in exchange for a story. Was the narrator putting the addressee of his story in the same painful situation as that in which he found himself, forced to listen to Eumolpus's verse in an unsuitable social setting? Or is that verse, which so affronts the taste of Encolpius and the other art lovers, really intended for a reader who might appreciate them?

The text repeats this episode but this time it is 295 lines of a poem entitled *On the Civil War* that are cited in full. The circumstances of this brutal *recitatio* are equally paradoxical. The three heroes, Encolpius, his friend Giton, and the poet Eumolpus, are caught in a storm off the coast of Croton. The ship is sinking. Eumolpus, shut away in his cabin, is writing his epic on a vast parchment, at the same time declaiming it to himself. His companions have to tear him by force from his writing. Having been rescued by a fisherman, they decide to walk to the town. In the course of this journey, after lecturing his companions on the writing of poetry, Eumolpus reads them the poem recently completed amid the waves: is this a parody or not?[75] The lacunas in the text are such that we have no way of knowing whether the narrator went on to describe the effects of this reading on the other two characters. But at least, here again, we can draw a comparison with Aristomenes' story: the epic ends when the journey does and the very last line is declaimed as they enter Croton.[76] An epic has thus on two occasions been read aloud, instead of a story, in unsuitable circumstances, that is to say not within the framework of a *recitatio*.

Elsewhere, the *Satyricon* does contain real stories and these are told in suitable situations. I have already referred to the tales of werewolves and *stryges* swapped by the freedmen at Trimalchio's banquet. Eumolpus himself, though an execrable poet, is a good storyteller. As we have seen, he excels at the "Milesian fable" or erotic tale. In the museum, he comforts Encolpius, who has just been deserted by Giton, by telling him the story of the ephebe of Pergamum; and on Lichas's ship, Eumolpus is equally successful with another erotic tale, "The Matron of Ephesus."[77]

It would be perfectly possible to take the *Satyricon* to pieces and classify all the different kinds of discourse that it contains. It would, after all, not be the first time that attention was paid solely to the statements in the book. All commentators agree that the writing of the *Satyricon* is carnavalesque; the text resembles Harlequin's costume, a patchwork of rags and tatters. They speak of a *satura*, a potpourri. One hypothesis that is common to all these commentators, whether or not they spell it out, is that the book serves a priori as a unificatory principle. To be sure. But to what end and for whom? Is it really possible to believe that one and the same reader would swallow, one after the other, the werewolves, the ephebe of Pergamum, the civil war, the diatribe against modernity in the arts, not to mention the many poems in the Alexandrian mode with which the text is studded? For if we consider this hodgepodge from the point of view of a speech act, the ravages are considerable. Speech acts of different kinds abound: we can pick out scholarly declamation, the marginal banquet, the erotic banquet, the exchange of love stories, and the public lecture. Each of these speech acts corresponds to a different addressee. The situation seems hopeless.

When reading the *Satyricon*, do not we ourselves skip Eumolpus's long poems? Unless, of course, we happen to be particularly interested in epics—in which case, we skip the rest.

One explanation might be that the *Satyricon* functions like *The Golden Ass*, but in a more complex fashion. Perhaps it is an anthology of models, a machine for producing discourse in a variety of contexts, held together by its fictitious form of a story. You can pick out whatever you want. This would explain how it is that it has already been taken apart so that all that remains of it for us are scattered and disjointed fragments.

Rome's Memory Evolving through Orality and Writing: In Praise of the "Remake"

With stories such as these, written down and twined together, we might have thought we had come upon proper literary books that might have given birth to the novel. But instead we find writing that is the prisoner either of orality or of studious production, for which no reading public exists.

The Golden Ass was a means of transferring from Greek orality to Latin orality. Writing constituted a space in which a matrix of stories in Latin came to be created, to be used in a variety of ways by storyteller-readers. The model of translation was inscription.[78] To translate was to read a Greek text in Latin, to produce an *interpretatio* of it.

The *recitatio*, for its part, made it possible for the work of rewriting and imitation begun by the Alexandrians and taken over by Rome to become integrated into social life, as a feature of the life of the Roman elite. The ritual itself consisted of an oral performance inserted between two feats of writing: first the *recitator* wrote his text, then, after the *recitatio*, there followed the correction of the text and its publication. The first bout of writing served simply to fuel the oral performance, the second commemorated that performance. Neither piece of writing was valued on its own account. The wider public would never read these books produced in the aftermath of a *recitatio*, always written within the framework of a fictitious speech act, the dry reading of which could only ever be critical and professorial.

On the other hand, sometimes books such as these could be given new life thanks to a theatrical oralization. For the real public was not a group of readers, for those did not exist, but one that came together in a theater or in a circus, to watch games. It was in the theater that the Romans applauded Virgil's *Eclogues*, not as they listened to a reading of his verse but as they watched a spectacle of dancing and singing based on the written text.[79] Which brings us back to an earlier practice. The purpose of the writing was to imitate something that had preceded it and to translate this with a view to a Latin oralization. Virgil can thus be regarded as Theocritus's translator. The Greek *Eclogues* were based on a fictitious speech act, the songs and poetic contests of Sicilian shepherds. Their adaptation to the theater made Virgil Apuleius's predecessor as an intermediary between Greek and Roman orality. Never mind if the first of those two oralities was fictitious: for the Roman reader it simply provided a context for the composition.

In the last analysis, it was the Latin theater that, as early as the third century B.C., opened up the way for this use of translation writing. Just as *The Golden Ass* was a Greek story told in Latin, the staged Roman games, known as "Greek games" (*ludi graeci*), were Greek comedies and tragedies in Latin, not Latin comedies and tragedies. The comic, or tragic, poet effected a transfer, an "interpretation" of the Greek comedy or tragedy that it represented, serving as a means of transmission between the two cultures. That is why the prologues give the Greek title of the play and, in many cases, the name of its author too. Translation writing was a necessary intermediary between a Greek speech act and a Roman one, for theater in Rome was very different from Greek theater. It was a ritual specifically linked with Roman religion, the patron god of which was Jupiter of the Capitol who, for the duration of these days of games, music, and dancing, established a reign of nonviolence and gratuitous gestures and words.

This Roman way of rewriting-translating Greek theater or other Greek poetic forms constituted a homage to the omnipotence of the speech act. A linguistic translation served no purpose at all unless it simultaneously effected a transfer from the one culture to the other. Besides, why translate? Urban Romans were bilingual and Plautus's public certainly understood Greek (many of his jokes were Greek puns). A straightforward Latin translation was neither more nor less easy to perform in Rome than the original Greek text, for neither could be turned into a real Roman spectacle, only into a fictitious Greek spectacle. What the Romans expected from their poets were "remakes."

That anachronistic remark is intended to encourage contemporaries to think again about the American practice of the "remake," which purists find so exasperating. To be sure, it does ride roughshod over romantic notions of work and author and it primarily serves economic ends. Nevertheless, it constitutes a symptom of the emergence of a new culture of "events." It assumes that a film has a limited number of addressees, depending on the time, the place, and the degree of their enthusiasm for the cinema. Let us consider the example of *Le retour de Martin Guerre*,[80] a superb story: it concerns the return of a soldier who passes himself off as another native of his village, even with the latter's wife. Everyone suspects that he is not the real Martin, but he is so much better than the true one was that nobody denounces the impostor. Rather than confess, he ends up being hanged for the murder committed by the man he is pretending to be. The French film was situated in the period of Occitanian history and its images gripped its public's imagination because it was a period rooted in the collective memory. But this film, which had been highly rated by the Hollywood professionals, could not be presented just as it was to American audiences. Hence the American remake, which takes place in the American South at the end of the Civil War—a mythical period if ever there was one both for American history and for Hollywood tradition, forever marked by *Gone with the Wind*. My reason for speaking up for the "remake" in both Roman theater and American cinema is my delight in cultures of "events," which restore the speech act to the place that the textualization of statements has denied them. The fact that, in both cases, it is popular culture that is involved here is not without significance.

The culture of the remake is a culture of events in which the theater recovers its importance. For there are two ways of looking at the contemporary direction of plays. Either the performance is truly the creation of the director, a real event for the public, which goes to see a spectacle in which an ancient text discovers a new necessity or, alternatively, the director effaces himself before the text, turning it into a straightforward reading, in which case the spectacle becomes a way of celebrating a monument. The important question is: is the theater a place to celebrate a piece of writing at a distance or is it a place for the creation of orality?

The Lie about the Novel

Rome, a civilization of books, thus produced a literature without readers. We have to face the fact: the Romans did not read novels; they did not like literature, except when they themselves had written it.

One teacher of French literature, a state employee, has written a delightful book entitled *Comme un roman* (Just like a novel).[81] He tries to find reasons for and ways of teaching children the pleasure of reading not only their set-text authors but novels in general. In a highly intelligent fashion, instead of treating reading as the nonevent that it sometimes is, just something that has to be done before schoolwork, he brings reading into the classroom: he reads aloud the books that the children are physically incapable of reading at home, where they fall asleep after just a few pages or are bored to tears. He creates a space for a socially integrated speech act, a place for ritualized exchange. He gives the children speech that they themselves are incapable of producing. He deciphers the book for them and gives them its music, rhythm, and flesh, turning reading into a mode of communication between him and them, like a spectacle or a concert. He is the subject of the speech act–reading—something that it is impossible for the author to be. The meaning of what he reads does not really matter; and never mind whether they understand or not. The narrative offered brings the happiness of a gift. A story is presented as if it were a festive meal, for a present is only a proper present if it is superfluous.

By doing this, Daniel Pennac reproduces in his classroom what he regards as the secret of the desire to read: the experience of being read to as a little child by one's father or mother, in bed, before falling asleep. The physical contact and the voice addressed solely to me, the child, in this unique intimacy, produce an atmosphere of sweet, warm milk. And before getting to the stage of reading to the child, the father or the mother would tell him or her a story. Reading followed on from those stories that led into it, just as a teacher can lure on children not yet ready for a book by telling them the story that he cannot yet read to them. Later, his pupils, like the little child, will try to prolong the happiness of the evening story or the reading in class by reading the book for themselves. But it is bound to be a frustrating substitute. However, the child falls into the trap. The best time was the beginning, the story told in a warm physical proximity, with arms free for hugs and the light turned out. Then came the story read from a picture book: the reader's arms were hampered by the book that he or she held and the light was on. Later, the child reads, seeking from the words a feeble recreation of that lost paradise. It is the price you have to pay to become a good student.

A story, that is to say a narrative with no meaning beyond its intrinsic one, derived its efficacy as a speech act from the situation of social communicativity in which it was told. To be sure the story was "a good yarn" and all good yarns in themselves give a certain pleasure, but that pleasure is inadequate unless it is completed by a particular kind of speech act, whether it be a matter of the story serving as a means of a mythical exploration, producing new understanding, or whether it serves to actualize love between parents and their child, or even merely to create a narcissistic relationship between the reader and himself. Without that extra dimension, reduced to itself, however, a story or a novel becomes an object to be commented on or subjected to endless interpretations that in themselves testify to the frustration of the reader. He feels obliged to discover behind—or within?—this "good yarn" some hidden meaning, philosophical depths, a political message, a moral lesson, or even some subconscious discourse.[82]

The search for meaning is brought on by the loss of the body of "another" and the isolation of the individual in a culture in which writing consummates his own body's separation from the relationship to "another" or others that used to be created thanks to the festivity amid which that union was manifested by intoxication, love, and wine. Certainly, once literature acquires the ability to overcome that absence that paves the way for endless commentaries, a rhetoric of reading develops that constructs the work through its own mediations. The book is restored as a book, for the reader really does become the subject of a solitary speech act that he has to construct for himself and that he can discuss with others. Literary books can only function in a culture of commentaries in which life reasserts its rights.

Reflecting on the encounter between Jean de Léry, a French Protestant and hence very much a man of books, and the Tupis of Brazil, in the sixteenth century, Michel Certeau, better than anyone, has drawn attention to the distortion produced by writing:

> Something was left behind there: Tupi speech. It is an aspect of "others" that cannot be salvaged, a perishable act that writing cannot convey. So it is that in the diadem represented by the narrative, speech is like a missing jewel . . . what creates an empty hole in time is the absence of meaning. . . . Nothing of it can be transmitted, brought back, preserved. . . . Writing commemorates a forgotten separation. It is the "form" of memory, not its "content": it is a faint reflection of a loss and a debt, but it neither preserves nor reconstitutes the initial content, since that is lost (forgotten) forever . . . the practice of writing is memory. But any "content" that might claim to indicate a place or a truth for it can only be a fabrication or symptom of it, a fiction.[83]

You could think you were reading a commentary on a poem by Catullus, in which all that writing can convey is the absence of a body, a loss of orality. But, above all, those few lines seem also to express the inanity of any attempt to discover in ancient texts an orality captured by words or the truth of live speech. These texts can convey to us nothing but evidence of antiquity's kind of relationship to writing. As for the rest, by which I mean the live culture of gestures and speech, the only way to discover about that is through a minute reconstruction in the manner of archaeologists and ethnologists, who find as much to interest them in heaps of rubbish as they do in tombs, and as much in culinary rituals as in great solstice festivals.

CONCLUSION

The Entropy of Cultural Changes

IF THERE IS ONE certainty that has emerged from our foray through the Greek and Roman cultures from the sixth century B.C. to the Roman Empire, it is the following: the writing-reading pair, always present, was always inadequate in itself, unable to accede to a culturally autonomous existence. Reading-writing was always put to serve some other social institution, the theater, correspondence, the education of children, political speech, religious rituals. That institution would recontextualize the written statement, frequently by integrating it into an oral practice. If our own culture recognizes "people who write," without needing to specify an object or an addressee, the "What do you do?"—"I write" exchange only makes sense because now a culturally autonomous social institution, namely literature, does exist and this legitimates literary writing, which is called into existence by literary reading. In antiquity, in contrast, you wrote something for someone specific; writing and reading did not constitute ends in themselves.[1]

Books never gave the ancients what intoxication and festivity brought them. Reading, a solitary act, brought them neither oblivion nor pleasure. What marks the break between them and us is surely the low status of fictional accounts. For us, these constitute an essential element in literary work; but in antiquity fictional accounts were merely auxiliaries to epic, tragedy, or tales. A book was like water that could do no more than slake a traveler's thirst.

Writing and Death

Ancient writing was a statement in quest of a speech act. Reading, in all its forms, including those of rewriting, ingesting knowledge, and oral recreation, was always a means of creating social symbolism through a pragmatic meaning that was in many cases quite distinct from the reading itself. That pragmatic meaning, which could only be produced in an event, furthermore often required the presence of speaking bodies. In the absence of those bodies, when reduced to a book, writing was fated to draw attention endlessly to that absence.

I refer here not only to the written texts that sheltered behind purportedly dictated fictitious words, but equally to those that were actually presented precisely as written texts. Poetic writing, or written poetic speech acts, which were never accorded any reality of their own by either the Greek or the Roman tradition, unlike in China, for instance, commandeered cultural models in which the inscription of letters onto some object was rendered necessary because of the future absence of the writer or because whoever should have pronounced the words in question orally had no voice.

Those models were the law, where the subject was the people; letter writing, in which distance rendered both the addresser and the addressee dumb and deaf; and the funerary stele, which had been commissioned by a person who was now dead. Thanks to the voice of the reader, the inscription spoke in place of the absent person. Writing that could make objects such as banquet cups speak thus served, through the medium of engraved stone, wax tablets, or painted papyri, to give speech to people who were absent or dead; it provided a voice for those without one or those who no longer possessed one.[2]

It is death par excellence that constitutes human absence, which is why writing was the best means of getting the dead to speak. That is also how it was that writing confirmed the mortality of human beings; the gods never wrote and Pythagoras, whose ambition was to become like the gods, never wrote either, any more than he ate meat, since those were two practices that integrated human beings into the temporality of death. Writings were like children in that they perpetuated their father by taking his place, which was why their father gave them his name. The successions of generations inscribed in genealogical time allowed men to escape from the biological time of animals; memory brought men closer to the gods in that it opened the gates of eternity to them, but that memory, whether entrusted to children or to writing, was still constructed upon human mortality. As with Promethean sacrifice, so it was with memory, since men ate cooked meat, which they shared with the gods—and this distinguished them from animals, which ate raw meat—yet by eating that animal flesh they ensured for themselves the physical mortality of animals.

On a funerary stele, the present tense of the inscription was the present of the reader; the writer, "he," was referred to in the third person and was situated in the past. That "he" was all that would remain forever of the writer, indefatigably repeated by passersby who were manipulated by the inscription that got them to speak. Though present in the words that were read out, he was kept at a distance by the use of that third person. It was his absence that was commemorated, his death that was repeated.

A piece of writing was thus seen as something left behind when life and the present moment had fled. By entrusting his memory to writing and, more generally, to being recorded, by taking an imprint of the event, just as the Romans preserved an imprint of the greatest of its dead in the wax of a deathmask, Western civilization set up a remarkable complicity between death and oblivion. At the center of culture it placed the dead, deathmask-books that spoke through the breath of the living.

Books, Letters, and Rumors

We have seen how close rumor and conversation were in Rome, enfolding the community in a murmur that spread from one mouth to another. However, that expanding diffusion did not spread indefinitely. As soon as the distance became too great, the thread of rumor snapped; communication through chat between neighbors (*sermo*) stopped at the end of the road and, to be relayed further afield, had to depend on letters and travelers' tales. But the epistolatory link was too loose: Ovid died on the shores of the Black Sea, deprived of the life and sociability of civilized speech and unable to give *recitationes*. He sent his works to Rome in the form of books, but books were no substitute for a living voice and his body, left mute for too long, was soon to abandon him.

Nevertheless, it certainly was by means of books and letters that Roman society under the empire sought to gain mastery over the new space over which the town ruled. Instead of simply gossiping in the dining rooms of

Roman society and telling jokes that would be found scribbled on the local house walls the following morning, men of letters published their witticisms in collections of epigrams or satirical poems that then circulated from Alexandria to Cologne and from Lyons to Gades. In similar fashion, fathers alarmed by the ever increasing proportions of global knowledge, instead of relying on the traditional institution of the family to pass on to their sons the culture that was indispensable for a life in society, produced chaotic books in which they collected together all the knowledge that they could possibly amass.

These writings, which took the place of rumor and were read in a murmur and whose style possessed the transparency of conversation, would soon fade away, as rumor itself did. New knowledge would then come to light and a new father would produce a new compilation—and all this learned chat would soon lose its freshness. Before long, nobody would remember who had produced it or what it was all about. None of these books purveying nothing but information were destined to last.

Whether operating as rumors or as tombstones, ancient books could not provide a basis for culture, but all the same it was upon books (*litterae*) that the empire depended to make Rome illustrious and to commemorate it, and to pass on a common culture to its children.[3] At a stroke, live culture thereupon disappeared, no doubt to survive in microsystems, but a culture such as that possessed no prestige.

Culture and Energy

Antiquity is not alone in having experienced this history of culture done to death by the dominant prestige of written texts. In most traditional cultures, as soon as texts formerly composed orally were fixed in writing, singers ceased to improvise and the festivities in which that improvisation has taken place disappeared. The same phenomenon can still be observed today. Whole sectors of cultural life collapse or are marginalized, surviving for a while only among shamefaced peasants, "out in the sticks."

Is it possible to press on beyond simply noting the phenomenon to an interpretation of these cultural changes on the basis of a theory on energy? When I suggested regarding the creation of theater in Athens and the replacement of epic myth by tragic myth as a phenomenon of cultural entropy,[4] I was already considering the possibility. The suggestion is based on the idea of hot cultures and cold cultures, for which, of course, there is no statistical evidence, but which nevertheless makes sense in the context of the Greek and Roman cultures.

When one compares, on the one hand, the daughters of Minyas or Apuleius's travelers "working" even as they tell their stories—in other words, not devoting their entire energies to this exchange of words—and, on the other, the symposion drinkers or the players of comissatio games, lying on their beds and throwing their entire persons into their singing, playing, and loving, it is clear that the amount of energy invested in the two different kinds of cultural activity is by no means even. The Greeks and Romans themselves conceived of love and intoxication as an inflagration, a fire that made the soul more mobile. But at the same time, the banquet was a part of leisure. It was never claimed to be an effort that tired the drinker: on the contrary, the ancients regarded it as a recreative activity in which, by dint of eating well and sharing in other pleasures, men recovered from and repaired the fatigue occasioned by political life. That may seem somewhat contradictory. More generally, the cultural activities of any society require from it a certain economic investment, which may either take the form of a supply of extra food or luxury objects, or that of time wasted and the use of servants of pleasure, or of special products such as wine. None of this expense brings in any return; it constitutes neither seed-corn nor commercial investment: once the energy of the party is exhausted, nothing will remain. Hot culture is pure waste.

"Maxwell's Demon" at the Banquet

Adopting this perspective, it may be tempting to weigh the quantity of energy expended by the group in its festivities against the energy received by each of those for whom the party was held, all of whom go home refreshed. And since the success of a party lies in the sociability that it succeeds in establishing between the participants, I would suggest that that refreshment stems from the harmony experienced within the festive microsociety. Thanks to the ritual, which functions like a machine, what the festivity does is convert economic energy into a social structure. It is the fastidious rituality that gives the festivity its maximum efficacy, since this is what allows each participant to be an actor in the cultural process and thus to find his precisely defined place in the system, to exist fully, to be irreplaceable. Theater was less ritualized than a banquet through the very fact that it left the public in the state of an undifferentiated mass, even in Athens, where the audience did participate collectively and practically both as spectators and vicariously, through the mediation of the chorus and the competition judges. On that account, it was a less effective transformer of energy than the symposion.

Now let us transpose these remarks into the framework of thermodynamics.[5] We know that thermodynamics is based on the principle according to which thermic exchanges always take place spontaneously from a hot source to a cold one, not the other way around. In other words, in a closed system, that is to say one in which there are no interventions from outside, a hotter body naturally imparts its heat to a colder one, whereas a colder body does not impart any of its heat to the hotter one. A closed, asymmetrical system such as this tends toward a state of equilibrium in which both bodies acquire the same temperature and so become undifferentiated from the point of view of their heat. This constitutes a state of maximum entropy, of thermodynamic death, since there is then no movement. To counter this paralysis, the system may open up, take in energy from outside and, by dint of activity—for instance, by means of a steam engine—it may convert that energy into a structure, reestablishing distinctions, known as dissymetries, which will impart new dynamism to the system. That activity is the work of "Maxwell's demon," the imaginary being that separates the hot from the cold in a liquid that is warm, in order to create a hot source that is distinct from the cold one and thereby provoke a flow of energy from the hot into the cold. The quantity of energy borrowed from the external world by an open system and spent by "Maxwell's demon" is always greater than the energy produced mechanically, the difference between them being accounted for by the dissipation of part of the energy, which is liberated but not recuperated: steam and smoke, the fatigue of the engine stoker, the overheating of the pistons.

Let us regard the banquet as an open system, with Dionysus playing the role of "Maxwell's demon." In other words, the rituality of the banquet makes it possible to convert the energy communicated by the wine into a social structure, through a circular flow from one participant to the next, kept endlessly going by the music, wine, and desire. A failed banquet, such as Trimalchio's, wasted all the energy invested in it. The disorder and social chaos, the lack of differentiation among the participants, and the impossibility of any reciprocal exchange except through storytelling all point to a high level of entropy in the system. The same could be said of the robbers' banquet in Apuleius.

Dissipatory Structures

I hope these somewhat disorganized remarks will suffice to justify my appeal to the model of thermodynamics, to help us think about the aspects of cultural history studied in this book. My intention is, of course, not to propose a strictly scientific new methodology, but simply to co-opt a concept from physics, already taken up by biology, namely the concept of entropy, in order to shake up a number of preconceived ideas. It is a ploy that has already been put to good use by a number of sociologists,[6] who have sought to question the overhasty assimilation of social order and equilibrium by showing, thanks to the model of entropy, that maximum social stability is a stability of chaos and corresponds to the maximum social entropy to which any human group naturally tends. To maintain itself as an organized system, a society needs to fight against entropy by means of laws, constraints, education, and culture: "Any factor that promotes social communication is by definition negentropic."[7]

Sociologists have not yet got around to establishing a hierarchy of the various negentropic social activities. I would like to suggest that those that pertain to the framework of pleasures and leisure—those that could be classed under the general heading of cultural negentropy—operate differently from the category of laws and constraints designed to maintain the social order: they introduce energy of a better quality into society, but only in particular circumstances.

To be more specific, it might well be interesting to think of the ephemeral microsocieties created by cultural activities—not only banquets of various kinds, but also *recitatio* gatherings, groups of travelers, women engaged in woolwork, a neighborhood rife with rumors, a theater public—as "dissipative structures" created temporarily by surges of energy and destined to disappear when those surges cease.[8] In those cases, the external framework was constituted by a disorganized society, such as Greece before Alexander, in which the constant wars between cities with low entropy established an amorphous equilibrium corresponding to maximum entropy.[9] The Greek world at that time was a liquid structured locally by fleeting surges, but never globally.

The effect of panhellenism was to introduce a degree of global structure and to lower the entropy of the Hellenic community. The panhellenic festivals remained dissipative structures at the heart of what was still a quite fluid Hellenic community. But political influences were beginning to insinuate themselves into the social scene. This evolution from a sociocultural order to a politicosocial one may usefully be imagined as a form of crystallization. "Liquid crystals have long-range order in some directions, but not in others; . . . there is . . . a global structure."[10] Clearly, if such a crystallization were to be total, it would be a tyrannical nightmare, as it would be composed solely of the dead, since a society necessarily implies movement—with entropy naturally increasing as one generation follows another—and it has to integrate new energies. This it manages to do by means of rites of passage. However, it is not hard to see that any attempts to structure society from a distance tend to "solidify" it, render it less fluid, and therefore make things more difficult for dissipative structures. As its numbers increase and it becomes more structured through and through, a society threatens its live cultures, by progressively paralyzing its dissipative structures. Thus, any crystallization of global structures implies death for minority cultures. Global disorder protects local order. When the Athenian aristocracy turned the symposion into a distinctive practice, a local structure created by extremely energetic impulses, what it was trying to do was resist the cultural solidification that was threatening its existence.

Dissipative structures affect all minorities, which, in order to survive culturally, have more need than others of ritual festivities that are socially closed yet open to new energies. This is certainly the case of gypsy flamenco. Such cultures need a minimum degree of fluidity in order to operate, but if they are unfortunate enough to be absorbed by the global structure and become a self-referential form of culture, they are bound to become bogged down in a more viscous system and to lose their negentropic power. That is how first the festival culture, than the culture of libraries and museums came to develop.

From Orality to Writing: A Degradation of Energy

Because it introduces dissymmetry into the description of cultural phenomena, the notion of entropy has, among other advantages, that of prompting one to reflect differently upon the switch from orality to writing, which today seems historically irreversible. All around us, today, we can see how orality is being increasingly pinned down, transcribed onto paper, wax, sensitized film, or magnetic disks and videos, to be stored in data banks. Traditionally oral cultures find themselves faced by the alternative of a surrender to writing or death: so traditional songs are transcribed and recorded. "In the long term, writing is bound to win, as our own experience shows, for it is on the side of power: not the vital, cosmic, liberating power of live speech, but the socialized, codified, dominating power of the imposed norm—the Law. In the even longer term, of course, its advantage may well be brought into question: our own contemporary experience would indeed suggest this."[11] This irresistible process may well put us in mind of the entropy of the universe. Writing, which has a high entropy, or virtually no negentropic power at all, naturally pursues oral culture, which has a low entropy and a strong negentropic power.

Writing is, so to speak, potential energy stored in a book, but energy that has been degraded into statements, captive energy like coal or petroleum. This energy is, it is true, the energy that is peculiar to language, the energy of social communication, which creates an exchange of speech, the energy that belongs to the constructive process created by the establishment of a dialogue. But if all that reading involves is a simple oralization of the words, it will not suffice to liberate that energy, for it will not create a social situation that would enable the statement to find its place as an event, integrate time, and be replaced within a real speech act. The fact is that, culturally speaking, solitary reading, the reading of a traveler in a train or a child in an attic, creates no structure at all; on the contrary, both the traveler and the child are using reading as a means of escape, of isolating themselves from their environment.

Reading needs to be integrated into a social institution that gives a statement immediacy by providing it with an appropriate speech act and thereby liberating its potential energy. These days, the theater may constitute the requisite social institution that makes it possible to recycle what has been written down in an effective manner. But we all know how much theatrical productions cost.

The Future Belongs to the Recycling of Written Texts within a Framework of Festivity

This book has examined a handful of social institutions of that kind in antiquity: the citations of the comissatio, the *recitatio*, the priest's *praeitio*, the *interpretatio*, and the translation through reading. The most effective from the point of entropy was what one might call the oral recycling of writing, as practiced by a reader of Apuleius, who at the same time himself became a storyteller. For what he did was reconstruct the dissipative structure of an oral composition. He restored a low entropy to the degraded energy that had been stored away in writing. However, that recycling was effected through cultural speech that retained a high entropy, since it was the speech of ordinary conversation (*sermo*), which possessed no more than a weak structuring power. Even more effective was recycling through *lusus*, the wordplay of the comissatio, using Greek poetry translated by writing and recontextualized in the banquet where it was recited.

The written traces of an oral performance may be regarded as residue from an event, preserved in the hope that the potential energy that they contain, although degraded, like that of the coals of an extinguished fire, may still come in useful. Such detritus consists of the intrinsic sense or what I have called the semantic meaning of the statement. In the case of myth, this would be the narrative fiction. The level of that potential energy depends on the extent to which the text is narrative or informative, which corresponds to the degree of energy liberated in the course of the oral performance: a story is less negentropic than Homeric epic, which, itself, is less negentropic than a banquet song. In contrast, the imitation of one written text by another written text, in the Alexandrian manner, liberates no energy at all; on the contrary, with each new rewriting, entropy increases. Conversely, statements that are unreadable, such as the song for Cleobulus and the word games of Catullus, a reading of which, of whatever kind, liberates no energy at all since they need to be totally recomposed, show us that, ideally at least, a symposion left no detritus, lost not an iota of the energy that it liberated: all the linguistic energy invested in the event was converted into structure; Dionysus truly was "Maxwell's demon."

When Paul Zumthor, hazarding a prediction, declared that the advantage of writing might well come to be brought into question, this was no millenarian wishful thinking, the hope of a return to the splendor of our oral beginnings. Rather it was prompted by a concrete observation of the comeback being made by a culture of events. I have mentioned the importance of the "remake" in American cinema, the success of marathon spectacles and huge concerts only given on one occasion, such as the performances of Jean-Michel Jarre. In parallel to these, however, this age of ours is frenetically engaged in setting up archives of the traces left by these happenings. Both phenomena reflect the angst felt in the face of the growth of cultural and social entropy and the chaos of urban indifferentiation.

Surely the future belongs to a recycling of written texts, their conversion into live energy. Just as Rome "recycled" the cultural monuments bequeathed by the Alexandrian culture through an interplay of translation and theater, our own postmodern culture might, similarly, take over all the "masterpieces of literature," as is being done today in francophone Africa, and reinvest them in music, dance, rap. . . .

APPENDIX

Some Curious Documents

Here are a number of translations of the song for Cleobulus (fragment 2 [357]), some into French, some into English, which reflect various tendencies of literary history. Except for the version by David Mulroy, not one of them respects the Greek cultural and religious context. The most curious of all is surely that by Marguerite Yourcenar. I have indicated in italics what appear to me to be the most glaring betrayals.

Yves Battistini, *Lyra erotica*, Imprimerie nationale (Paris, 1992), 245

> Seigneur, puisqu'avec toi Eros le séducteur
> et les nymphes aux yeux *indigo*
> et l'Aphrodite de *pourpre*
> ont leurs ébats, toi qui hantes
> aussi les hautes cimes des montagnes
> *je te supplie à genoux*, et toi, viens à moi
> d'une âme bienveillante pour entendre
> ta prière et qu'elle plaise à ton coeur:
> de Cléobule fais-toi bon
> conseiller, que mon amour
> ô Dionysos, par lui soit accuelli.

The change in the position of the knees is odd: a Greek suppliant never fell to his knees as a praying Christian would. Instead, he clasped the knees, or the chin, or the altar, of the god whom he was addressing. As a consequence of this change, the wine cup has disappeared. The same substitution occurs in the translations by Mario Meunier and J. M. Edmonds. Furthermore, this translator shows no discrimination where colors are concerned but liberally spatters his text with purple and indigo.

Marguerite Yourcenar, *La couronne et la lyre* (Paris: Gallimard, 1979)

PRIERE A DIONYSOS

Dieu dansant *au fond des forêts*
Avec les Nymphes *aux bras frais*
Avec Cypris *au coeur tendre,*
Dieu qui bois le moût à longs traits,
Dieu séducteur, daigne m'entendre!
Mon souhait est de ceux qu'un amant peut former:
Fais que mon Cléobule, enfin, se laisse aimer.

The original Greek has been virtually rewritten so that, without the reference, one would be forgiven for wondering if this really was supposed to be the song for Cleobulus. The addition of "enfin" in the last line puts this prayer into the context of the romantic and narrative temporality of a love story in which the young Cleobulus has up until this point been resisting the singer's advances. The translation thus removes the song from ritual time and situates it in an imaginary biographical time. The translator is apparently ignorant of the fact that *le moût* is the juice of squashed grapes that is as yet unfermented. What could this *moût*, which for Athenians would be quite undrinkable, be doing in a banquet? One also wonders why the translator has replaced the god of wild mountains by a drinking god, thereby destroying the religious meaning of the prayer. As for the cool arms (*bras frais*) of the Nymphs and the tender heart (*coeur tendre*) of Cypris, I will leave the reader to muse on the lady's erotic imagination.

The substitution of a moralizing interpretation of the "fine song" for its ritual efficacy is typical of a general tendency to smother original texts in a coating of humanistic moralizing, felt to be more universal.

Mario Meunier, *Sappho, Anacréon et Anacréontiques* (Paris, 1941)

> O roi, avec qui Eros vainqueur, —
> les Nymphes *aux yeaux bleus*—et
> la brillante Aphrodite, —se plaisent
> à jouer!—Détourne-toi—des hauts
> sommets des monts, —*je t'en prie à*
> *genoux!*—Sois-moi propice, viens
> avec nous, —et favorablement—
> écoute ma prière. —Sois pour Cléobule
> —un sage conseiller, —et fais,
> Dionysos, —qu'il agrée mon amour!

Again, Christian knees instead of Greek ones! The English translations are no less fantastical.

C. M. Bowra, *Greek Lyric Poetry* (Oxford: Oxford University Press, 1961), 283

> Master, with whom Love the subduer and the *blue-eyed* Nymphs and *rosy* Aphrodite play, who hauntest the high peaks of mountains, I beseech thee. Come to us with kindly heart, and let our prayer please thee and hearken to it. Be a good counsellor to Cleobulus and may he, O Dionysos, receive my love.

J. M. Edmonds, *Lyra Graeca*, Loeb Classical Library (London: Heinemann, 1979), 138

> O Lord with whom played Love the subduer and the dark-eyed Nymphs and *rosy* Aphrodite as thou wanderest the tops of the lofty hills, to thee I *kneel*; do thou come unto me kind and lending ear unto a prayer *that is acceptable*, and give Cleobulus good counsel, O Dionysus, to receive my love.

David Mulroy's translation, on the other hand, betrays none of the cultural data implicit in the statement. It is far and away the best.

David Mulroy, *Early Greek Poetry* (Ann Arbor: University of Michigan Press, 1992), 128

Lord who revels
on mountaintops
with conquering Eros
dark-eyed Nymphs
and blushing Aphrodite
I clasp your knee
Be kind, hear
and accept my prayer:
Counsel Cleobulus
well; make him
welcome my love
O Dionysus.

NOTES

Introduction: Toward Another Use of Antiquity

1. *Homère et Dallas. Introduction à une critique anthropologique* (Paris: Hachette, 1991).

2. The expression was suggested by the Mauss group, and the idea has been developed by Alain Caillé, *Critique de la raison utilitaire* (Paris: La Découverte, 1989).

3. Eric A. Havelock, *Origins of Western Literacy* (Toronto: OISE Press, 1976). Despite the undeniable interest of this book, the author continues to regard alphabetic writing as a memorization technique that replaced oral memory.

4. See in Anne-Marie Christin, ed., *Ecritures II* (Paris: Le Sycomore, 1985), the articles by Dominique Charpin, Jean-Marie Durand, and Pascal Vernus; cf. also the introduction in Marcel Detienne, ed., *Les savoirs de l'écriture en Grèce ancienne* (Lille: Presses universitaires de Lille, 1988).

5. Jack Goody, *The Logic of Writing and the Organization of Society* (Cambridge: Cambridge University Press, 1986).

6. Gregory Nagy, *The Best of the Achaeans* (Baltimore: Johns Hopkins University Press, 1979).

7. Plato, *Phaedrus*, 275ff., and the commentary on it in Jacques Derrida, *Dissemination*, trans. Barbara Johnson (London: Athlone Press, 1981).

8. P. M. Fraser, *Ptolemaic Alexandria*, 3 vols. (Oxford: Oxford University Press, 1972), 1:314.

9. Claude Calame, *Le récit en Grèce ancienne* (Paris: Klincksieck, 1986), and Havelock, *Western Literacy*, 13.

10. Marcel Detienne ("L'espace de la publicité") and Giorgio Camassa, in Detienne, *Les savoirs de l'écriture en Grèce ancienne*, 29–81 and 130–55, respectively.

11. On the representation of reading in ancient Greece, see the key work by Jesper Svenbro, *Phrasikleia: An Anthropology of Reading in Ancient Greece*, trans. Janet Lloyd (Ithaca, N.Y.: Cornell University Press, 1993).

12. Seneca, *De brevitate vitae,* 8.3.

13. Dominique Charpin, "L'appropriation de l'oral," in Danielle Hébrard and Annie Prassolhoft, eds., *Cahiers textuels* (Paris: Université de Paris-VII, 1990), 58.

14. Michel Charles, *La rhétorique de la lecture* (Paris: Le Seuil, 1977).

15. Ibid., 79.

16. Ibid., 9, 61.

17. Ibid., 61.

18. Ibid., 62.

19. The essential conceptual references are Svenbro, *Phrasikleia;* Nagy, *The Best of the Achaeans,* and *Pindar's Homer: The Lyric Possession of an Epic Past* (Baltimore: Johns Hopkins University Press, 1990); Paul Zumthor, *Introduction à la poésie orale* (Paris, 1983), and *La poésie de la voix dans la civilisation médiévale* (Paris, 1984); Dominique Maingueneau, *Pragmatique pour le discours littéraire* (Paris: Bordas, 1990); François Recanati, *Les enoncés performatifs* (Paris: Ed. de Minuit, 1981); Calame, *Le récit en Grèce ancienne;* Bernard Cerquiglini, *Eloge de la variante* (Paris: Le Seuil, 1989); Goody, *The Logic of Writing and the Organization of Society;* John Schied and Jesper Svenbro, *Le métier de Zeus. Mythe du tissu et du tissage dans le monde gréco-romain* (Paris: La Découverte, 1994); and last but not least, endless conversations with Jean-Louis Durand, both a Greek and an African scholar, and a dissector of orality as it is practiced today.

20. Pietro Pucci, *Odysseus Poloutropos: Intertextual Reading in the Odyssey and the Iliad* (Ithaca, N.Y.: Cornell University Press, 1987).

21. Cerquiglini, *Eloge de la variante,* 19, 91.

22. The expression is used by Cerquiglini (ibid.).

Part I. The Culture of Intoxication

1. For a recent example of a "romantic" interpretation of the poetry of Anacreon, in which the author declares that he sings out of amorous frustration, converting his failures as an aging lover into works of art in which he expresses "his personal vision of love," see Patricia Rosenmeyer, *The Poetics of Imitation: Anacreon and the Anacreontic Tradition* (Cambridge: Cambridge University Press, 1992), 44.

2. The expression served as a title for a round table conference at the Beaubourg center (22 April 1986), the proceedings of which were published by the University of Paris–VII, under the direction of Danielle Hébrard and Annie Prassoloff in *Cahiers textuels* (1990).

3. The best book in French on the symposion is François Lissarague's *Un flot d'images. Une esthétique du banquet grec* (Paris: Adam Birò, 1987). The whole of the present chapter is directly inspired by it. For a historical view, see Pauline Schmitt-Pantel, *La cité au banquet* (Rome: CEFR 51, 1992). See also the collective work edited

by O. Murray, *Sympotica: A Symposion on the Symposion* (Oxford: Clarendon Press, 1990).

4. Athenian banquet song, anonymous, preserved by Athenaeus, 15.695d, no. 19, and translated into French by Lissarague, *Un flot d'images*, 11.

5. Valeria Ando, "Vin et *mania*," in B. Fournier and S. d'Onofrio, eds., *Le ferment divin* (Paris: Maison des sciences de l'homme, 1991), 167–79.

6. J.-P. Vernant, "The Society of the Gods," in *Myth and Society in Ancient Greece*, trans. Janet Lloyd (New York: Zone Books, 1988), 101–19.

7. Eros is the god who gives boys erections, a straight and turgescent *phallos* being one of the manifestations of this god; cf. Marcel Detienne, *Dionysos à ciel ouvert* (Paris: Hachette, 1986), 89f.

8. Solon, frag. 20, ed. Diehl, cited by Plutarch, *Septem sapientium convivium*, 155F.

Chapter 1. The Song for Cleobulus

1. Frag. 2.

2. 2.62. Dio Chryostom was a rhetor of the late first century.

3. Translator's note: the English translation is based directly on the author's French translation from the original Greek.

4. Patricia Rosenmeyer, *The Poetics of Imitation: Anacreon and the Anacreontic Tradition* (Cambridge: Cambridge University Press, 1992), 43.

5. François Lissarague, *Un flot d'images. Un esthétique du banquet grec* (Paris: Adam Birò, 1987), 27, 37. Faced with a fragment of a drinking cup on which a picture of a Satyr is recognizable, for example, the iconologist compares it with other pictures featuring Satyrs. He works on a series of "vases with Satyrs" and defines a semantics of Satyrs in the symposion, on the basis of which he can then interpret every new image featuring a Satyr. This is the method followed by the iconologists of the Centre Louis-Gernet (J.-L. Durand, F. Frontisi-Ducroux, F. Lissarague, A. Schnapp).

6. The proposis has been studied by Giuseppe Giangrande in "Sympotic Literature," in *Epigramme grecque, Entretiens de la fondation Hardt* 14 (1967): 121, 147f.

7. Athenaeus, 11.498, and *Schol. Pindar Olympians*, 7.5.

8. Lissarague, *Un flot d'images*, 58 and fig. 41.

9. Anacreon, frag. 76.

10. Dionysus Calchus, cited by Athenaeus, 15.669e.

11. Anacreon, 78.

12. Meleager, *Palatine Anthology*, 5.137.

13. *Anacreonteia*, frags. 450 and 60.32–33.

14. Later, we shall see how speech articulated in singing is like water in wine; it

tames the song but, on its own is like water that is drunk with no intoxication, cf. below, pp. 184–85.

15. Pindar, *Olympian Odes*, 7.1–10, trans. John Sandys (adapted), in *The Odes of Pindar*, Loeb Classical Library (Cambridge, Mass.: Harvard University Press, 1946).

16. Pauline Schmitt-Pantel, *La cité au banquet* (Rome: CEFR 51, 1992), 23.

17. Marcel Detienne, in *Dictionnaire des mythologies* (Paris: Flammarion, 1981), 2:65, 70.

18. Thus, J. M. Edmonds, the editor of *Lyra Graeca*, vol. 2, Loeb Classical Library (Cambridge, Mass.: Harvard University Press, 1979), translates *porphyrē* as "rosy," as indeed does C. M. Bowra. On these literary misunderstandings, see the appendix to the present work. As is well known, Greek does not really have any terms for colors, it simply registers luminosity: *kyanos* designates whatever is somber or gray, such as death, or underwater caves, for example, while *porphyrē* qualifies whatever shines in the sun, such as snow, the sea, rich purple cloth.

19. Cf. Simon Goldhill, "The Dance of the Veils: Reading Five Fragments of Anacreon," *Eranos* 85 (1987): 14.

20. Lissarague, *Un flot d'images*, 120, 128–30, and Athenaeus, 15.694a–696a.

21. Cf. below, pp. 84f.

22. On the song as a sacrificial offering, cf. Pindar, *Olympians* 5.1–6, in which the poet offers his ode to the goddess Camarina.

23. For example, Lissarague, *Un flot d'images*, 58, fig. 41, with commentary on p. 59. I am following the methodological conclusions of the iconologists of the Centre Louis Gernet.

24. "A statement is called performative if it simultaneously satisfies two conditions: 1. interpreted literally, it describes the present action of the speaker; 2. the specific function of its speech act is to perform that action"; Oswald Ducrot, *Dire et ne pas dire* (Paris: Hermann, 1972), 69.

25. François Recanati, *Les enoncés performatifs* (Paris: Ed. de Minuit, 1981), 87.

26. The altar is the place-cum-instrument of sacrifice, the spot where men and gods meet, when meeting in the context of sacrifice; cf. M. Detienne and J.-P. Vernant, eds., *La cuisine du sacrifice en pays grec* (Paris: Gallimard, 1979). When the relationship between man and god takes the form of a possession, there is no altar, so the receptacle for the god, in this case the cup, takes its place.

27. Possibly, the use of the verb *gounoumai*, instead of the more common *iketeuō*, is a way to get the text to make the gesture of supplication more explicit. Furthermore, the term *gonu* 'knee' might be one of the terms of human anatomy that were used to name various parts of a vase; cf. Lissarague, *Un flot d'images*, 56 and 57, fig. 38.

28. Such a hypothesis is put forward by J. M. Edmonds in the Loeb *Lyra Graeca*, 2:139, n. 2, which mentions a possible "letter to Cleobulus." Many commentators

take the prayer to Dionysus to be merely a poetic figure of speech, a "manipulation" of the reader (*sic*), a flirtatious ploy, a way of indirectly addressing the boy.

29. Those are the interpretations most commonly suggested; cf. Rosenmeyer, *The Poetics of Imitation*; David Mulroy, *Early Greek Lyric Poetry* (Ann Arbor: University of Michigan Press, 1992); Giangrande, "Symptotic Literature," 114; Simon Goldhill, "The Dance of the Veils," 11ff.

30. Lissarague, *Un flot d'images*, 59f. On objects that speak: Jesper Svenbro, *Phrasikleia: An Anthropology of Reading in Ancient Greece*, trans. Janet Lloyd (Ithaca, N.Y.: Cornell University Press, 1993), 26ff.

31. F. Lissarague, "Paroles d'images," in Anne-Marie Christin, ed., *Ecritures II* (Paris: Le Sycomore, 1985), 71–89.

32. Ibid., 85.

33. Lissarague, *Un flot d'images*, 129.

34. In default of making that journey, read, on the phenomenology of flamenco, Frédéric Deval, *Le flamenco et ses valeurs* (Arles: Aubier, 1989); for a history of flamenco together with a collection of the texts of the songs, see Danielle Dumas, *Coplas flamencas* (Paris: Aubier-Montaigne, 1973).

35. Deval, *Le flamenco*, 62.

36. Ibid., 9.

37. Ibid., 14.

38. Ibid., 16.

39. Cf. below, p. 77.

40. Deval, *Le flamenco*, 30f.

41. Dumas, *Coplas flamencas*, 62f.

42. Ibid., 195.

Chapter 2. The Invention of Anacreon

1. Gregory Nagy, *Pindar's Homer: The Lyric Possession of an Epic Past* (Baltimore: Johns Hopkins University Press, 1990). This entire chapter is based on Nagy's book, from which it borrows the historical information and, essentially, the analyses, on occasion carrying them further to suit my present theme. References to individual pages would have been so numerous that I am citing Nagy's work at this point, once and for all, in acknowledgment of my debt.

2. Pauline Schmitt-Pantel, *La cité au banquet* (Rome: CEFR 51, 1992), 46f.

3. J.-P. Vernant and P. Vidal-Naquet, *Myth and Tragedy in Ancient Greece*, trans. Janet Lloyd (New York: Zone Books, 1988), 23–28.

4. On writing as a representation of speech, see above p. 00, and François Lissarague, *Un flot d'images. Un esthétique du banquet grec* (Paris: Adam Birò, 1987), 129.

5. On this point, see the various works of Annie Belis.

6. Introduction to the edition of Archilocus by A. Bonnard and F. Laserre (Paris: Belles Lettres, 1958), lxii f.; and P. M. Fraser, *Ptolemaic Alexandria*, 3 vols. (Oxford: Oxford University Press, 1972), 1:313.

7. Jesper Svenbro, "La cigale et les fourmis. Voix et écriture dans une allégorie grecque," *Opuscula Romana* 7 (1970): 7–21.

8. Jesper Svenbro, *Phrasikleia: An Anthropology of Reading in Ancient Greece*, trans. Janet Lloyd (Ithaca, N.Y.: Cornell University Press, 1993), 12–15.

9. Bernard Cerquiglini, *Eloge de la variante* (Paris: Le Seuil, 1989), has shown that the medieval poems were "variations," and that the variants from one manuscript to another resulted neither from a mistake on the part of the copyist nor from an alteration made by a singer.

10. *Palatine Anthology*, 7.28.

11. All the ancient texts, both Greek and Latin, on the life of Anacreon have been collected in the Loeb Classical Library's *Lyra Graeca*, ed. J. M. Edmonds (Cambridge, Mass.: Harvard University Press, [1924] 1979), 2:121–36.

12. *Suda*, s.v. Anacreon.

13. Maximus of Tyr, 37.5.

14. Aelian, 9.5.

15. Plato, *Hipparchus*, 228b.

16. *Schol. Prometheus Bound*, 128.

17. Pausanias, 1.25.1.

18. Maximus of Tyr, 21.7, trans. Edmonds, *Lyra Graeca*, vol. 2, Loeb Classical Library (Cambridge, Mass.: Harvard University Press, 1924) (adapted).

19. François Frontisi and François Lissarague, "De l'ambiguité à l'ambivalence: Un parcours dionysiaque," *AION* (1983): 11–32; I am summarizing the analyses of these two iconologists.

20. Also known as the *barbiton*, commonly used in Dionysiac banquets; cf. Annie Belis, "Les instruments de la Grèce antique," *Dossiers d'archéologie* 142 (1989): 41–47.

21. Ibid., 32.

22. Anacreon, frag. 124.

23. *Palatine Anthology*, 7.31.2.

24. Cf. below, pp. 95f.

25. Aulus Gellius, 19.9.

26. François Lissarague, "Le vin des satyres," in *Le vin des historiens*, symposium on Vin et Histoire, 1989 (Suze-la-Rousse, 1990).

27. *Iliad*, 18.485.

28. Bergk, *Fragments lyriques* (Teubner: Leipzig, 1882), 3:298, no. 3, and *Lyra Graeca*, vol. 2.

29. On this Roman banquet, see below, pp. 104f.

30. Nagy, *Pindar's Homer,* 384f.

31. For that, see ibid., and Vernant and Vidal-Naquet, *Myth and Tragedy in Ancient Greece,* 23–48, and Henri Jeanmaire, *Dionysos. Histoire du culte de Bacchus,* 5th ed. (Paris: Payot, [1951] 1991), 36f.

32. E. R. Dodds, *The Greeks and the Irrational* (Berkeley: University of California Press, 1951).

33. J.-P. Vernant, "Le Dionysos masqué des *Bacchantes* d'Euripide," *L'Homme* 93 (1985): 39–42, and Françoise Frontisi-Ducroux, *Le dieu-masqué. Une figure de Dionysos d'Athenes* (Paris: La Découverte-EFR, 1991), 225f.

34. Frontisi-Ducroux, *Le dieu-masqué,* shows that Dionysus, the masked god, is an Athenian invention.

35. Jeanmaire, *Dionysos. Histoire du culte de Bacchus,* 220–49.

36. Charles Segal, "Vérité, tragédie et écriture," in Marcel Detienne, ed., *Les savoirs de l'écriture en Grèce ancienne* (Lille: Presses universitaires de Lille, 1988), 330–58, and Diego Lanza, "Le comédien face à l'écrit," in ibid., 359–86.

37. Aeschylus, *Choephori*; Sophocles, *Electra*; Euripides, *Electra.*

38. Cf. Introduction, pp. 14–15.

39. I shall be developing this hypothesis, in more general terms, in the Conclusion and all the bibliographical references will be given there.

40. Nagy, *Pindar's Homer,* 107, 384–413, on the aristocratic resistance to the theatrocracy and its consequences.

41. Athenaeus, 15.694a–696a.

42. Ibid., 13.1, 24, 16, 19.

43. Lissarague, *Un flot d'images,* 129f.

44. Ibid., 131, figs. 105, 106.

45. Frédéric Deval, *Le flamenco et ses valeurs* (Arles: Aubier, 1989), 18f.; and Antonio Mairena, *Mundo y formas del cante flamenco* (Granada, 1979); and Danielle Dumas, *Coplas flamencas* (Paris: Aubier-Montaigne, 1973), 199.

46. Plato, *Ion,* 534a–534d.

47. See Nagy, *Pindar's Homer,* 51, 91–101, on the precise meaning of these two terms.

48. *Ion,* 534a–b.

49. On *Ion* and the rhapsode as a reader, cf. Michel Charles, *La rhétorique de la lecture* (Paris: Le Seuil, 1977), 74f.

50. Aristotle, *Poetics,* 1447a8–47b28. All the quotations and their translation come from the Loeb Classical Library's edition, translated by W. Hamilton Fyfe (Cambridge, Mass.: Harvard University Press, 1946). However, the term *mimēsis* is rendered by "representation," which is preferable to "imitation," since the Aristotelian concept of *mimēsis* is certainly at the origin of the ideology of representation.

51. My reading of Aristotle owes much to the exhaustive book of Jacqueline Lichtenstein, *La couleur éloquente* (Paris: Flammarion, 1989), in particular 55–82.

52. Aristotle, *Poetics*, 1450b15. The same point is made at 1453b1–7.

53. Ibid., 1462a4f.

54. Ibid., 1462a12.

55. Ibid., 1451b27–33.

56. Ibid., 1456a25–26.

57. Aristotle, *Rhetoric*, 3.1.1–3.

58. On the Museum and the library of Alexandria, cf. Fraser, *Ptolemaic Alexandria*; Luciano Canfora, *La véritable histoire de la bibliothèque d'Alexandrie* (Paris: Desjonquières, 1986); *Autrement*, "Mémoires" series, no. 19 (November 1992): "Alexandrie, IIIe siècle av. J.C.," and *Autrement*, "Mutations" series, no. 121 (April 1991): "La bibliothèque"; Marc Baratin and Christian Jacob, eds., *Alexandrie ou la mémoire du savoir* (Paris: Bibliothèque de France, forthcoming).

59. He was tyrant of Athens from 317 to 307 B.C.

60. On Greek Hellenistic culture and its diffusion in the Greek and Roman worlds through education, cf. Jean Sirinelli, *Les enfants d'Alexandre* (Paris: Fayard, 1993).

61. Michèle Blanchard and Alain Blanchard, "La mosaïque d'Anacréon à Autun," *REA* 75 (1973): 268–79.

Part II. The Culture of the Kiss

1. Armelle Rahje, "Le banquet homérique en Italie centrale à la période orientalisante," in Oswyn Murray, ed., *Sympotica: A Symposion on the Symposion* (Oxford: Clarendon Press, 1990), 279f.

2. Pierre Flobert, "Le témoignage de la langue latine sur la vigne et le vin dans l'Italie antique," in *Actes du congrès de l'Association Guillaume Budé, Bordeaux 1988* (Paris: Belles Lettres, 1989), 447–49.

3. Michel de Certeau, *L'invention du quotidien, I. Arts de faire* (Paris: Gallimard, Folio, 1990).

4. For a discussion of this point, see Pauline Schmitt-Pantel, *La cité au banquet* (Rome: CEFR 51, 1992). In this prudent and meticulous work, the author shows how dangerous it is to generalize about any of the forms taken by banquets (p. 37: "There were as many kinds of banquets as there were cities") in Greece, and she in particular opposes the thesis of O. Murray according to which the symposion was a common model, by pointing out, irrefutably, that there could be no symposion without Dionysus.

5. This is again the view of O. Murray, "Symposion and Genre in the Poetry of Horace," *JRS* (1985): 39–50.

6. It is totally misleading, of course, even though the term does indeed come from the Latin root meaning to cut up, or share that is to be found in *caro, carnis* 'slice of meat': cf. John Scheid, "Les Romains au partage," *Studi storici* 4 (1985): 945f.

7. For a fuller analysis of the presence of the bard and the Muses in a Homeric *dais*, see Florence Dupont, *Homère et Dallas. Introduction à une critique anthropologique* (Paris: Hachette, 1992).

8. Aulus Gellius, *Attic Nights*, 19.9.

9. That is the method adopted by Georges Dumézil in *Fêtes romaines d'été et automne* (Paris: Gallimard, 1975); on wine and Jupiter, cf. 83–98.

10. Pliny the Elder, *Natural History*, 14.88, 119.

11. This prohibition has been the subject of a number of interpretations. The one presented here reflects the view of Olivier de Cazanove, *RHR*, no. 8 (1988): 413f., and "*Exesto*, l'incapacité sacrificielle des femmes," *Phénix* 41 (1987): 159f.

12. Varro, *RR*, 75; Pliny the Elder, *Natural History*, 14.55, 23.40.

13. Pliny, *Natural History*, 14.58. The remark was made to Alexander.

Chapter 3. The Games of Catullus

1. This poem has given rise to as many commentaries as the song for Cleobulus. I will cite only Charles Segal, "Catullian *otiosi*: The Lover and the Poet," *Greece and Rome* 17 (1970): 25–31; and Luciano Landolfi, "Il *lusus* simposiale di Catullo e Calvo improvvisazione conviviale neoterica," *Quaderni Urbinati di cultura classica* 53 (1986): 77–89.

2. We know that this Caius Licinius Macer Calvus was, as his name suggests, from an old Roman family and that he was a distinguished orator. He wrote an elegy on the death of his wife Quintilia—possibly a funerary epigram (Propertius, 2.34.89–90)—and on that occasion Catullus dedicated a poem of consolation to him (Catullus, 96).

3. On the poet of the banquet and the orator, cf. Catullus's epigram dedicated to Cicero: Catullus, 49.

4. On orators finding relaxation in light poetry, cf. for example Pliny the Younger, *Letters*, 7.9.12.

5. On this playful world of improvised poetry and on the many values of poetic *lusus*, cf. Catullus, 58.17, 156; 61.132, 210, 211, 232. Pliny the Younger, *Letters*, 7.9.9–10, defines *carmina* that distract one from one's cares as *lusus*. As for a *delicatus*, he is described as *quasi lusui dicatus*, Festus (Paul), 61.12, ed. Lindsay. These word games took the form of *uersiculi*, short, light verses. The vocabulary is circular: games, pleasures, love affairs, and love poems all imply one another.

6. It seems that this way of improvising *uersiculi* in a banquet, writing on a

tablet, then reading them out to those present, was a current practice in Rome; cf. Petronius, *Satyricon*, 55.

7. Virgil, *Eclogues*, 3.80–89. It is known that the *Eclogues* were pure fictions, written for Roman intellectuals and modeled on the *Eclogues* of Theocritus, another working writer. The characters are operetta shepherds and the spectacle of their supposed virtuosity is without interest as normally the contest is one of improvisation, whereas in the *Eclogues* the text is written in advance. The sole raison d'être of the *Eclogues* was to present examples of improvisations within the framework of twinned songs: in other words to constitute a technical instruction book. On the *Eclogues* in the theater, cf. below, p. 242.

8. Landolfi, "Il lusus," 86.

9. Cicero, *De oratore*, 2.191.

10. The imaginary society of Roman comedy attributed this "charm" to young people as a characteristic of their age group, which thinks only of the pleasures of banqueting and love. All those who wish to be accepted in their group have to become *lepidi*, even old men, as is shown, for example, by the character of Periplectomenus in Plautus's *Miles Gloriosus*.

11. We are dealing here with a civilization in which eroticism between men is interpretable in not sexual but juridical terms. Anything was permissible to a free man on condition that the body in question was that of a slave. On the other hand, the bodies of free individuals, boys, girls, men, and women (apart from one's wife) were all protected by strict laws. There was therefore no censure, as we know it, directed against homosexual desire, only against its fulfillment: it was a situation that allowed for all kinds of flirtations and embraces of a tender and physical nature between free men.

12. François Lissarague, "Paroles d'images," in Anne-Marie Christin, ed., *Ecritures II*, (Paris: Le Sycomore, 1985), 71–89.

13. On the interpretation of epigrams, cf. Jesper Svenbro, *Phrasikleia: An Anthropology of Reading in Ancient Greece*, trans. Janet Lloyd (Ithaca, N.Y.: Cornell University Press, 1993), 26–43; on revengeful graffiti in Rome, cf. Paul Veyne, *La société romaine* (Paris: Le Seuil, 1991), chap. 2 (1983), 57–86; on the aesthetics of the epigram, cf. Pierre Laurens, *L'abeille dans l'ambre* (Paris: Belles Lettres, 1989).

14. Catullus, 17.1–3. The Latin text is uncertain.

15. Ibid., 47.4. The god Priapus is represented with an enormous phallus, which, to the Athenians, made him a monster of great ugliness. Here, that ugliness is increased by the circumcision, which, in Rome, was regarded as a mutilation that inhibited any loving relationship.

16. Ibid., 37.10. A number of graffiti recovered from Pompei are to be found in Philippe Moreau, *Sur les murs de Pompei. Choix d'inscriptions latines* (Paris: Le Promeneur, 1993).

17. Cf. above, p. 54.

18. The text is cited in Svenbro [1990], who also provides a commentary, and has been reproduced in the *Palatine Anthology*, 7.213.

19. Catullus, 1.1, 8.2.

20. Ibid., 14b. Books did have some *lectores*, that is to say, as E. Valette-Cagnac has shown, in *La lecture à Rome*, EPHE thesis, 5th section (Paris, 1994); they would be read not in public readings but by individual readers, as if these were the sole addressees.

Chapter 4. Kisses in the Greek Manner and Roman Cuisine

1. Aulus Gellius, *Attic Nights*, 19.11. The attribution is disputed (cf. K. J. Dover, *Greek Homosexuality* [London, 1978], who shows that this couplet was certainly considered to represent "Platonic" pederastic love). Apuleius, *Apologia*, 10–12, shows that in the second century, Plato was regarded as the official patron of the love of boys that found expression in comissatio games.

2. I shall not venture into the question of the Greek interpretation of this distich which may, of course, have a philosophical meaning in the Platonic doctrine and also an anthropological one, but shall limit myself here to its Roman exegesis.

3. On this question of Roman translations of Greek texts that provided references to cultural practices, cf. also below, pp. 220f.

4. On Latin terms for "kiss," cf. Philippe Moreau, "Osculum, basium, sauium," *Revue de philologie* 52 (1978): 87–97.

5. But in many circumstances it was not erotic at all: in the context of family or friendly relationships, or when it sealed a peace treaty.

6. The use of the verb *duco* with the meaning "to absorb" is limited to air and to fine wines. Cf. Cicero, *De natura deorum*, 2.18, 136, and Horace, 1.17.22, and 4.12.14.

7. *Labia*, *labra*, and the diminutive *labella* are all formed from the same root as the verb *lambo* 'to lick' or 'to lap'.

8. Cf. above, pp. 109–10.

9. Seneca, *Letters*, 10.83.16.

10. Poem by Quintus Lutatius Catulus, cited by Aulus Gellius, *Attic Nights*, 19.11.

11. Jesper Svenbro, *Phrasikleia: An Anthropology of Reading in Ancient Greece*, trans. Janet Lloyd (Ithaca, N.Y.: Cornell University Press, 1993), 187f.

12. Achilles Tatius (an author of the second century A.D.), *Leucippe and Clitophon*, 2.37. The translation is based directly on the French translation by P. Grimal, *Les romans grecs et latins* (Paris: Gallimard, La Pléiade, 1963). This novel, written in

Greek in the second century by an Alexandrian, at this point presents the words of a defender of the pederastic *eros*, having previously allowed a defender of feminine eroticism to speak.

13. Seneca, *Letters*, 83.19–20.

14. For example, Marcel Detienne, *The Gardens of Adonis: Spices in Greek Mythology*, trans. Janet Lloyd (Princeton: Princeton University Press, 1994).

15. Catullus, 5: "Da mi basia mille . . . ," and 7.

16. Petronius, *Satyricon*, 127. The expression is somewhat unclear. If *robur* is the hard heart of oak, *uoluptatem robustam* should really mean "the heart of pleasure." The English translation used is that by Michael Heseltine, in the Loeb Classical Library series (Cambridge, Mass.: Harvard University Press, 1979).

17. Petronius, *Satyricon*, 129.

18. Ibid., 79.

19. Ibid., 11.

20. Ibid., 132.

21. Petronius, frag. 54. The question of the attribution is not important here.

22. This is the adjective earlier used by Circe of those who wish to copulate in earnest.

23. In *The Satyricon* in particular there are comic scenes in which the characters have to strain hard to achieve an orgasm; cf., for example, chaps. 23 and 140.

24. Achilles Tatius, *Leucippe and Clitophon*, 2.37.

25. Cf. above, "The Blood of the Earth," p. 109.

26. Petronius, *Satyricon*, 128.

27. Cf. also Catullus, 69.

28. Ibid., 97.

29. Ibid., 99.7–10.

30. Ibid., 33.

31. Ibid., 39. The inhabitants of Spain, a Roman province, were known as Celtiberians.

32. Ibid., 80.

33. Ibid., 16. His words echo priapic inscriptions used to threaten the plunderers of gardens. Priapus was opposed to Eros in the sexual domain, as he was a god without enjoyment.

34. An idea also to be found in Martial, Ovid, and Pliny the Younger.

35. C. Lévi-Strauss, "Le triangle culinaire," *L'Arc*, "Lévi-Strauss," 19–29.

36. The most recent analyses on this subject are the following: Paul Veyne, "La famille et l'amour sous le Haut-Empire romain," *Annales ESC* 33 (1978): f.; "L'homosexualité romaine," *Sexualités occidentales, Communication* 35 (1982); Michel Foucault, *The History of Sexuality*, vol. 3, *Care of the Self* (London: Allen Lane, 1988); and Eva Cantarella, *Seion la nature, l'usage et la loi: La bisexualité dans le monde antique* (Paris: La Découverte, 1991). These authors certainly show that the categories "homosex-

ual" and "heterosexual" are inadequate in connection with the men of antiquity, but their substitution of the categories of "active" and "passive" do not improve matters. Only Aline Rousselle, in *L'histoire de la famille*, vol. 1, ed. Martine Segalen (Paris: Armand Colin, 1986), introduces an anthropological and historical point of view on the question, by reconstructing the day-to-day eroticism of life in a Roman household.

37. Veyne, "La famille et l'amour sous le Haut-Empire romain," 51; and "L'homosexualité romaine," 29.

38. Catullus, 15.

39. Petronius, frag. 53.

40. Plautus, *Charancon*, 37–38.

41. Seneca the Orator, *Controversies*, 4, preface 10.

42. Valerius Maximus, 6.1.7.

43. Plutarch, *Cato the Younger*, 25.

44. Foucault, *History of Sexuality*, chap. 5.1. Pliny the Younger, *Letters*, 7.4.6.

45. Plato, *Laws*, 836f.

46. *Palatine Anthology*, 12.133.

47. Ibid., 5.261.

48. Ibid., 5.244.

49. Philostratus, *Images*, 1.2.298, translation and commentary by François Frontisi and François Lissarague, "Da l'ambiguité à l'ambivalence: Un parcours dionysiaque," *AION* (1983): 28. These authors are amazed by this description, which does not correspond to the Anacreontic dancers of the Attic vases.

50. Cited by Stobaeus, *Eclogues*, 64–65. English translation based on the French translation by F. Buffière, in *Eros adolescent* (Paris: Belles Lettres, 1980).

51. Suetonius, *Claudius*, 33.

52. Aulus Gellius, *Attic Nights*, 19.9. Cf. above, p. 107.

53. Cicero, *Cato maior*, 46.

54. Cf. above, p. 108.

55. Cicero, *Laws*, 2.15.

56. Used and cited above, p. 72.

57. Apuleius, *Apologia*, 9. This trial took place between A.D. 148 and 161, under the reign of Antoninus.

58. I am following the correction *donaci* in the edition by Paul Valette (Paris: Belles Lettres, 1960).

59. On the *recitatio* 'public reading' practiced by authors under the empire, cf. below, pp. 223f.

60. One does come across Romans reading to themselves love poetry that excites them, as we have seen with Pliny the Younger, *Letters*, 7.4.6, reading a loving epigram by Cicero.

61. Cf. below, pp. 223f.

62. Plato, *Symposium*, 176e.

63. Ibid., 214b.

64. Cf. below, pp. 183f.

65. Plato, *Symposium*, 215b, and 220a.

66. Ibid., 173c.

67. Plato's text explicitly states "aneu organōn psilois logois," 215c and d.

68. On bookish knowledge that is absorbed like food, cf. E. Valette-Cagnac, *La lecture à Rome*, EPHE thesis, 5th section (Paris, 1994), 86f.

69. Macrobius, *Saturnalia*, preface, 1–6.

70. Plutarch, *Table Talk*, 6, preface, 686a–e.

71. Athenaeus, *Deipnosophists*, 1.1 (3rd century).

72. Pliny the Younger, *Letters*, 3.5.

73. Petronius, *Satyricon*, 28–78. In this episode, the erotic rivalry between Encolpius and Ascyltos is suspended, and Giton, the cause of their rivalry, plays the role of a slave, although he is never represented as one in any of the other episodes.

74. Ibid., 59.

75. Ibid., 52.

76. Seneca, *Letters*, 27.5–6.

77. Cf. below, pp. 198f.

78. Michel de Certeau, *L'invention du quotidien, I. Arts de faire* (Paris: Gallimard, Folio, 1990), introduction, xxxvf.

Part III. The Story Culture

1. Seneca, *Letters to Lucilius*, 25.7.

2. Ernout-Meillet, *s.v. circulus*: "qui circumeundo artem exercet uel qui homines circum se colligit."

3. Pliny the Younger, *Letters*, 2.20.1.

4. On Mnemosyne, cf. the early and somewhat uneven book by Marcel Detienne, *The Masters of Truth in Archaic Greece*, trans. Janet Lloyd (New York: Zone Books, 1996).

5. Cf. Introduction, p. 14.

6. On the central place of sacrifice in Greek civilization, cf. M. Detienne and J.-P. Vernant, eds., *La cuisine du sacrifice en pays grec* (Paris: Gallimard, 1979), and on the episode of the Cyclops in the *Odyssey*, Pierre Vidal-Naquet, *The Black Hunter*, trans. Andrew Szegedy-Maszak (Baltimore: Johns Hopkins University Press, 1986), 15–38.

7. On the Satyrs, cf. François Lissarague, "Le vin des satyres," in *Le vin des historiens*, symposium on Vin et Histoire, 1989 (Suze-la-Rousse, 1990), 49–62, and "La sexualité des satyres," *Métis* 2, no. 1 (1987): 63–90.

8. This way of looking at things is quite common in traditional societies in

which, very often, a people's name means, quite simply, "men." Our own humanism has reversed this attitude: instead of declaring "we are the human race," we say "the human race is [like] us." We have not necessarily gained anything by making this change.

Chapter 5. *The Golden Ass* Stories

1. On journeys and legends and the opening up of spaces, cf. Michel de Certeau, *L'invention du quotidien, I. Arts de faire* (Paris: Gallimard, Folio, 1990), 160.

2. Christian Jacob, *Géographie et ethnographie en Grèce Ancienne* (Paris: Armand Colin, "Cursus" collection, 1991).

3. Apuleius, *The Golden Ass,* 1.20.

4. Ibid., 2, 20.

5. Jean-Marie Andre and Marie-Françoise Baslez, *Voyager dans l'antiquité* (Paris: Fayard, 1993).

6. Apuleius, *The Golden Ass,* 1.2, 20. The translation used is that by J. Arthur Hanson, in the Loeb Classical Library.

7. This is a term used in particular by Massimo Fusillo, *Naissance du roman* (Paris: Le Seuil, 1989).

8. Achilles Tatius, *Leucippe and Clitophon,* 8.4. The English translation is based on the French translation by P. Grimal, in *Les romans grecs et latins* (Paris: La Pléiade, 1958).

9. Heliodorus, *Aethiopica,* 5.16. The English translation is again based on that by Grimal, *Les Romans.*

10. Laurence Kahn, *Hermès passe, ou les ambiguités de la communication* (Paris: Maspero, 1978); on the speech of Hermes and exchange, cf. 119f. and 135f.

11. Achilles Tatius, *Leucippe and Clitophon,* 2.4.

12. Ovid, *Metamorphoses,* 4.4–56.

13. Ovid's account (ibid.) frequently makes the point that the telling of these stories neither interrupts nor slows down the work in progress: 4.36, 54, 275.

14. Ibid., 271, 53, 276, 285.

15. Ibid., 272.

16. Ibid., 389–415.

17. Apuleius, *The Golden Ass,* 10.2–12.

18. The buskin is the emblematic shoe of tragedy, the slipper that of comedy.

19. Apuleius, *The Golden Ass,* 4.26–27.

20. Ibid., 4.27.8.

21. *Les mille et une nuits,* trans. Antoine Galland, ed. Jean Gaulmier (Paris: Flammarion, 1965). The references are to this edition.

22. Ibid., 35.

23. Apuleius, *The Golden Ass,* 3.24.

24. On Priapus, cf. Maurice Olender, *Priape et Baubô* (Paris: Flammarion, 1994).

25. *The Golden Ass,* 2.25, 4.6.

26. On stories about metamorphosis, cf. F. Dupont, "Se reproduire et se métamorphoser," *Topique* 9–10 (1973): 23–32.

27. Ovid, *Metamorphoses,* 10.570f. (Hecuba); 1.233–34 (Lycaon); 2.340f. (Heliades); 1.705–12 (Syrinx).

28. *The Golden Ass,* 4.6f.

29. Ibid., 4.9.

30. The "fine death" has been studied in depth by J.-P. Vernant, *L'invidu, la mort, l'amour* (Paris: Gallimard, 1989), chaps. 2, 3; and above all by Nicole Loraux, *The Invention of Athens,* trans. Alan Sheridan (Cambridge, Mass., 1986).

31. *The Golden Ass,* 4.11. The exaggerated style is probably intended to be humorous; but that does not affect the preceding analysis, the main point being that a particular type of discourse is immediately recognizable.

32. Marcel Detienne and Jesper Svenbro, "Les loups au festin, ou la cité impossible," in M. Detienne and J.-P. Vernant, eds., *La cuisine du sacrifice en pays grec* (Paris: Gallimard, 1979).

33. For every ritual performance constitutes a negotiation between a particular situation and the rules governing its celebration.

34. On the figure of Trimalchio as a fantasy for the use of free Romans, cf. Paul Veyne, "Vie de Trimalchion," *Annales ESC* (1961): 213–47, reprinted in Veyne, *La société romaine* (Paris: Le Seuil, 1991), 13–56.

35. Cf. above, pp. 162f.

36. Petronius, *Satyricon,* 61.

37. G. Dumézil, *Idées romaines* (Paris: Gallimard, 1969), 255–56.

38. *The Golden Ass,* 7.31.

Chapter 6. Writing Sandwiched between Two Voices

1. Catherine Salles, *Ecrivain, livre et public dans le mode occidental d'Auguste à l'avènement d'Hadrien,* thesis (Paris, 1981), and *Lire à Rome* (Paris: Belles Lettres, 1992).

2. Guy Achard, *La communication à Rome* (Paris: Belles Lettres, 1991), 183–98.

3. These two terms are borrowed, respectively, from Gregory Nagy (recomposition) and Paul Zumthor (*mouvance* 'shifting'), who use them to describe oral poetry.

4. This expression is adapted from that used by Michel Charles, *La rhétorique de la lecture* (Paris: Le Seuil, 1977), 61f.: "a machine for producing readings." I have indicated, in the Introduction, how important I consider this work to be.

5. On *sermo*, the language of communication, cf. Achard, *La communication à Rome*, 113f.

6. Pierre Cordier, *Introduction à une approche pragmatique de l'épistolarité des "Lettres à Lucilius,"* DEA, Paris-IV (Paris, 1990), and "La lettre et l'*amicitia*," in *Paroles romaines* (Nancy: PUN, 1994), chap. 2; cf. above, pp. 118–19.

7. Jesper Svenbro, "The Reader and the *eromènos*: The Pederastic Paradigm of Writing," in *Phrasikleia: An Anthropology of Reading in Ancient Greece*, trans. Janet Lloyd (Ithaca, N.Y.: Cornell University Press, 1993), 187–216.

8. CIL 13.10017.

9. E. Valette-Cagnac, *La lecture à Rome*, EPHE thesis, 5th section (Paris, 1994), 305–6, shows that it is not simply a matter of drawing a distinction between reading for others, that is to say aloud (*recitatio*) and reading to oneself (*lectio*), which is soundless. Quietly murmured reading, inaudible except to a listener very close to the reader, is also possible and bestows a different kind of reality upon the text. For example, Seneca, *Letters*, 10.5: men who offer up prayers which they wish to keep secret, yet without losing the elocutory force of orality, whisper (*susurrant*). The sound is loud enough to be heard by passersby but they cannot make out the words, so they draw nearer; at which point those who are whispering fall silent.

10. Cf. above, pp. 198f.

11. Studied from this point of view, in Greece, by Svenbro, *Phrasikleia*, chap. 3, 44–46, and in Rome by Valette-Cagnac, *La lecture*, 344–78.

12. Svenbro, *Phrasikleia*, 56–61.

13. Paul Valette (Paris: Belles Lettres, 1940), and Victor Betolaud (Paris: Garnier, 1870).

14. Svenbro, *Phrasikleia*, 75–76.

15. Ibid., 54–56.

16. Africanist ethnologists have shown how passing from orality to writing entails a qualitative change in the text. Cf. *Graines de paroles. Puissances du verbe et traditions orales* (Paris: Editions du CNRS, 1989), in particular the article by Maurice Houis, "Pour une taxinomie des textes en oralité," 167–83.

17. Pliny the Younger, *Letters*, 2.19.2f.

18. On the book as food for speech, cf. Valette-Cagnac, *La lecture*, 86–179; and above, "Erudite Banquets and the Books That Provided the Nourishment," pp. 160f.

19. M. Fusillo, *Naissance du roman* (Paris: Le Seuil, 1989), 185.

20. Cf. below, pp. 222f.

21. *The Golden Ass*, 6.25.

22. Cf. above, pp. 193f.

23. Editions Jean-Claude Lattès (Paris, 1979). A more recent popular edition has turned it into a pornographic text, so that this *Lucius* has been published in

black covers in the series Les classiques interdits. The frontispiece shows a blown-up photograph of a woman's camisole; the shiny, black rayonne material with an edging of lace allows a glimpse of the very white skin of a breast. On the fourth page of this publication the following words appear: "Ranging from pink to black, the many reflections that love has produced, does produce, and will always produce in men's imaginations, seen through the most famous and curious of texts. Banned for many years, they remained accessible only to a limited number of free spirits. Now they are available to all."

24. Petronius, *Satyricon*, 111, 85.

25. Thierry Eloi, "Amoureux des fragments de discours. La parole plurielle du héros romanesque dans le *Satiricon*," in *Paroles romaines* (Nancy: PUN, 1994), chap. 10.

26. The first selection of Milesian stories, collected in Greek by Aristides, in the first century B.C., was translated in Rome by a contemporary of Cicero, a Roman noble by the name of Lucius Cornelius Sisenna.

27. John Scheid and Jesper Svenbro, "Paroles tissées. Sur le tissage langagier à Rome," in *Paroles romaines*.

28. Ibid., 150.

29. Valette-Cagnac, *La lecture*, 380f.

30. Valerius Maximus, 4.10; an example cited and commented on by Valette-Cagnac, *La lecture*, 417–18, whose analysis I have followed here.

31. Horace, *Epistles*, 2.1.108–9, and Seneca the Orator, *Controversies*, 4, pref. 2.

32. On the *recitatio*, cf. Valette-Cagnac, *La lecture*, 443–503, on which most of the present chapter is based; and F. Dupont, "Une nouvelle parole, entre écriture et oralité, sous l'Empire: La *recitatio*," paper presented at the colloquium on The Roman Cultural Revolution. Princeton, N.J., March 1993; Eckard Lefevre, "Die römische Literatur zwischen Mündlichekeit und Schriftlichkeit," in Gregor Vogt-Spira, ed., *Strukturen der Mündichkeit in der römischen Welt* (Tübingen, 1990).

33. Achard, *La communication à Rome*, 183–98, refers, with reason, to the "despotism of the written text."

34. Ovid, *Tristia*, 4.10.45–50, 57–58: in his exile among barbarians, Ovid complains of being unable to give a *recitatio*, owing to the lack of culturally competent listeners. For him, this is the equivalent of social death.

35. Pliny the Younger, *Letters*, 7.17.1–4.

36. On the *sermo* as purely communicatory speech: Cicero, *Orator*, 61, 113.

37. Françoise Desbordes, *Idées romaines sur l'écriture* (Lille: Presses universitaires de Lille, 1990), 78f.

38. Cf. above, p. 158. But there is one difference: the banqueters of Aulus Gellius were only commemorating recognized monuments from the past, whereas here it is a matter of appreciating new works.

39. Pliny the Younger, *Letters,* 5.17.1.

40. For example, Pliny the Younger, 1.8.2 and passim; Horace, *Ars poetica,* 419–52; Seneca, *Letters to Lucilius,* 122.11; Pliny the Younger, 8.12.1.

41. Pliny the Younger, 3.15.3; that is why the listener must try not to be seduced by the music of the words.

42. Ibid., 2.10.1f., 2.19.1f.

43. Martial, *Epigrams,* pref. 12, and Pliny the Younger, passim.

44. Horace, *Epistles,* 1.2.1.

45. Pliny the Younger, 9.34.1–2.

46. Ibid., 1.13.

47. Ibid., 5.10, and *Letters to Trajan,* 94, 95.

48. *Letters,* 9.34.

49. Juvenal, 7.436–47.

50. Ibid., 1.1–18.

51. Horace, *Satires,* 1.4.

52. Martial, 5.78, 25f.

53. Yan Thomas, "Se venger au forum: Solidarité familiale et procès criminel à Rome," in Raymond Verdier and Jean-Pierre Poly, eds., *La Vengeance. Vengeance, pouvoirs et idéologies dans quelques civilisations de l'antiquité* (Paris: Cujas, 1984), 65–100.

54. Pliny the Younger, 5.17.1.

55. Ibid., 1.13.1.

56. Ibid., 2.3.1–4, and Quintilian, 10.1.

57. Quintilian, 12.11.17–22.

58. Ibid., 12.11.22.

59. Horace, *Epistles,* 1.2.1f.

60. Ibid., 2.1.112.

61. Pliny the Younger, 1.20.9.

62. Ibid., 2.10.3.

63. Ibid., 2.9.4.

64. Horace, *Odes,* 3.30.

65. Ibid., and Pliny the Younger, 2.9.2.

66. Cf. above, p. 210.

67. Tacitus, *Dialogus,* 10.3.

68. Pliny the Younger, 7.20.1–2.

69. Pliny the Younger, 3.18.

70. Ibid., 2–3.

71. Ibid., 8–9.

72. On the concept of ideograms and pictograms, cf. Jean-Marie Durand, "Trois approches de la notion d'idéogramme sumérien," in Anne-Marie Christin, *Ecritures II* (Paris: Le Sycomore, 1985), 25–42.

73. Petronius, *Satyricon*, 89.

74. Ibid., 91.

75. P. Grimal has persuasively argued that it could not be a parody: *La guerre civile de Pétrone dans ses rapports avec la Pharsale* (Paris: Les Belles Lettres, 1977).

76. Petronius, *Satyricon*, 124.

77. Ibid., 110–13.

78. John Scheid and Jesper Svenbro, *Le Métier de Zeus. Mythe du tissu et du tissage dans le monde gréco-romain* (Paris: La Découverte, 1994): weaving is an image that combines both practices.

79. Suetonius, *Life of Virgil*, 102–3; Servius, *Ad Buc.*, 6.11; Tacitus, *Dialogus*, 13.

80. Directed by Daniel Vigne.

81. Daniel Pennac, *Comme un roman* (Paris: Gallimard, 1992).

82. To look no further than *The Golden Ass*, see the strange book by Marie-Louise von Franz, *Interprétation d'un conte, L'Ane d'or* (Paris: Fontaine de Pierre, 1978).

83. Michel de Certeau, *L'ecriture de l'histoire* (Paris: Gallimard, 1975), in particular 215–331.

Conclusion: The Entropy of Cultural Changes

1. Bernard Sarrazin and Robert Sctrick, eds., *Lire pour lire. La lecture littéraire* (Paris: Université de Paris-VII, Textuel, 1990) contains valuable analyses of literary reading as practiced today, as an end in itself.

2. Jesper Svenbro, *Phrasikleia: An Anthropology of Reading in Ancient Greece*, trans. Janet Lloyd (Ithaca, N.Y.: Cornell University Press, 1993), 140f.

3. In Augustine's *Confessions*, it is interesting to read the account of his education at school.

4. Cf. above, pp. 82f.

5. For an uninformed reader, the best account of Carnot's second principle is to be found in P. W. Atkins, *The Second Law: Energy, Chaos and Form* (New York: Scientific American, [1984] 1994).

6. Michel Forse, *L'ordre improbable. Entropie et processus sociaux* (Paris: PUF, 1989).

7. Ibid., p. 87.

8. Ibid., p. 105, and Atkins, *The Second Law*.

9. As with the Indian societies described by Pierre Clastres as "societies for war," in *Remarques d'anthropologie politique* (Paris: Gallimard, 1980), 171f.

10. Atkins, *The Second Law*, 181, 183.

11. Paul Zumthor, introduction to *Graines d paroles. Puissance du verbe et traditions orales* (Paris: Editions du CNRS, 1989).

INDEX

Library of Congress Cataloging-in-Publication Data
Dupont, Florence.
[Invention de la littérature. English]
The invention of literature : from Greek intoxication to the Latin book / by Florence Dupont ; translated by Janet Lloyd.
p. cm.
Includes bibliographical references (p.) and index.
ISBN 0-8018-5864-X (alk. paper)
1. Classical literature—History and criticism—Theory, etc. 2. Literature and society—Greece. 3. Literature and society—Rome. 4. Greece—Civilization. 5. Rome—Civilization. 6. Rhetoric, Ancient. I. Title.
PA3009.D8613 1999
880′.09—dc21 98-42865
CIP

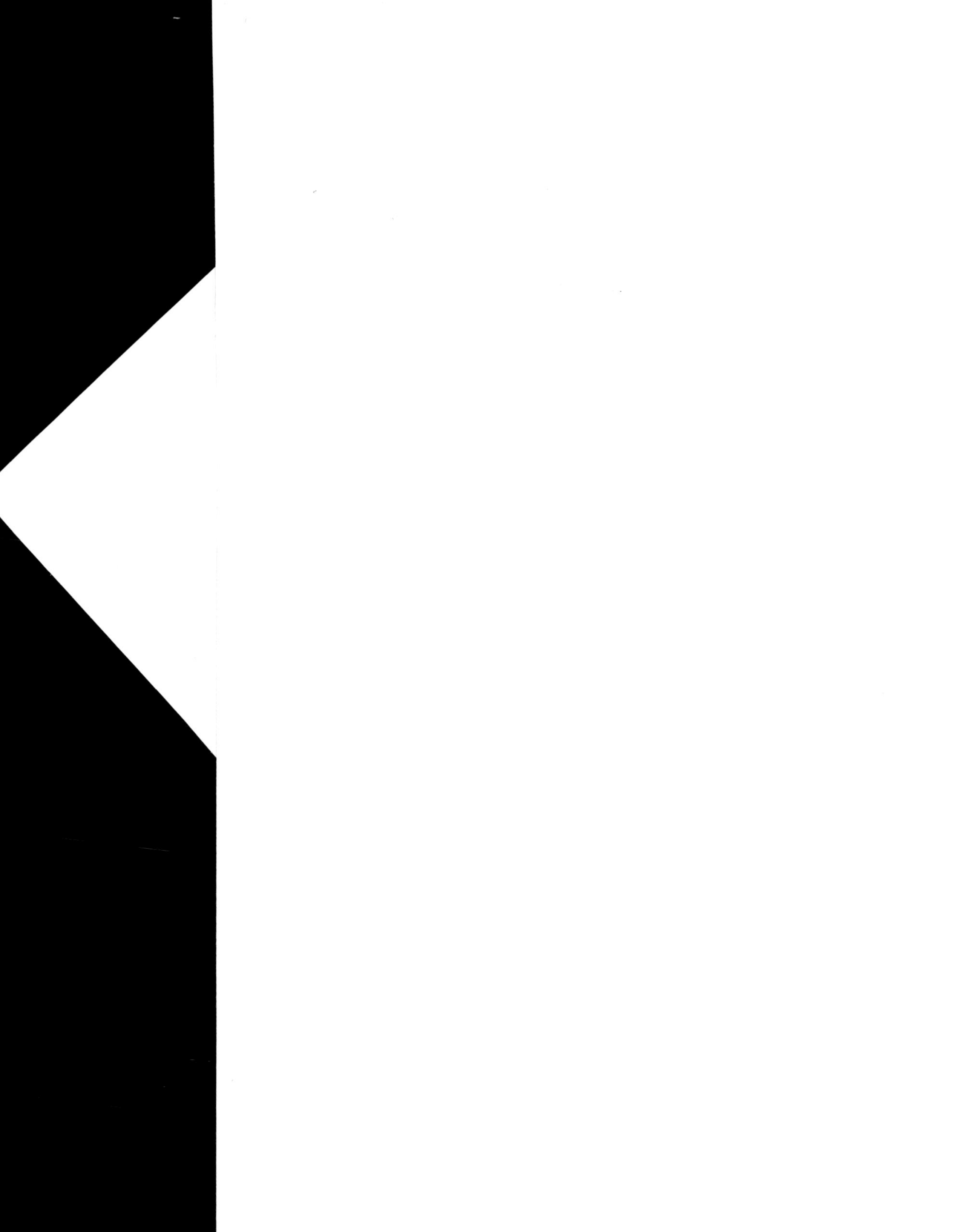

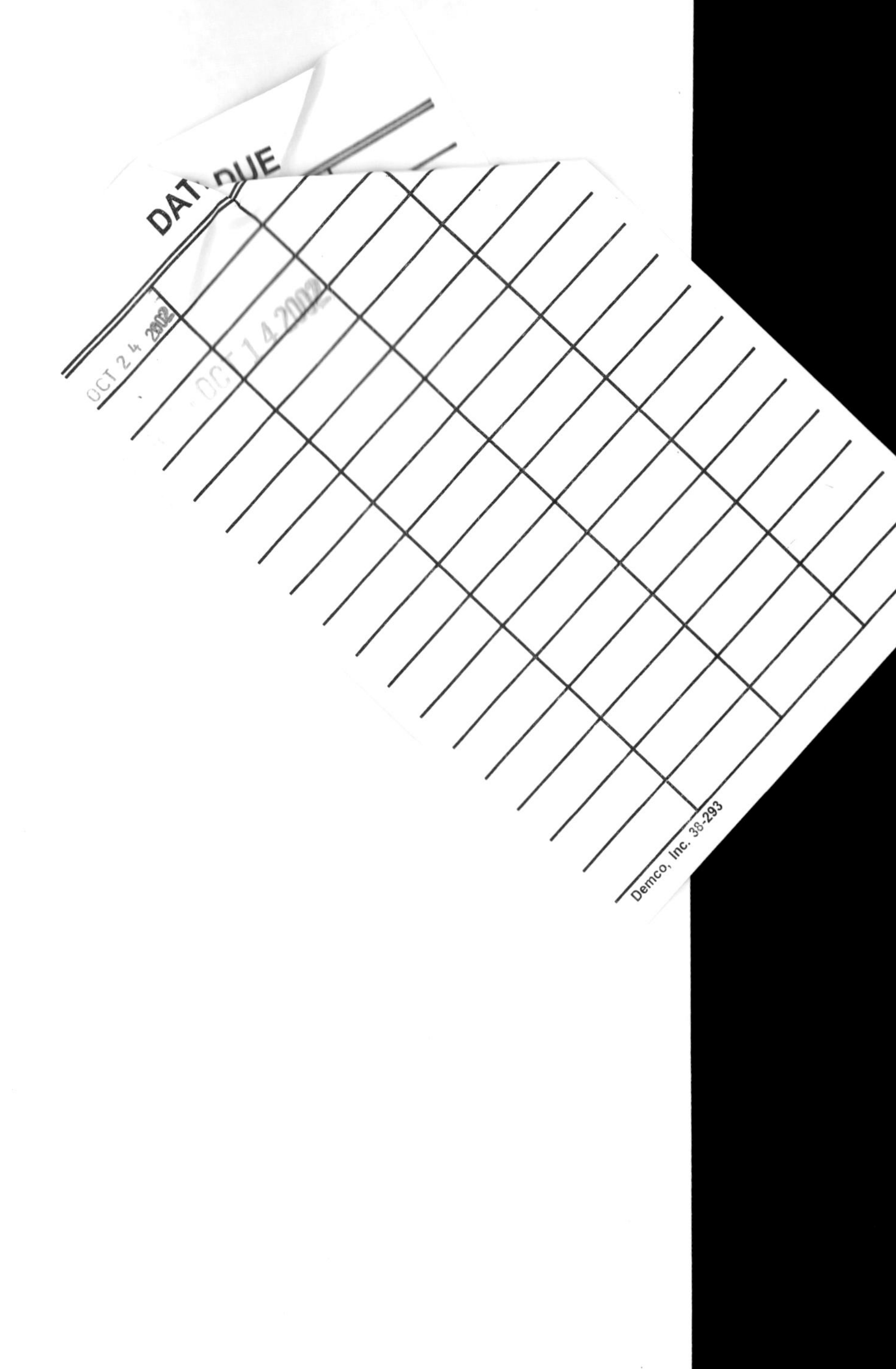